ZORRO'S SHADOW

HOW A MEXICAN LEGEND BECAME AMERICA'S FIRST SUPERHERO

STEPHEN J. C. ANDES

CHICAGO
REVIEW
PRESS

Portions of this book have previously appeared in articles published by the author
at Medium.com and in "Welcome to the Hotel Zorro! Such a Lovely Place,"
PostScript: Essays in Film and the Humanities 38, no. 1 (Fall 2019): 52–55.

Library of Congress Cataloging-in-Publication Data
Names: Andes, Stephen J. C. (Stephen Joseph Carl), author.
Title: Zorro's shadow: how a Mexican legend became America's first
    superhero / Stephen J. C. Andes.
Description: Chicago, IL: Chicago Review Press, [2020] | Includes bibliographical
    references and index. | Summary: "Historian and Latin American studies
    expert Stephen J. C. Andes investigates the legends behind the mask of Zorro,
    describing how the stories of William Lamport and Joaquín Murrieta influenced
    the development of the masked hero in black, and revealing Zorro as the Latinx
    inspiration for today's iconic superheroes"—Provided by publisher.
Identifiers: LCCN 2020017269 (print) | LCCN 2020017270 (ebook) | ISBN
    9781641602938 (trade paperback) | ISBN 9781641602945 (adobe pdf) | ISBN
    9781641602969 (epub) | ISBN 9781641602952 (kindle edition)
Subjects: LCSH: Zorro (Fictitious character) | McCulley, Johnston,
    1883–1958—Characters—Zorro. | Lombardo, Guillén,
    1615–1659—Influence. | Murieta, Joaquín, –1853—Influence. | Superheroes.
Classification: LCC PS3525.A17725 Z53 2020 (print) | LCC PS3525.A17725
    (ebook) | DDC 813.52—dc23
LC record available at https://lccn.loc.gov/2020017269
LC ebook record available at https://lccn.loc.gov/2020017270

Cover design: Jonathan Hahn
Cover photo: Guy Williams as the title character of the TV series *Zorro*, 1957.
    Photo by Silver Screen Collection / Getty Images
Typesetting: Nord Compo

Printed in the United States of America
5 4 3 2 1

For my favorite *zorritos*: Opal, Silas, and Mercer

CONTENTS

PREFACE

Who Is America's First Superhero?

AMERICA'S FIRST SUPERHERO WASN'T SUPERMAN. It was only in 1938 that he ripped open his first suit shirt and got confused for a bird and/ or a plane.

And it wasn't Batman either. He's only been brooding in Gotham City's dark corners, surprising hapless criminals, foiling dastardly schemes, since 1939.

Wonder Woman? Nope. Feminist icon with Amazonian roots—only since 1941.

The Shadow? Uh-uh. His maniacal laugh and power to cloud the minds of men have only been around since 1930.

What if I told you Zorro was America's first superhero? The masked man in black first appeared in 1919. But unlike the superheroes above, he got his start not in comics—they hadn't really been invented yet—but in the pulps. Pulps were magazines with fiction stories, hugely popular in America from the 1880s to the 1920s. Adventure tales. Crime detective stories. (The term *pulp fiction* came from the low-grade "pulpy" paper many of the magazines were printed on.)

Zorro's dual identity fit right into this genre. By day, he was the foppish aristocrat Don Diego Vega. By night, he was Zorro—Spanish for "fox"—a crime fighter and avenger who fought corrupt governors and army captains in Spanish California with his signature sword, bullwhip, and lightning-fast reflexes. He carved his calling card—a letter *Z*—on the foreheads of evildoers as punishment and as a reminder: Zorro was there, watching from the shadows, an avenging ghost who could appear wherever and whenever he willed. He did it all with a general joie de vivre that would be lost on most superheroes today. Zorro was looking out for the weak and oppressed of Old Spanish California. And he was having a really good time doing it: "Ha ha!"—*parry, thrust*—"Ho ho!"—*feint, counter, jab*—"Take that, *mi amigo*! Justice for all!"

Sure, Zorro didn't have supernatural or superhuman powers, but neither does Batman. And yes, Zorro wasn't properly a comic book hero until later, after Batman, Superman, and Wonder Woman had built the superhero genre in that medium. But Zorro laid the blueprint for the comic book—and movie blockbuster—superheroes we know today. He wore a mask. He had a signature costume. Zorro had an alter ego, a dual identity. He battled archvillains. A loyal sidekick? Yes, he even had one of those. Zorro, and all of his superhero accoutrements, came twenty years before Superman, Batman, and Wonder Woman.

Zorro is America's first superhero.

And there's more.

What if I told you that Zorro—America's first superhero—is proof that the whole superhero genre owes an enormous debt to Mexican American legends? Zorro is a product of Latinx history and experience. And, in turn, Zorro inspired the superhero genre. Logic tells us, then, that Latinx culture helped produce the American superhero. The American superhero is not just a product of Anglo, white American culture. The superhero is multicultural. The superhero is, in fact, a product of American diversity.

Imagine that.

I know what you're thinking: *But Zorro is Spanish, right? Not Mexican.*

True. Zorro exists in the popular imagination as a whitewashed Spanish version of Mexican legends, but the character still remains connected to those Mexican legends. They've just been covered up. It's time they were unmasked. It's taken one hundred years for this history—this masked history—to be revealed.

I've got the secret history of Zorro![1]

Zorro helped create the American superhero, and the history of Latino American people helped create American culture.

It's as plain, and as permanent, as Zorro's Z.

PART I

GHOSTS

An era can be considered over when its basic illusions
have been exhausted.

—Arthur Miller

1 | THE STATUE

Research Log #1
Reforma Boulevard, Mexico City
9:33 AM

IS ZORRO REALLY JUST FICTION? I couldn't get the question out of my mind as I walked the crowded streets of Mexico City.

The American writer Johnston McCulley wrote the first Zorro story one hundred years ago. He called it *The Curse of Capistrano*. The pulp magazine *All-Story Weekly* serialized it in five installments: August 9, August 16, August 23, August 30, and September 6, 1919. That's the origin of Don Diego Vega and his fictional alter ego, Zorro. Zorro was born in the mind of a white guy from Chillicothe, Illinois. End of story.

Or not . . .

I've been on a journey to find the origins of Zorro for the past two years. I've read McCulley's earliest stories; devoured the Zorro comic books of Everett Raymond Kinstler, Don McGregor, and Matt Wagner; and seen all the Zorro feature films, from Douglas Fairbanks to the Republic Pictures matinee serials to the spoof *Zorro: The Gay Blade* (1981)—and, of course, the Antonio Banderas and Catherine Zeta-Jones reboots (1998's *The Mask of Zorro* and 2005's *The Legend of Zorro*). I began my journey with Zorro already established as a cultural icon.[1] I've been a little obsessed, I suppose.

And of course, I've done my research. Scholarly books and articles piled up on my desk. I was, at first, skeptical of Zorro's status as a superhero. *What superpowers does Zorro have?* As I explored the literature on superheroes, I discovered two important facets to the question: first, not all "superheroes" have superhuman abilities, and second, Zorro is more of a prototype superhero, one whose abilities were enlarged in the heroes he inspired—for example, the Shadow, the Phantom, the Green Hornet, and Batman.[2]

My investigation into the origins of Zorro also led me to ask myself, *Is Zorro really just fiction?* Because if Zorro was a prototype for later superheroes, could Zorro himself have had a prototype? My research began to suggest that he was based on a historical figure.

At first, I was dubious that Zorro was anything more than a romantic fiction, but as it turns out, I'm not the only one to look for the inspiration for the man behind the mask. As I studied further, two real-life inspirations for Zorro emerged.

The first inspiration I encountered was Joaquín Murrieta (ca. 1824–1853), a notorious *bandido* who terrorized southern California in the days of the gold rush.[3] Tales of Murrieta have been much sensationalized, but many associate him with the masked crusader.[4] In the Zorro movies with Antonio Banderas, Catherine Zeta-Jones, and Anthony Hopkins, Hopkins even portrays an aging Zorro who bequeaths the mask to *Alejandro* Murrieta, played by Banderas. I began to think that all I had to do was prove that Murrieta was the basis for Zorro to make the Latinx origins of the superhero genre clear.[5]

Until I encountered inspiration number two: William Lamport, an Irishman of undeniably European origin. I discovered that the second real-life character who allegedly inspired the Zorro stories was the so-called Irish Zorro—an Irish Spanish adventurer who lived in the seventeenth century (1611–1659). He emigrated to Mexico and was captured by the Mexican Inquisition for a conspiracy to rebel against the Spanish Crown. He proclaimed Mexican independence more than 150 years before independence happened in 1810. He was burned at the stake.

His legend lived on, however, and in 1872 a Mexican author of romantic fiction named Vicente Riva Palacio wrote a novel based on his life called *Memorias de un impostor: D. Guillén de Lampart, rey de México* ("Memoirs of an Imposter: D. Guillén de Lampart, King of Mexico"). The theory, recently popularized by an Italian historian named Fabio Troncarelli, is that Johnston McCulley based his Zorro on Palacio's novel.[6] An interesting literary and cultural similarity was apparent between Lamport and Zorro.[7] Marketing for Troncarelli's book made a splash, especially in Europe. Headlines carried zingers like PADDY O'ZORRO, the WEXFORD WOMANIZER, and various other alliterative titles, ad nauseam.

But could it be true? Was Zorro based on a seventeenth-century Irishman?

This brought me to Mexico City, where I hoped to find out if there was anything to the idea. I decided to start my investigation with Lamport, because if Lamport turned out to be the real inspiration for Zorro, my whole claim that America's first superhero is based on Latinx history and experience would be on far shakier ground. I'm a historian, so I had to do my due diligence, to deal with the European Zorro—establish his merits, see how the evidence stacked up—before I could compare him with Murrieta. For the moment, then, I left aside Joaquín Murrieta's claims to the mask.

———————

Before I found Lamport's statue, I considered the fictional Zorro as I'd come to understand him. I realized if I was to judge whether Zorro was based on Murrieta or Lamport I'd have to get a clear idea of who the fictional Zorro is.

Here's the rundown.

McCulley's Zorro came to the attention of Hollywood not long after the first stories appeared in 1919. Douglas Fairbanks Sr., star of the silent film era, snapped up the Zorro story and made the first film adaptation in 1920. He called the film *The Mark of Zorro*. Fairbanks gave Zorro more than a dose of athleticism—he jumped, he strutted, he did his own stunts. Fairbanks also gave Diego Vega his dandy characteristics. For instance, in the film, Fairbanks uses a handkerchief scented with perfume to protect his aristocratic nose from the unpleasant smells of plebeians; McCulley wrote that tidbit into later Zorro stories.[8] So influential, in fact, was the movie on the early development of the character that editors renamed *The Curse of Capistrano* as *The Mark of Zorro* in later printings.[9] McCulley continued to write new Zorro stories for the pulps. He would publish four serialized Zorro novels plus another fifty-eight short stories before his death in 1958.[10]

McCulley set his stories in California under Spanish rule, but he wasn't clear or consistent about the timeline. It could be the early 1800s or the 1820s, but they were all centered on Los Angeles, or Nuestra Señora la Reina de los Angeles, as it was known then. "The Zorro franchise," writes Eric Trautman, "exists in a historical vortex; from the beginning, it was more of a fantasy version of Mexico than a historically accurate one."[11] Our hero was the son of a wealthy hacienda owner. He masqueraded at night with mask and cape to fight government and military corruption. His enemies were always upstart, unscrupulous *comandantes* who mistreated Indians and women. By day, Zorro was the foppish Diego Vega, who read the poets and couldn't be bothered to ride a few miles to court his love interest. He wouldn't be caught dead, so he said, playing a guitar under the window of a pretty senorita.[12]

All McCulley's Zorro stories contained similar elements and themes. Heroism, love, honor, justice, truth—these were the staples of McCulley's Zorro, mixed with action, adventure, and derring-do. Zorro had to take up his sword because those responsible for justice were not handing it out. Thus, the caballero, the gentleman—a man of blue blood, pure and noble—became the avenger of the weak.

In retrospect, it's all pretty paternalistic: white rich guy has to be the hero. But then again, that's also Batman in a nutshell.

This is the Zorro we know. Created one hundred years ago, he's been the product of fiction—pulps, movies, serials, TV, comics, cartoons, satires, pornos, reboots, new stories, and crossovers. The legend of Zorro is a product of twentieth-century media. And Zorro always seems to reappear. His story is durable. Like other pop cultural icons, Zorro's symbolism is not fixed but open to change as contemporary consumers look for what they need in him. Bandits, from Robin Hood to Mexico's narco-saint Jesús Malverde, have always performed a function for their audiences.[13] They are symbols of hope, symbols of justice, symbols of vicarious adventure.

It's important, after a century, to delve into Zorro's origins. If we're going to create an icon that represents our hopes and symbols of justice, that sparks our imagination, we need to deal with the ghosts of Zorro's past, put them to rest, and move on toward a more inclusive future. Telling better stories starts with telling the old, uncomfortable stories from the past.

———————

I snapped out of my academic reverie and focused on the object before me: the statue of William Lamport. I stood in front of an enormous monument to Mexican independence looking for the Irishman. The monument looked a bit like the July Column in Paris, or Nelson's Column in London's Trafalgar Square. The Mexican victory column is called El Ángel de la Independencia ("The Angel of Independence"). It's 311 feet high, with a golden angel on top. It stands in the center of the city's main boulevard, Reforma, which is lined with shops, banks, and tourists, and at the time, with Día de los Muertos a few days away, the orange marigolds of the dead—the *cempasúchitl*—were in full bloom.

I scurried across the road toward the monument, which works as a convenient roundabout in the center of the boulevard. Stairs climb toward the base of the stone tower. Everywhere, groups were taking pictures. I circled the monument once—names of Mexican independence heroes and cultural icons adorn the stone; robed and seated women representing Law, Justice, War, and Peace guard each corner of the column's base. One statuary installation is of a child leading a lion, as if to say that the birth of the Mexican nation came with untamed power. Miguel Hidalgo, the priest who set off insurrection in 1810, Vicente Guerrero, and others stand on the pedestal before the column rises to a staggering height.[14]

Where is the Irish Zorro?

I saw a door that led into the monument. There's a mausoleum inside where, until recently, the actual remains of many of the independence heroes were interred.

The door was locked.

I peered through a darkened window and saw it—or him, I should say: William Lamport in marble, perfectly straight, staring up at the horizon. A partially opened interior door blocked half of the statue. I saw someone's foot and part of a leg jutting out of the door. I knocked.

I knocked quite a bit. From the shadows I saw a police officer—or security guard, it was hard to know which. He motioned at me that they were closed. I knocked again, adding a contrite facial expression. He kindly opened the heavy brass door.

The police officer emerged with a full bulletproof vest and a smile. He wore horn-rimmed glasses and stood about five foot two. He said in Spanish that I couldn't come inside and that the mausoleum was closed for the next year for renovations.

A year?

I explained my story. I was researching William Lampart. *Is that his statue?* I asked. I whipped up my courage and asked if I could take a picture. He kindly let me do so.

We talked, the police officer and I, about William Lampart, known as Don Guillén de Lampart in Mexico. He told me about several books on Guillén.

"This is sort of funny," I said, "but have you ever heard that Guillén de Lampart was the inspiration for Zorro?"

"Yes," he looked at me with a broad smile. "There are some who say yes, and some no. There's quite a controversy about it."

The police officer gave me a five-minute dissertation on the different theories. "Perhaps," he said, "as the legend of Guillén de Lampart went farther north it changed, and over time became the legend of Zorro."

Is it me, I thought to myself, *or is this police officer really well informed?*

I thanked him profusely for his time. A crowd had gathered around us. My thoughts spun in many directions.

What am I missing? I wondered. *What in William Lampart's history ties him to the legend of Zorro?*

2 | THE PYRE

IN 1659, WILLIAM LAMPORT stood not far from where I was that day, but he could never have imagined that there would one day be a statue in his honor. At the time, honor was far off from Lamport indeed. He wore a conical pasteboard dunce cap painted with demons suffering the torments of hell. His cloak had a black cross of Saint Andrew, and it, too, carried demonic images—fitting clothing for one condemned by the Inquisition.[1]

In his lifetime, Lamport was a scholar, a sailor, a soldier, a seducer, and a spy. Like Zorro, Lamport escaped secret dungeons, but in contrast to our masked hero, the Irishman advocated radical social revolution. Zorro always fought for the oppressed of Spanish California, but he was no insurgent. "Zorro is not one to urge rebellion," a pirate named Bardoso says of the masked man in one story.[2] Lamport, however, freely promoted rebellion, sedition, and the abolition of slavery; the Irishman proclaimed himself king of Mexico, but was then recaptured and sent again to more dungeons. He spent almost twenty years in isolated torment.

He went a little mad.

In prison, Lamport claimed to see visions of angels, and he wrote almost one thousand psalms to God. He was called an impostor, a liar, and a heretic, and the Inquisitors made sure to condemn all his aliases. "Don Guillén Lombardo de Guzmán," reads one document, "properly Guillermo Lamport; or Lampart."[3]

And there were other identities besides his name—ones given him by the Inquisitors: "Don Guillén Lombardo de Guzmán . . . is condemned . . . for having been, and being, a heretic, apostate, henchman of the sects of the heresies of Calvin, Pelagius, Hus, Wycliff, Luther, of the Illuminists [*Alumbrados*] and of other heretics and also theorist and inventor of new heresies, arrogant and pertinacious."[4]

The Inquisition called him "seditious, reckless and scandalous." He questioned the divine right of kings and the authority of the pope over temporal affairs.[5] He insisted "on the right of the oppressed to overthrow tyrants by force."[6] He was "suspect in the faith." They claimed Lamport's psalms to God, which he penned while in prison using ink made from candle smoke and honey, were sacrilegious.[7] Lamport, in short, according to the Inquisition, was an "unrepentant heretic." The Inquisitors railed at Lamport for never bowing before the Virgin Mary and the crucifix in his dungeon cell. These were but small symptoms, they argued, of the man's larger spiritual sickness.

"I have venerated them!" Lamport shouted back at the time of his sentencing, "Not that you have even noticed! But I do not respond to the accusations of demons. You are demons. All of you: the visitor, the notary, this seditious lawyer and these individuals who circulate through the tribunal calling themselves inquisitors, secretaries, and scribes."[8]

This outburst was just further proof to the Inquisitors that William Lamport deserved to die. And so, on November 19, 1659, several guards fastened Lamport by an iron collar to an eight-foot stake. Some forty thousand people watched—priests, princes, and paupers alike. The woodpile under him was covered with pitch, but he paid no attention. He looked up; his gaze was fixed on a dark sky, which threatened rain. He searched the horizon as though expecting help to come, some unseen ally to free him.[9]

The fictional stories of Zorro are full of last-minute escapes, but history would not be so kind as to afford a deus ex machina for Lamport. The Irishman's salvation did not come.

3 | THE LEGEND OF DON GUILLÉN DE LAMPART

WHO REMEMBERED WILLIAM LAMPORT? He was dead, ashes; the Inquisition even buried the Irishman's remains in a secret location so that no one would remember him.

But someone did remember Lamport, and the legend of Don Guillén de Lampart developed. Although his story became bound up in the saga of Mexican independence, there's no compelling evidence that Johnston McCulley used Lamport as inspiration for Zorro. He had plenty of other models to draw from in crafting his masked crusader—especially nineteenth-century adventure novels.

I went to the Mexican Archivo General de la Nación and found the actual Inquisition files on William Lamport. It's a large fortress of stone, that archive, a former prison called Lecumberri Palace, which now houses paper captives instead of living inmates. In several huge tomes I saw the script go from that of a learned scribe to tiny handwriting. It was Lamport's own confession—his testimony to the Inquisition where he laid out his life story.

Lamport's history is intriguing, to say the least. There are tales of how he was kidnapped by pirates. He was sent to colonial Mexico as a spy for the Spanish Crown. He had to live a double life for a time. In Lamport's life, there are some similarities with Zorro, but nothing truly striking. It seems as likely that McCulley used D'Artagnan from *The Three Musketeers* or Edmond Dantès from *The Count of Monte Cristo* as a model for Zorro as that he used Lamport.

Leaving the Archivo General, I made my way back to the Angel of Independence monument to take stock.

I realized there's a gap, or a pair of them, in the story. The William Lamport burned in 1659 *somehow* became the legend in marble before me. And, what's more, the marbled statue version of William Lamport *somehow* became the inspiration for the Zorro stories. The theory of the Irish Zorro only works if one can fill in these gaps: William to statue—statue to Zorro. It all depends on that vague, yet crucial, *somehow*.

For the first gap, I knew there's an image of Lamport that fits between the Inquisition's pyre of 1659 and the construction of the Lamport statue. And it's less of a *somehow* and more of a *someone*: the Mexican author Vicente Riva Palacio. If William Lamport is indeed Zorro's inspiration, then Vicente Riva Palacio is the missing link.

One hundred and sixty-two years after Lamport's death, Mexico finally gained its independence from Spain. Mexican independence came in 1821 under three guarantees: religion, independence, and unity. The new government abolished slavery and the caste system. The new nation inherited a society plagued by racism, put in place by Spanish colonialism. Legally, the caste system disappeared. In practice, white creoles—Spaniards born in Mexico—simply replaced *peninsulares* at the top of the hierarchy, while mixed-race Mexicans, Natives, and those of African descent remained in subservient positions. The military, a bastion of meritocracy, offered a place where mixed-race Mexicans could rise to political power.[1]

Vicente Guerrero, a man of Afro-mestizo heritage, was just such an individual. A hero of independence, he and his fellow liberals—men who desired free trade, greater political participation, and a break from the colonial past—struggled to forge a new nation. Conservatives, men who wanted to protect colonial landholding, colonial privileges, and the power of the colonial church, aimed to forge the new nation in their own way. The liberals and conservatives fought each other for Mexico's future. Vicente Guerrero became president in 1829, but conservatives ousted him in a coup and executed him in 1831.[2] Just a year later, Guerrero's grandson, Vicente Riva Palacio y Guerrero, was born. He inherited his grandfather's political vision—the reform of Mexico's political institutions, progress through scientific knowledge, and disdain for the tyranny of colonialism.

It was in school, as a young man, when Riva Palacio first heard of Don Guillén Lombardo. He later wrote:

I was a child, and I was studying Philosophy in the Colegio de San Gregorio, when one of my classmates, more or less my age, told me, that many years before the priest Hidalgo had proclaimed the Independence of Mexico, a man, of the Irish nation, had tried to rise up as a king of Anáhuac [a mythical name for Mexico], liberating Mexico from Spanish domination; but the conspiracy had been discovered, and the Irishman had been put to death by the hands of justice.[3]

The young Riva Palacio believed the simple story. "The narration impressed me so much," he wrote, "that throughout my life, wherever I heard speak the history of Mexico, or when I meditated upon it, the memory of the Irishman came instantly to my memory."[4]

As Riva Palacio grew, the intermittent civil war between conservatives and liberals continued. Riva Palacio, like his grandfather, entered public life via the military in a context of bloody conflict. He fought for the liberals and their leader Benito Juárez, the future president of Mexico. The liberals separated church and state and wrote a new constitution. Conservatives, for their part, were down but not out. They looked to Europe for help. Conservatives, with support from the Catholic Church, conspired with the French under Napoleon III to set a Hapsburg monarch on the throne of Mexico. Maximilian I, an Austrian noble, ruled Mexico between 1864 and 1867. Riva Palacio, now a general, was given command of the army in central Mexico. He helped defeat the French invaders and rode victorious at the front of his division into Mexico City. The liberals arrested Maximilian and had him shot. Benito Juárez became president of the so-called Restored Republic. Riva Palacio entered politics and briefly served as a justice on Mexico's supreme court.

But Riva Palacio's next battle was mainly taken up with his pen. He established several opposition newspapers, *La Orquesta* and *El Ahuizote*, lambasting the political cronyism and political incumbency that followed Mexico's government after Benito Juárez died in 1872. Riva Palacio went to jail for a short time when he criticized the administration of Manuel González, an interim president who served at the whim of Mexico's real strongman, Porfirio Díaz. Riva Palacio was eventually released and subsequently took up a post as ambassador to Spain. President Díaz, apparently, decided that Riva Palacio was better off sent to foreign shores rather than be left close enough to continue his campaign of dissent. Riva Palacio died in Spain in 1896.[5]

As a novelist, Riva Palacio looked to Mexico's past in order to find a way forward to Mexico's future. From the late 1860s, his writing took a historical turn. He composed a series of historical novels based on sources he'd obtained from the Mexican Catholic Church. Many of these sources came to Riva Palacio through government channels. Beginning in the 1850s, Benito Juárez oversaw a project of secularization whereby the church had to give up property and influence, as well as the materials found in their archives. Riva Palacio obtained some seventy volumes of records created by the Mexican Inquisition. In them he found material for his most celebrated novels: *Monja y casada, vírgen y mártir* (1868); *Martín Garatuza* (1868); and *Las dos emparedadas* (1869).[6] Riva Palacio wrote:

> You may ask, dear reader, why I speak in the majority of my novels of the Inquisition? I would respond, that in the entirety of the epoch of Spanish domination in Mexico, the novelist or the historian cannot take the slightest step, without encountering the Holy Tribunal, that it encompassed everything and invaded everything; and if it causes displeasure to find it in a novel, would it not have caused the same in those who lived in those times, encountering the Holy Office at each and every step of their life, from the cradle to the grave, from the memory of their antecedents to the future of their most remote generation?[7]

To avoid a dark future in Mexico, according to Riva Palacio, one ruled by obscurantism and superstition, meant exposing the Inquisition as Mexico's bête noire, an obstacle to progress and freedom, in Mexico's colonial past.

The subjects of Riva Palacio's novels were lifted from actual court proceedings and processes found in the Inquisition files. He wrote about real people, but set them in fictional plots. As with the historical novels of nineteenth-century Europe, Riva Palacio used fiction to tell the truth about Mexico's colonial tragedies. He sought, like Jules Verne, Cyrano de Bergerac, Walter Scott, and Alexandre Dumas to "popularize scientific knowledge, avoiding the pitfalls of the fastidious."[8] He could reach more people if his stories entertained as well as informed. People read fiction, and, like many nineteenth-century writers, Riva Palacio believed that history was prone to just as many half truths as novels. Novels could reach into the soul, expose the interior world of the emotions, which were just as real as, and in many ways more real than, a strict recitation of facts.

Novels in the romantic tradition evoked the truth of feeling, and feeling could move people to action where dry, dusty tomes could not. He wanted readers to be captured by the way his protagonists had constantly faced resistance to knowledge. They were persecuted for it. He told, for instance, the story of Martín Garatuza, a trickster and charlatan who disguised himself as a priest in order to gain prestige, money, and power. Garatuza was a real individual, who faced trial by the Inquisition in the seventeenth century. But under Riva Palacio's pen he became a picaresque character who managed to outwit the Inquisition through pluck and derring-do.[9] Martín Garatuza, writes Riva Palacio in the novel of the same name, "displayed all the sagacity of the she-fox."[10] (*El zorro* is the Spanish word for "fox," and Riva Palacio referred to Martín Garatuza by the name—although in the feminine form, *zorra*.) Garatuza also took on the alter ego of a priest. Perhaps there is something of Garatuza in Johnston McCulley's Zorro?

If the name and the alter ego were present in Riva Palacio's novel *Martín Garatuza*, the other elements of Zorro were missing. But then it happened: Riva Palacio finally found his Irishman, whom he had been looking for since his youth. And when he found the Irishman, he found a character that seems very Zorro-like to the modern reader. "I was looking for I don't know what," Riva Palacio recalled, but "ready like the astronomer who while viewing the heavens sees a shooting star, when I encountered a very voluminous case mounted against D. Guillén de Lampart, for being an astrologer, seditious, a heretic, etc., etc."[11]

Riva Palacio devoured the Inquisition documents. It was the Irishman he'd heard about as a child in school—he had found him. Don Guillén's story, the actual historical documents, had so much of the novelesque already in it: "The well plotted and well executed romantic escapes told by the French novelists," noted Riva Palacio.[12] Don Guillén, he felt, was Mexico's *The Count of Monte Cristo* and *The Three Musketeers* all in one. Riva Palacio set out to tell Don Guillén's story that way, as a romantic adventure, but one written to tell of the perennial battle between the forces of superstition and tradition and the forces of light and knowledge. In Don Guillén we see Edmond Dantès betrayed and imprisoned for long years; we see the swashbuckling D'Artagnan in Don Guillén's brisk readiness, with his skilled swordsmanship.

Under Riva Palacio's pen, William Lamport, the Irishman, became Don Guillén de Lampart—a man of many disguises, masquerading as a wealthy creole by day and a hero who participates in a conspiracy to overthrow colonialism by night. He's adept with the sword, but also writes poems. Riva Palacio made Don Guillén love not just one woman but four, which ultimately becomes his undoing as one of the spurned women denounces him to the Inquisition. Don Guillén's best friend is named Diego—and Zorro's alter ego is, of course, Diego; together the two friends form part of a secret society devoted to knowledge and freedom very much reminiscent of the Freemasons. They're called the Order of the Sun in Riva Palacio's novel. Riva Palacio was himself a Freemason, as were many of Mexico's political and literary liberals.

Riva Palacio created the enduring image of William Lamport, always called Don Guillén in his novel—and always, *Lampart*, with an *a*, instead of *Lamport*, with an *o*. Don Guillén has knowledge and wisdom. He knows languages, thirsts for scientific progress, and longs for freedom from Spain's yoke. Bits and pieces of this Don Guillén are present in the historical William Lamport. But the Don Guillén of Riva Palacio's creation looks more like Riva Palacio than the actual seventeenth-century Irishman. Riva Palacio was an army general and a man of letters, a Freemason, a man who criticized the Mexican political establishment. The Don Guillén of his making could've passed as a late nineteenth-century liberal, but one set in Mexico's colonial past. By nature, Don Guillén exists in the novel as a forerunner, a precursor, because Riva Palacio's Don Guillén was something of an anachronism. For all of William Lamport's radicalism, he belonged to his own time and wouldn't have had the same sensibilities as Riva Palacio. But Riva Palacio depicted him that way, nonetheless.

The image stuck. At the turn of the twentieth century, as Mexicans considered the one hundredth anniversary of independence, they looked to Riva Palacio's portrait of Don Guillén for inspiration.[13] Don Guillén became a hero—the first to proclaim independence from Spain, but a man before his time, and therefore a template of a man willing to die for the values twentieth-century Mexicans held dear. This Don Guillén, very much the man of Riva Palacio's imagination, would be added as a gatekeeper to the pantheon of national heroes at the centenary celebration of 1910 and, thereafter, added to the mausoleum under the Angel of Independence monument. His bodily remains were absent, of course, though his independent spirit was captured in marbled defiance.[14]

Vicente Riva Palacio is the *somehow* between William Lamport, the heretic burned in 1659, and Don Guillén de Lampart, statue and symbol of the longing for the daybreak of Mexican independence that pervaded even the darkest hours of the colonial night. But is Don Guillén—the Don Guillén created by Riva Palacio—also the inspiration for Zorro?

———————

I watched Mexico City traffic clutter and snarl around the monument. Many of the apparent similarities between Lamport and Zorro are generic. Don Guillén is a swordsman, he leads a double life, he has a certain success with women. But these elements are basic tropes of many adventure novels.

My doubts increased about the connection between Lamport and Zorro. What about the time and place discrepancy between Don Guillén—seventeenth-century Mexico City—and Zorro of Spanish California around the year 1800? There's no evidence McCulley even read Riva Palacio. There's no evidence McCulley, born in Illinois, ever visited Mexico or that he knew Spanish, except for the few words he sprinkled throughout his novels. And here's the kicker: the novel by Riva Palacio has never been translated into English and was not widely available in the United States at the time McCulley was writing his first Zorro stories. For McCulley to use the Irishman as inspiration for Zorro, he probably needed to actually know about the real Lamport. It's not at all likely that he did.

The theory put forward by Italian historian Fabio Troncarelli is that McCulley must have read about Lamport because both Riva Palacio and McCulley were Freemasons.[15] This, according to Troncarelli, is the *somehow* between Don Guillén of the independence statue and Zorro. McCulley, I found out, was indeed a member of a Colorado Springs Lodge, but he joined the Freemasons in 1925—after he'd already written *The Curse of Capistrano*.[16]

As I sat on the monument steps, Troncarelli's theory would have me play the role of Robert Langdon in Dan Brown's *The Da Vinci Code*—searching for hidden masonic symbols within McCulley's Zorro stories. I realized I forgot to look for any symbols on the statue of Don Guillén. Troncarelli argues that Zorro's trademark *Z* is actually a masonic symbol of enlightenment. This, as Troncarelli's argument goes, is the link between Don Guillén's thirst for scientific knowledge and Zorro's crusade to put right the wrongs of Old California. Zorro isn't just leaving a calling card, he's heralding a new order through his mark. It's an interesting theory, I admit. I really want to believe it. It would make a good movie.

But what if there's an easier explanation for the similarities between Lamport—especially Riva Palacio's Lamport—and McCulley's Zorro than the Freemason theory?

Occam's razor—the simplest answer is often correct. It occurred to me Riva Palacio actually does describe some of his influences in crafting Lamport: French and English adventure novels. In other words, part of the reason why Lamport and Zorro appear so similar is because both Riva Palacio, who romanticized Lamport using adventure novel tropes, and McCulley, who also read nineteenth-century adventure novels, were both reading from the same script.

In the 1800s, British and French novelists were writing romantic tales with swashbuckling heroes—tales of cape and sword. We could list, among these tales, Sir Walter Scott's *Waverley* (1814), *Rob Roy* (1817), and *Ivanhoe* (1819). In France, we find Alexandre Dumas and his *The Three Musketeers* (1844) and the sequels. Also, Dumas's own *The Count of Monte Cristo* (1844) provides an important prototype for a hero who has to masquerade as someone he's not in order to exact revenge on his enemies. None of these characters have superhuman powers. But they do have extraordinary skills, and they often have to carry out their schemes for justice in secret, and there's always an element of derring-do about them.

A recent book by Tom Reiss, *The Black Count*, describes the real-life adventures of Thomas-Alexandre Davy de La Pailleterie, the father of the famous novelist Alexandre Dumas. Thomas-Alexandre was born in France's Caribbean slave colonies and was the child of a white planter father and a black mother. Remarkably, Thomas-Alexandre emigrated to France and rose in the French revolutionary army. He was hailed for his remarkable sword skills, his intimidating physique, and his "superhuman" ability to lift a horse off its feet with just his powerful legs. Reiss argues, in the book, that Thomas-Alexandre inspired his son's most famous novels and provided the template for *The Count of Monte Cristo*. Napoleon, apparently, envied Thomas-Alexandre and left him to rot in a dungeon in Italy after the Egyptian campaign—a plot that sounds a lot like the Monte Cristo novel written by Alexandre Dumas. Reiss notes:

> In *The Count of Monte Cristo*, Dumas would give his betrayed pro-
> tagonist not only the fate of his father's final years but also a fictional
> taste of a dark sort of triumph. In the novel's hero you can see the
> premise of every modern thriller from Batman comics to *The Bourne
> Identity*. No other adventure novel of the nineteenth century carries
> its resonance. After escaping the dungeon and securing the treasure of
> Monte Cristo, Dantes builds a luxurious subterranean hideout in the
> caves of the island. He becomes master of all styles of combat, though
> he mainly uses his mind to defeat his enemies, bending the law and
> other institutions to his superhuman will. Knowing that the world is
> violent and corrupt, the Count becomes master of violence and cor-
> ruption—all with the goal of helping the weakest and most victimized
> people of all. The Count is the first fictional hero to announce himself
> as a "superman," anticipating Nietzsche—not to mention the birth
> of comics—by many years.[17]

Riva Palacio and McCulley both drew from Dumas, in other words. It's not that Riva Palacio influenced McCulley. They seem so similar because they both took elements from Dumas.

And perhaps there's good reason to look for elements of Zorro, especially Zorro's diverse origins, in Dumas's *Count of Monte Cristo*. Any discussion of Zorro, or America's first superhero, should probably start with this novel, based on the real-life adventures and tragedies of the novelist's father. And note: the first character to describe himself as a "superman" was created by a writer of mixed heritage, one who had to constantly battle racist reviews because of his Afro-Caribbean background. Even nineteenth-century adventure novels set in Europe, and written by European writers, owe an unacknowledged debt to diversity. It's true that Lamport became a Mexican icon of independence, which brings Lamport closer to Zorro. But, a character like Joaquín Murrieta, whose life and legend actually took place in California, where Zorro also was set, seems like a simpler explanation than does trying to explain why or how McCulley transferred the story of Lamport to California. It just doesn't really make sense.

The basic fact is that there's no evidence that McCulley read Riva Palacio, but both men did read Alexandre Dumas. What I needed to find out was whether McCulley would've been exposed to the legend surrounding Joaquín Murrieta.

As I collected my things, as I made my way from the monument and into the heart of the city, I felt I'd done my due diligence with Lamport. His story became important for Mexican independence—there was a Mexican element to it, but not really a Mexican American aspect. And Zorro's Latinx origins were part of the history of the United States. McCulley didn't read Riva Palacio. And McCulley had other models to draw from in crafting Zorro. Essentially, if Lamport is taken out of the equation, we still arrive at Zorro.

For instance, besides Dumas, there are also several other literary models that are clearly visible in Zorro and in the American superhero. One early precursor was birthed in penny dreadful publications in England. (Penny dreadfuls were so called because of their price and their content, like America's later pulp fiction.) The penny dreadful character Spring-Heeled Jack appeared in 1837. He was an urban legend, a frightful character described as diabolical, with clawed hands and eyes of burning fire.[18] He was known for his extraordinary leaps and ability to jump—from which came the "spring-heeled" sobriquet. But he could also appear as a gentleman, alluding to the importance of disguise. But Jack was a villain, a terror. He wasn't known for Robin Hood–style adventures. He looks a lot like Batman, really.

The next precursor is *The Scarlet Pimpernel*, first a stage play (1903) and then a novel (1905), by Baroness Emmuska Orczy. The novel's protagonist is Sir Percy Blakeney, a foppish British aristocrat who uses various disguises to save French aristocrats from the guillotine in the era of the French Revolution. Blakeney is the first millionaire-by-day and hero-by-night sort of character.

Masquerading as the Scarlet Pimpernel, a name that comes from a particular flower left as his calling card, Blakeney disguises himself as an old woman, as well as a *Merchant of Venice*–style Shylock character, in order to throw off the cunning French inspector on his trail. (Note the heavy anti-Semitic theme in Orczy's story.)[19] The Scarlet Pimpernel uses his wits, not any cunning swordplay, to beat his enemies. The novel is told from the perspective of Blakeney's French wife, who believes her husband is a huge wimp. Eventually, the Scarlet Pimpernel saves his wife and her brother from arrest and the guillotine, and the world is put to rights.

There's a lot of the Scarlet Pimpernel in Zorro. In 1919, Johnston McCulley wrote the first serialized novel with the character Zorro—the "fox." McCulley's Zorro clearly pulled from Dumas's and Orczy's creations—the larger-than-life hero, the disguise—but McCulley's Zorro did something different, something new, that arguably set the blueprint for the superhero genre.

First, Zorro had an identifiable disguise that he always wore: the mask, the cape, the black outfit, the hat, the sword, the whip. He rode a black horse called Tornado, which is basically the model for Batman's black Batmobile.

Second, Zorro had a manservant, Bernardo, who knew of Zorro's identity and aided him in his adventures. Bernardo becomes the other half of the first "dynamic duo," as well as a literary device whereby the hero is able to narrate his thoughts to the reader through exposition to his sidekick.

Third, Zorro's alter ego as Don Diego de la Vega provides a more thoroughly dual identity. The Scarlet Pimpernel's alter ego comprises many different disguises—an old woman, for example. But Zorro has a costume! He's Zorro when he puts on a certain identifiable outfit. Zorro is much closer to the costumed superheroes of the comic books than is the Scarlet Pimpernel.

Fourth, Zorro exists in the geography of the New World, in California of the Spanish era, and sometimes in the era of Mexican California (c. 1821–1846). He's the first hero, with a mask and a dual identity, who has his adventures in America. *The Count of Monte Cristo* and *The Scarlet Pimpernel* both operate in Europe.

Fifth, Zorro's influence can be seen in later comics characters: the Shadow, Batman, the Green Hornet, etc. The cocreator of Batman, Bob Kane, always pointed to Zorro as one of his inspirations. Kane's testimony articulates that Zorro played a large role in his ideas about Batman.[20]

Zorro should be considered among America's first superheroes. He laid an important template for later comic book heroes, and he was uniquely "American" in his origin. And, despite the European connection via Dumas or Orczy, Zorro also owes a debt to Latinx culture. That's what the next part of my journey would be about. I decided to go to the desert to find the birthplace, a thousand miles to the north of Mexico City, of Joaquín Murrieta, a Mexican bandit known as an outlaw to Americans but called a patriot by his countrymen. Joaquín Murrieta, not Lamport, was the missing element to Zorro that has been left out of the history of the character. If I could show that—if I could unmask that fact—then I could demonstrate that the American superhero, too, owes an unacknowledged debt to Latinx history.

4 | WELCOME TO THE HOTEL ZORRO!

THE POOLSIDE PATIO LIGHTS dimmed as I sipped at my Don Julio Blanco.[1]

I decided to stop here on my way to find the birthplace of Joaquín Murrieta. *The show's about to begin.*

There were about forty of us sitting at tables that skirted the blue waters of the pool. Cabana thatch shaded the last rays of dusk. We ate river lobster and fresh fish from the nearby Río Fuerte. We were tourists. From Venezuela. From all over Mexico. Some Canadians. Recently retired schoolteachers from Mexico City tittered and laughed at one table.

And then there was me. I'd been on a road trip through Mexico, searching for the Mexican origins of Zorro. It had brought me here, to El Fuerte, a little colonial town in the northwest state of Sinaloa, and to the Posada del Hidalgo Hotel. Its main attraction is Zorro.

Don Diego de la Vega, Zorro's alter ego, was born in this very hotel—well, before it was this hotel, but you get the point—according to the legend being promoted. (It's even fully written out on one wall, this legend.) You can stay in the room of Zorro's birth. (It was booked. I got the Governor's Suite.) At night, as the legend goes, you can hear the defiant cackles of *el Zorro*, the fox, the famed bandit hero of El Camino Real. His spirit (conveniently enough for the Balderrama Hotel chain, which owns Posada del Hidalgo) has returned to the place where he first drew breath.

I love this place.

The rest of the Don Julio went down in one long, delicious pull.

Lights flickered. Rumbles came from an overwhelmed speaker system. Fuzz and feedback. Simulated lighting and thunder. A strong flamenco guitar sounded its opening *thrumb-thrumb*, all open E chord.

Ah, sweet pathos, I thought. *It's everything you want in music, booze, and romance.*

A haughty laugh came from somewhere in the shadows of the now-darkened poolside patio.

It's Zorro, it's Zorro! excited looks passing between tourists seem to say.

And then the kicker. A thin layer of stage fog filled the poolside. (*Stage fog! I know, right?!*) I almost fainted.

Out of the shadows and the smoke came the caped avenger, Spanish rapier in hand. There, the flat-rimmed gaucho hat; there, the mask, the disguise tied around flashing eyes; there, the pencil-thin mustache! Another haughty laugh escaped as *el Zorro* ran the length of the pool. He stood, now, in full power pose. Hands on hips—very pelvis forward, I should add—chest puffed, head cocked back in mirth, abandon, mischief, and . . . *dare I say it? I was really feeling that moment* . . . pure goddamn sex appeal.

The stage smoke wisped away, the music faded, and all eyes were riveted on this man.

Listen up, pinches gringos! I told myself, *this is the* REAL *Zorro!*

This might be a good spot to point out that Don Diego de la Vega was not actually a historical person. I mean, did someone born in El Fuerte have a name that combined Diego and de la Vega? Perhaps, yes. It's a common Spanish name. But what I mean—and what I was trying to ponder as *el Zorro* stood in front of us like some mythic archetype of beauty, sex, and death—is that no historians actually believe or have argued that Diego de la Vega was a real dude. But that's exactly what the hotel is, indeed, arguing.

Diego de la Vega is literally a character of fiction. Whatever potential inspirations for Zorro there may be in the desert of Sonora, where Joaquín Murrieta was supposedly born, Zorro first appeared as a character in 1919. But the hotel has created a so-called *real* backstory for Diego de la Vega. He was born in 1795, the hotel's promotional pamphlet tells us. (It's in Spanish and English.) He was born in a room in the Casa Vieja, the old part of the building structure, which was later remodeled and expanded into the hotel we were now in, this minute, watching *el Zorro* stand backlit with concert fog. It would be as if the owner of a New York hotel decided Bruce Wayne, Batman's alter ego, was actually a real guy and said, *Yup, Bruce Wayne was born here, and we own his ass!* And then, added to this, there was not even a hint of irony anywhere at the Posada del Hidalgo. No winks. No nods. Just pure credulity.

Ok, I thought, *I can dig it—that just adds to the charm!* Did I say I really loved this place?

The historian in me wanted to know how all this happened. I was honestly curious and, of course, really entertained, but I was trying to wrap my head around it. I tried a really long *how* question: *How* did an American pop culture / pulp fiction star (Zorro, that is) become a comic book character, then a TV show icon, then a late-'90s movie reboot (true, with a nod to Hispanic heritage in Antonio Banderas)—but all, in the main, examples of classic cultural appropriation—then get reintroduced in Mexico, sold as a hotel attraction, packaged as authentic history, and then promoted back to tourists who first became aware of Zorro by the aforesaid media cultural appropriation bonanza?

I was severely out of breath, and I really had no clue. But as Zorro stood before us, I decided to do some investigating. Because this *Mexican* Zorro strutting here was real. He had a sword and a debonair mustache, and he was not going away.

Later, after the Zorro show, I would search the Zorro hotel, feeling slightly devious in doing so. *Does someone know that I know that Zorro wasn't actually born here?* There's a wall covered in historical documents, I'd find out. Like, completely covered. Some docs are from the sixteenth century, describing the original settlers to El Fuerte. Some are documents from the early 1900s, listing all the workers who helped build the structure that has become the hotel. There are some old newspapers as well. Nothing historically verifies the legend purported by the hotel—that Don Diego de la Vega was born here. I suspect the wall of documents is supposed to add an aura of historical authenticity. It's a nice touch, but really proves nothing.

Later, I would discover the prime mover of the whole thing: the hotelier Roberto Balderrama Gómez. His family has been an institution in Sinaloa for one hundred years. I would find a photo of the family patriarch, Próspero Balderrama. Roberto, one of his sons, inherited his father's enterprises and expanded them into a chain of six hotels. In the 1990s, Roberto received a national tourism prize from the Mexican president.[2] In 2008 *el Zorro* was named the emblem and symbol of El Fuerte. It was all thanks to Roberto, his savvy marketing, and his desire to make sure El Fuerte stayed on the touristic map. In one 2008 newspaper article framed on the wall, a local businessperson says: "I plan to go to the hotel soon to get information so I can orient tourists better, as right now I don't have Zorro merchandise, but it really interests me to sell it and to learn about our history so we can educate our visitors."[3]

I would be struck, later, with sheer wonder thinking about how no one questioned the Zorro backstory. Local businesspeople, the town mayor, employees, guests—everyone wanted to believe Zorro was born in El Fuerte. And it made sense. I couldn't blame them. Why shouldn't Zorro be owned by this little colonial town of El Fuerte, instead of a media outlet in the United States? Or why shouldn't Zorro be the secret identity of a Mexican hotel employee instead of the product of an Anglo-American pulp fiction writer?

As Zorro strutted before us poolside, however, it felt like justice. *Zorro is Mexican!*

Our Zorro began to speak. He had one of those nifty headset mics so his voice carried. He told us the legend, that Zorro was born in this very hotel. His mother died when Dieguito was just ten years old. Diego's father, Alejandro de la Vega, moved with his son to Alta California. Years later, the citizens of El Fuerte heard of the exploits of *el Zorro* in California, never knowing that their native son was the one fighting for justice in the land to the north. But now, as our Zorro told us poolside, this history had become known *by an unknown chronicler!*

Who this unknown chronicler is, I'll never be able to uncover, I mused. Was it Roberto Balderrama himself?

Before ending his speech, our Zorro commented: "The man in the mask represents all those who work in this hotel and the working person of Mexico." I was taken off guard by the statement. He was self-consciously using Zorro as a symbol for justice in Mexico.

I really love this friggin' place.

As the show ended, the man playing Zorro began to take pictures with the audience. He flirted with the retired schoolteachers. I, too, took a picture with Zorro.

And then it was over. People returned to their drinks, to their rooms, to the pleasant evening that stretched over El Fuerte. Me and my buddy who was traveling with me had to move our Sprinter van. We wanted to find secure parking, so we asked the nice woman at the front desk, and she called an attendant. A man appeared dressed in his hotel uniform. Unruffled, and with pencil-thin mustache, the attendant helped us move our van. It was totally the guy who played Zorro at the show. He didn't let on at all that it was him. I wanted to say something, some acknowledgment of his absolutely baller performance as Zorro—that I was glad he'd taken Zorro back from the gringos, made the symbol his own. But the moment passed.

Ten minutes later, outside, we saw him, Zorro, the hotel employee, leaving work for the evening. I called to get his attention.

"You know, it's weird," I told him. He looked at me puzzled. "When Zorro appeared at the show," I told him, "I didn't see you. You were nowhere to be found."

He smiled. He realized the pencil-thin mustache gave him away. He stood for a moment in the same power pose. He spun on his heels, laughed, and walked off toward his early 2000s Nissan Sentra. Another day of work done. He was headed home.

Zorro, in the flesh.

5 | BACK TO THE DESERT

Research Log #2
Sonoran Desert
10:01 AM

ZORRO'S ORIGINS STARTED HERE. There was no guarantee, but hope moved me forward.

It was high desert and hot—115 degrees and baking. The kind of shimmering heat that lifts wavy lines off the highway's asphalt. Mirage-inducing heat. The AC in our Sprinter van was at full blast, but beads of sweat still formed on my forehead. I'd taken to carrying a handkerchief to minimize the drip.

This was the landscape that I imagined Zorro riding in. My flights of imagination always pushed me back toward a lone rider barreling straight for me, but then going on past before I lost him in the distance. I didn't imagine that Zorro's origins might actually be in the landscape of my fantasy. Northern Mexico. Sonora.

I'd left William Lamport behind in Mexico City. The Irish Zorro was no Zorro at all. I'd taken a detour at the Hotel Zorro, and now I was tracking down another lead. In the course of my research, another name continued to come up: Joaquín Murrieta.

Three months earlier, I was sifting through e-mail. Most of it junk. But then an e-mail came from a traveling music theater group. A production called *Los Valientes*, or *The Courageous Ones*, in English. It celebrated the lives and legacies of three Latin American men: First, Oscar Romero, the assassinated archbishop of San Salvador. Romero stood up to the military dictatorship in El Salvador and was killed for it while saying mass. He was made a saint by Pope Francis. Second, Diego Rivera, famed Mexican muralist, radical, and artist who represented the "new Mexico" in the wake of the 1910 revolution. And third, Joaquín Murrieta. The publicity statement said this: "Los Valientes is a live music theatre work based on the lives of three legendary Latinos: Mexican painter Diego Rivera, martyred Archbishop Oscar Romero, and Mexican-American outlaw Joaquín Murrieta—some say the Zorro character was based on this historical figure." The publicity for *Los Valientes* almost took it as given. Murrieta as Zorro. I began rapidly looking for any and all research I could find on Murrieta.

Did everyone else believe Murrieta was Zorro?

I soon discovered there were far more people who mentioned the link between Murrieta and Zorro than mentioned the one between William Lamport and Zorro. And that made sense from a geographical perspective. Zorro's world was Southern California, the same for Murrieta. But I found that Murrieta himself was a ghost. His life and origins appeared just as murky, just as obscure, as the origins of Zorro.

Damn, I remember thinking. *I'm looking for one ghost to find another.*

Usually, when cited by authors, the link between Murrieta and Zorro was really vague: Joaquín Murrieta, the California bandit, *who some say* was the real-life inspiration for Zorro . . . Or, *scholars say* . . . Or, *tradition has it that* . . .[1] Little to no citations provided a concrete link from Murrieta to Zorro. And yet, Murrieta kept being tenuously linked to Zorro. The Murrieta possibility brought me to the desert to try to find out for myself.

I looked out the window of the Sprinter van—"Vandit," my buddy dubbed his multipassenger vehicle. The landscape seemed empty of people. There were no houses, no towns, nothing but tall cactus and hills in the distance.

The best resources on Murrieta pointed me to a little town called Trincheras in the northern Mexican state of Sonora. It hardly shows up on the map. Caborca, a larger city, lies about an hour northwest of Trincheras. I was following the Trincheras lead provided in a book written by a now-dead amateur historian named Frank Latta. Latta was obsessed with finding the real Murrieta.[2] He sifted through a hundred years of lore and legends surrounding the career of the California desperado, who lived from 1830 to 1853. But even

Murrieta's date of birth is not agreed upon. Latta read newspaper accounts, which were often sensationalized. Many of them appeared to conflate Murrieta with four other bandits named Joaquín at the time, as well as another noted outlaw, Three-Fingered Jack.

Latta persisted. He read what was available on Murrieta at the California State Archives—the mustering of, and reports on, the California Rangers; a few letters from Captain Harry S. Love, the leader of the troop sent to capture Murrieta; and affidavit after affidavit of individuals who swore under oath that they recognized a decapitated head put in a pickling jar filled with whiskey as belonging to Joaquín Murrieta. Captain Love had reportedly caught the Joaquín Band, as it was known, and killed Joaquín. To collect the bounty on Murrieta, Captain Love had Murrieta's head lopped off and placed in the jar. Captain Love wanted to collect his bounty, and the head in the jar was proof, backed up by a dozen affidavits.

Frank Latta visited the sites of Murrieta's career, including where Murrieta supposedly died at the hands of California Rangers in 1853.[3] (Even that was disputed by Latta as he interviewed descendants of Murrieta's family who said Murrieta escaped and went to Texas, where he lived the rest of his days.) Latta's research led him to Murrieta's origins in Trincheras, Mexico. In 1936, Latta drove in a Model T Ford across the US-Mexico border and into the heart of the baking-hot desert—the one I was driving through.

Latta followed rumors of Murrieta's living relatives still residing in northern Mexico. He decided to try to meet them. His lead was that a tiny, now no-longer-existing settlement just north of Trincheras still contained traces of the man who had left northern Mexico with his fiancée to find his fortune in California. Latta met dozens of people, including ones who echoed the report that Murrieta had fled to Texas. Many of the townspeople had the surname Murrieta. They all told him plainly: Yes, Murrieta, el famoso, the famous Joaquín, was born here. But no, they told Latta, Murrieta wasn't a bandit. They said he was el patrio—the patriot.[4]

Latta amassed hundreds of pages, stories, interviews. He returned to Trincheras in the 1970s and found that the old generation had died. But younger members of the Murrieta clan still held on to the memory. Latta self-published his research in a seven-hundred-page tome called Joaquín Murrieta and His Horse Gangs. Three years after publishing what amounted to his life's work, Latta died.

I'd come to see if there was still memory of Murrieta in Trincheras. Our Sprinter van pulled off Caborca / México Highway 2 and the safety of a marked road. We drove on. A paved narrow road met us; to the left and right were low-branched and stunted Sonoran desert scrub. A cloudless sky. Ahead in the distance was Cerro de Trincheras, a major archeological site. People have lived here for thousands of years. Trincheras was founded in 1775 as a kind of Spanish fortification that linked this land to settlements stretching all the way to San Francisco, California. It was all part of Spanish Mexico; then, after 1821 and independence, part of the new Mexican Republic. It was only in 1850 that Alta California officially became part of the United States. And then the Mexicans who had once migrated freely between northwest Sonora and the fertile San Fernando Valley, over five hundred miles to the north, were cut off—"strangers in their own land," according to one historian of the era.[5]

All this went through my head as I disentangled from my thoughts. And I almost missed it: out my window, off the road, was a kind of raised, paved gazebo, but thirty feet wide and fifty feet long. A minute after we passed it, Jason, my traveling companion, looked at me.

"Should we go back?"

"Yeah," I said. "We'd better."

We reversed course and found a barbed-wire cattle fence around the gazebo site. There was a tiny votive chapel at the back.

What are we looking for?

There was a gap in the cattle fence, and I gingerly avoided the razor wire. I kicked up a cloud of dust and finally made it to the raised platform.

Then I saw it: a wide plinth with a plaque all the way in the back. I began a quick, excited trot toward it.

It came into view. It was in Spanish, of course, but I quickly translated:

District of Altar—Municipality of Trincheras
Historic Plaque
Here, in the now gone Villa de San Rafael del Alamito, Joaquín
Murrieta was born between the years 1824–1830. His parents
were Don Juan Murrieta and Doña Juana Orosco. He fought in
California against the North American troops who mutilated
Mexico. The Anglo-Saxons called him Robber and Assassin, but
Californians knew him simply as "The Patriot."

I looked above the plaque. My heart stopped. There, etched in black, not an official marking, surely, but made by some unknown hand, was a long letter Z. It looked like a graffiti version of the Zorro trademark.

Somebody, here in Trincheras, believes Joaquín Murrieta is Zorro.

But, I thought to myself, to make that link between Murrieta and Zorro, I had to know more about the story of *el patrio*, Joaquín Murrieta—the real Murrieta.

———————

I knew there was more to discover than just this plaque in the desert. I made my way down from the gazebo and carefully threaded my way through the razor wire. I climbed back into the Sprinter van and started driving toward Trincheras. It only took a few minutes to chug our way over hard-packed dusty dirt roads, crossing a dry riverbed, and then to reach the entrance of the small town. Another plaque about Murrieta—*el patrio*—greeted us as dirt road bled into paved street. A large three-foot-tall lettered sign that read TRINCHERAS confirmed our arrival. It was afternoon and hot and the plaza was empty.

As I shut off the engine, I thought of Chilean poet Pablo Neruda's admonition about Murrieta—"Whoever approaches the truth or legend of this bandit will feel the charismatic force of his gaze."[6] Neruda wrote a play about Murrieta in the 1970s. If Neruda had felt compelled to use Murrieta as muse, and confessed to having trouble writing his story, what hope was there for me? I shook off the thought and got out of the van. As Neruda's line kept cycling in my head, I tried to find someone to talk with. I walked into the municipal government building, which skirts the small, deserted central plaza.

A man sat in his darkened office. It was the guy's lunch break, so I realized he was pretty nice to talk to me.

"You wanna see Rogelio," the man told me.

"Rogelio?" I asked.

"*Sí*, Rogelio Marcial León Ruiz," he said. "The town historian. He's just down the way, in the building at the foot of Cerro de Trincheras. In the archaeological zone."

"That way?" I pointed to the only land formation with any elevation in the area.

"Yes, that way." He nodded.

He smiled at me and returned to his darkened office and what remained of lunch.

I sat in a sparsely furnished office at the archaeological site. There was a small museum outside the office documenting the earliest indigenous inhabitants of the region. I asked the person at the front desk for Rogelio León Ruiz, hoping I had remembered his name correctly. I told her, as an afterthought, that I was a historian, to add a note of legitimacy to the whole thing. She gave me a little grin and then went to find the man I was looking for. I realized as she left that I was wearing flip-flops, shorts, a Star Wars shirt, and a trucker hat turned backward. I took off my hat, but then put it on again.

Rogelio León Ruiz, a man of about forty-five, introduced himself. He didn't seem fazed by my Star Wars fanboy look. He had on jeans and a tucked-in button-up shirt. He seemed unsurprised when I told him I was researching Joaquín Murrieta. Joaquín is, after all, pretty famous around here. He ushered me into his office where I now sat trying to put together an impromptu interview. Outside the window I could see the desert scrub as it ascended to the top of the Cerro de Trincheras.

Rogelio, as he told me I should call him, explained that when he was around twenty-three the town designated him *"el cronista de Trincheras"*—the chronicler, or town historian, for Trincheras. The town had a long memory, and Rogelio was one of the keepers of it.

He laughed. He said he always liked history but never figured he'd have a profession devoted to it—let alone be the guy tapped to preserve the history of the region. I asked about Murrieta.

"Yes," he said, "there are many people in the area with the surname Murrieta." He pointed me to a book, written by a Mexican historian named Manuel Rojas.[7] I later discovered that Rojas and Frank Latta, the American amateur historian who did scores of interviews in this region from the 1930s to the

'70s, are the two researchers who have best documented the oral memories of
Murrieta in and around Trincheras.

Oral history often doesn't match written documents. Memory is a record
of evolving identity, not always a replica of the past. And so, the first thing
I learned from Rogelio Ruiz, the town historian, was that the memories of
Murrieta in Trincheras are family memories. It's the history of aunts, uncles,
cousins, mothers, brothers, and fathers. Family lore is complicated. Thus, the
second thing I learned in Rogelio's office was some basic caution. Finding the
"real Murrieta" was not really my project. It was a fool's errand, really.

I decided to unlock myself from the charismatic gaze of Murrieta and
focus on how Murrieta's legend helped give birth to Zorro—how, in other
words, Murrieta's legend is a carrier of the very real experience of Mexicans
and Mexican Americans in California, and how that history became the building blocks for Zorro. I remembered another quote from Neruda's *Splendor
and Death of Joaquín Murieta*. The bandit, wrote Neruda, "took to the road
of my book and galloped off with his life and drama."[8] It was tantalizing, I've
got to admit, to follow the trail of Murrieta. But I was searching for another
highwayman in black. I listened to Rogelio Ruiz as he told me more about the
memories with which he had been entrusted.

6 | MEXICAN ARGONAUT

FROM THE BEGINNING, Joaquín Murrieta was the stuff of legend. Many books have been written about the life and death of the famous bandit. Some go to great lengths to prove—with unearthed documents, with razor-sharp historical reasoning, and sometimes with pure I-really-want-this passion—that Joaquín Murrieta was a unique, single, identifiable human being. *Look,* they say, *I found this certificate of baptism that includes a Joaquín Murrieta.* Or, *Here's an early newspaper account from California that mentions a Joaquín "Muliati"—certainly this refers to a phonetic rendering of "Murrieta" by a gringo newspaperman who didn't know Spanish. See,* these sorts of books seem to say, *Joaquín Murrieta was a real boy!* in full Geppetto enthusiasm. The book in Rogelio's office, by Manuel Rojas, is one of these sorts of books. It sets out to prove that Murrieta was a real guy who was from Trincheras. And there's a lot of merit to it. It's just really hard to know whether it's all true.

Because, for instance, there are other books that take the opposite approach. These are the hard-boiled histories, many written by mid-twentieth-century skeptics, jaundiced and world-weary, that have no faith in the veracity of Murrieta as a single, verifiable human life. *See, sweetheart,* I imagine these authors saying in their best Sam Spade–affected accent, *Joaquín Murrieta is just fiction, just a literary MacGuffin, the stuff that dreams are made of.* Writers like Joseph Henry Jackson, a preeminent California literary critic, fit this category.[1] In 1944, in the era of Sam Spade and hard-boiled detectives, Jackson argued that Joaquín Murieta (note the spelling with one *r*) was only picked out as someone real—picked out from among the many Joaquíns in the California press at

35

the time—by John Rollin Ridge's 1854 novelization of Joaquín's life. "But it was Ridge's *Life* of that outlaw," Jackson wrote, "as preposterous a fiction as any the Dime Libraries ever invented, that sent this vague bandit on his way to be written into the California histories, sensationalized in magazine pieces and books in several languages, and eventually to be made the subject of a 'biography' which was brought to the motion-picture screen." Californians had a dearth of heroes. "California badly needed a folk hero," Jackson reasoned, "and had none."[2] Joaquín Murrieta filled that gap. Murrieta, then, wasn't a real boy, but his story is really important.

He's got a point. The story of William Lamport actually has more documents to back up his "real boy" status than does Murrieta's. Although closer to us in the present, Murrieta's documentary record is pretty spotty, and most of what we know about him comes not from Joaquín himself but from sensationalized newspapers and John Rollin Ridge's 1854 dime-novel-as-history. Yet Joseph Henry Jackson's point, one we should listen to, is that California needed a hero and Joaquín Murrieta fit that need.

California needed a hero that somehow spoke to the reality that some got rich and others stayed poor in the goldfields—that "gettin' rich" was often achieved through injustice, repression, and flat-out rascality. Jackson says that Joaquín "was the hero who sprang spontaneously to life whenever and wherever some people had much and others had nothing. He was, in every land, the man who took from the rich and gave to the poor." In one "Dashing Outlaw," then, we find all the "hidden defiances," the "private longings," the pure gumption to do something about it.[3] Joaquín Murrieta was the *Breaking Bad*-style Walter White of 1850s California—the guy who wasn't gonna take it anymore and who decided to give it back in equal measure. Murrieta was the antihero, and people dug that idea. They needed it. Whether Murrieta was real was another matter entirely. The Latinx people whose stories he represented were real.

Between the Pinocchio-real-boy school of thought, on one side, and the Sam Spade, Joaquín-is-the-stuff-that-dreams-are-made-of argument on the other, there is another option. There are always agnostics. Perhaps, these Murrieta agnostics argue, Joaquín Murrieta was real, but how do we *really* know? Too much time has passed and too many legends have been written about Joaquín for us to find the "real Joaquín." It's this third position that is important for our history of Zorro. Why? Because "legends," as one historian writes, "are a source text on which other stories are based."[4] Legends are the well of water we draw out of to quench our thirst for meaning in the here and now. Legends are used to confirm or critique the present, depending on the point of view of the storyteller. It will come as no surprise, then, that in the hands of predominantly Anglo-American storytellers, the legend of Murrieta came to confirm the present—that American annexation brought liberty to California; that, if any wrongs were done, these were perpetrated by "bad apples," not the institutions of American government, law, or policy. And as the legend of Murrieta was a source text, a well of water from which to draw out other stories, Zorro continued the tradition of confirming the predominant story. Zorro rarely came to critique the myth of the West, one populated by noble pioneers, bad Indians, and grateful Mexican Americans.

So, even as the agnostics suggest that we can't really know if Murrieta was real, his story is a distillation of real experience. There were really Mexicans in California who suffered under the United States' annexation of California. There were really laws, official policies, that increased racial violence in the goldfields of the southern mines—really, too, recalcitrant, unyielding resisters to the whole show, and many of them took to banditry. Joaquín Murrieta is a better model for Zorro than is William Lamport. Murrieta represented the real-life history of California, its haves and have nots, the desire for an avenging hero to put right the injustice of the era; Murrieta's story was popular, retold, plagiarized, then repackaged to serve the needs of the present in California. Lamport's story was retold in Mexico City, but that's not where Murrieta became famous, and it's not where Zorro was born. The legend of Zorro, like the legend of Murrieta, begins in California under Spanish colonialism.

———————

More than one hundred years after William Lamport was burned at the stake in Mexico City, the Spanish colonial government was finally making plans to settle California. And it was at that time, in the mid-1700s, that the story of Joaquín Murrieta, and el Zorro, began.

It took the Spanish two hundred years, by the mid-1700s, to finally make headway through the mountains, through the deserts, and, most importantly, through the patchwork of indigenous empires that ruled what is today northern

Mexico, the American Southwest, and Alta (Upper) California.[5] It was a long slog indeed, for the Spanish.

But they made progress. A system of Catholic missions and presidios (forts), were established in the present-day Mexican states of Sinaloa, Sonora, and Chihuahua. El Fuerte, in fact, the town where I visited the Zorro hotel, was one such colonial outpost. Francisco de Ibarra, Spanish conquistador, founded El Fuerte in 1563. It served as a gateway to the northern territories, which were buffeted and endangered by Native raids. In 1772, Capitán Bernardo de Urrea, military comandante of the presidio in El Fuerte, was transferred, "for his services to the King of Spain," to the presidio under construction in Altar, Sonora.[6] That under-construction presidio was the first Spanish settlement in the community where I had talked to Rogelio Ruiz.

In 1804 a new military commander replaced Urrea in charge of Altar, and the population of Trincheras, not far from Altar, developed along with the now-disappeared settlement of San Rafael del Alamito. That new military commander—who founded San Rafael del Alamito, who developed several goldfields in the area, who discovered fertile lands in which to plant crops and good pastures in which to graze livestock, and who decided to stay—was named Capitán José María Murrieta. According to local memory, he was the grandfather of Joaquín Murrieta, el famoso—the famous Murrieta.

Trincheras has an authentic claim to Murrieta. There are actual records that back up his existence. The problem, for historians, is whether the real Murrieta of Trincheras was the same Joaquín who came to infamy in California. As Rogelio Ruiz, the town historian, related the memories of Trincheras, I became converted to, at the very least, a Murrieta agnostic.

As Capitán José María Murrieta settled into the area around Trincheras, Sonora, the Spanish Crown extended its reach into what was then called Alta California. Spain established a presence in California through Franciscan missionaries. Spain had European rivals in North America, including France, England, and czarist Russia. The French moved west from the Louisiana Territory, and so the Spanish put efforts into founding some missions and sparsely populated settlements in Spanish Texas. The English and the Russians took aim at the Pacific

Northwest, with the Russians especially eyeing potential colonization efforts in Alta California. This could not happen, according to the Spanish Crown, and therefore the Franciscans were called up from the bench, so to speak. Until then, the Spanish procedure of conquest consisted of a very uncomplicated threefold process: show up, claim it for Spain, and move on. But that was simply no longer enough, thought the Spanish Crown, given the increasingly fraught venture of colonial land grabbing.[7]

Many Zorro stories draw on this real-life history of colonial competition. Usually the plot involves some unscrupulous Spanish official conspiring with other European powers to weaken Spanish rule in Alta California. One of the early Zorro comics, in fact, "The Mask of Zorro" (*Dell Four Color* #538, March 1954), presents Zorro as a friend of the governor, ready to assist in foiling a Russian plot.

"We are threatened by the Bear that walks like a man!" says Zorro.

"No, Zorro, you must be mistaken!" the governor replies, dressed in a smoking jacket by his cozy fire in his study. "The strangers are only interested in trading and trapping!" the governor tells Zorro, who has appeared uninvited in his study.

"And perhaps one thing more," Zorro says as he takes off his mask.

"And what is that?"

"It might be the conquest of California!" Zorro says ominously as the reader cuts to another scene, discovering that, indeed, corrupt Spaniards are in league with the Russians to "destroy liberty by ripping aside the MASK of ZORRO."

Clearly the story of colonial competition was useful to Zorro writers in painting the Russians as enemies of liberty as far back as the days of Old California, just as they wanted to present them within in their own contemporary Cold War present. While the Russians never presented that great of a risk to the Spanish in California, the fictional portrayal is rooted in real history.

As with colonial competition, so with Franciscan friars. The Franciscans were a real presence in Alta California. And Johnston McCulley's Zorro stories describe the Franciscans, in characters like Fray Felipe, as defenders of the Indians and agents of civilization in Alta California. The history, of course, diverges from the fiction, but McCulley drew on the real history of Alta California in crafting the setting for his Zorro stories. "In charge of this hacienda was one Fray Felipe," writes McCulley in *The Curse of Capistrano*, "a member of the [Franciscan] order who was along in years, and under his discretion the neophytes made the estate a profitable one, raising much livestock and sending to the storehouses great amounts of hides and tallow and honey and fruit, as well as wine." Fray Felipe complains to Don Diego of his troubles with the military commanders of the region:

> It is but another instance of injustice. For twenty years we of the mis-
> sions have been subjected to it, and it grows. The sainted Junipero
> Serra invaded this land when other men feared, and at San Diego de
> Alcala he built the first mission of what became a chain, this giving
> an empire to the world. Our mistake was that we prospered. We did
> the work, and others reap the advantages. . . . They began taking
> our mission lands from us, lands we cultivated, which had formed
> a wilderness and which my brothers had turned into gardens and
> orchards. They robbed us of worldly goods. And not content with
> that, they now are persecuting us. The mission empire is doomed,
> *caballero*. The time is not far distant when mission roofs will fall in
> and the walls crumble away.[8]

Father Junípero Serra, OFM, was indeed the founder of a mission empire of sorts. A Franciscan priest, born on the Spanish island of Majorca in 1713, Serra was just the guy the Spanish Crown needed. He was certainly pious, taking his vows for the priesthood at the age of seventeen, but he was also smart, a good speaker, and—most importantly—born with an uncommon dose of indefatigability. By the age of thirty-one he was a university profes-sor. Yet, he wanted more. He managed to get his Franciscan superiors to send him to the New World. He spent the next twenty years preaching in the Mexican state of Querétaro, as well as teaching at the Franciscan college in Mexico City.

Junípero Serra was zealous, to say the least. He self-flagellated nightly in order to purify himself. Serra referred to himself as a "sinner" and a "most unworthy priest." "He wore sackcloth spiked with bristles," as one historian describes, "or a coat interwoven with broken pieces of wire, under his gray friar's outer garment."[9] To be fair, Serra wasn't the only fervent Catholic of his day to indulge in extreme self-mortification. But Serra was even reprimanded by his superiors for it. He was known to hold a crucifix in one hand while standing at the pulpit with a large stone in the other. To stress the importance of repentance, he'd smash the stone against his breast until he was out of breath and ready to faint.

Serra soon got his chance to take his missionary zeal to Alta California. The Spanish named him father president of the missionary efforts there. He set out north with five other Franciscan friars, including his most trusted friend and protégé, Father Francisco Palóu (1723–1789). Palóu kept a record of the journey and became Serra's first biographer. The friars had only one supply ship and two passenger ships. There were, in the caravan, soldiers, muleteers, and Native Americans from the missions in Baja California.

Father Palóu kept a journal of their arduous journey to what is now San Diego. "The blazing sun made the journey very painful," he wrote. "For the last four nights a roaring lion [puma] quite close by kept us awake," he noted at one point. "May God guard us from it, as He has till now."[10]

Serra quite literally hobbled into what the Spanish called San Diego de Alcalá. Serra limped along on a foot festering with a wound that almost killed him. Three hundred men had made the trip; only about half that number survived. Many of the Christian Natives from Baja California died along the way or had deserted. The soldiers denied them rations when supplies ran low. Some of the contingent died of scurvy.

Despite hardship, Serra erected a cross, celebrated mass, and made sure to get his records in order for the new Christian baptisms he knew he would soon record in his ledger. A few months later, however, with no baptisms yet inscribed, a group of Natives from the area attacked the small Spanish outpost. While Serra grabbed hold of a Jesus figurine in one hand and a Mary figurine in the other, several soldiers opened fire on the Natives. The fledgling mission barely survived.[11] They were only saved from starvation and annihilation when a supply ship arrived. By November 1769, Serra had reached San Francisco Bay, although a mission wouldn't be established there until 1771.

Until his death in 1784, Junípero Serra oversaw the founding of nine mission outposts. There was San Diego de Alcalá in 1769; San Gabriel Arcángel in 1771, outside of what is today Los Angeles; but also missions in San Juan Capistrano and all the way to the north in San Francisco de Asís. The Spanish established twenty-one missions in all by 1823, each linked by El Camino Real, the King's Highway.

In contrast to McCulley's sanguine description of the missions, the Native peoples didn't receive the Franciscans with open arms. Approximately three hundred thousand Native peoples lived in the region now called California when the Spanish arrived in 1769. By the time Mexico took control of the region, that number had decreased to two hundred thousand. Disease, over-work, and the severing of social support networks—issues that had decimated the indigenous population of Central Mexico after the conquest—worked in the same way in California.

Some one hundred different languages and distinct ethnic groups inhabited Alta California; almost 70 percent of those languages were mutually unintelligible between groups. California was one of the most culturally, ethnically, and linguistically diverse regions encountered by the Spanish during the colonial era. Father Serra, and those after him, encountered massive resistance to their efforts to convert and "civilize" these groups.

The Chumash, a people group located in the region of what is today Santa Barbara, was but one example. Serra wrote of the Chumash as "lively, agree-able, and mutely asking for the light of the Gospel." However, anthropologists have discovered that many Chumash saw the friars as "sons of mules," since they rode on the backs of the animals in the same way that female Chumash carried their own children.[12] There was a lot of mutual misunderstanding, in other words.

But that wasn't the worst of it. Even when the friars managed to convert Native peoples, the behavior of the soldiers stationed at the missions and the pre-sidios did the Christian cause no favors. At the San Gabriel mission, close to Los Angeles, one friar noted the soldiers' reputation for raping indigenous women. "I feel very deeply," the friar wrote, "about the fact that what the devil does not succeed in accomplishing among the pagans is accomplished by Christians. . . . The uprisings which have occurred in some of the *rancherías* (villages) closest to us were due to the fact that the soldiers had dishonored the wives of some of the Indians."[13] And then, what the devil didn't do, and the soldiers didn't do, the friars did. Father Serra wrote to one fellow missionary, "I am willing to admit that in the infliction of the punishment we are now discussing [whipping], there may have been some inequalities and excesses on the part of some fathers and that we are all exposed to err in that regard." Yet, Serra contented himself in believing, "I feel sure that everyone knows that we love them."[14]

Weirdly enough, Father Serra had a point. One military governor after another in Alta California under Spanish rule tried to steal Native land and generally treated the Native peoples worse than did the friars. One military governor, Pedro Fages, constantly butted heads with Serra.[15] The idea of giving retiring soldiers land in the region appealed to Fages. This, in fact, became the backstory for Don Diego's father, Alejandro de la Vega, in the Zorro stories—a retired commander who becomes a landlord. Serra opposed the measure, even going to Mexico City at one point to appeal to the viceroy.

Another Spanish military governor, Fernando de Rivera y Moncada, endeavored to force the mission Natives to labor in his building and infrastructure projects. This, too, echoes in several Zorro plots. In the more recent telenovela *Zorro: La espada y la rosa* (2007) the main villain is named Moncada, while Zorro's love interest is a relative of Moncada. Moncada, too, is the name of the main villain in Isabel Allende's 2005 novel *Zorro*. In other tales, Zorro has to defeat a military comandante, even while courting the comandante's niece, as in the Tyrone Power film *The Mark of Zorro* (1940). In the original pulp novel, McCulley presents a hierarchy of corrupt Spanish military characters, from the boastful Sergeant Gonzales, sometimes called García, to the conniving and sexually abusive Captain Ramón, to the far-off governor who appears only at the last instant and has to bow to the demands Zorro makes as representative of the benevolent landowners and defender of the abused Franciscans and peasants. The root of this main plot comes from the history of Alta California. And, comparatively speaking, the friars were better "friends" of the Natives than were the military or the other colonists.

Johnston McCulley's Zorro stories are found here, then, in the days of the Spanish missions in Alta California. But, the romantic Spanish missions of McCulley's imagination didn't exist. And yet, the context rings true in McCulley's rendering of Zorro. More true, in fact, than does William Lamport's Mexico City, despite the influence of Mexican author Riva Palacio on Lamport's legend. If Lamport seems like Zorro, it's mainly because Riva Palacio and McCulley both drew from and were influenced by the conventions of the romantic adventure novels by Alexandre Dumas and others.

McCulley's choice of setting in Alta California has more than a passing similarity to the actual history of the region. There was, in fact, antagonism between the Franciscan friars and the military governors of Alta California; there was also a desire on the part of the friars to protect the Native Americans, albeit a protection steeped in paternalism, racism, and the basic intolerance of the era. McCulley set Zorro in Alta California and drew on the real—though romanticized—history of the region. McCulley didn't have to import Lamport as a hero for his story. He had only to look to California for a hero, but one drawn from several decades after the Spanish missions, when California became, first, part of Mexico and then, after, part of the United States. That hero was Joaquín Murrieta.

———————————

Rogelio Ruiz, the town historian in Trincheras, pointed to more than just memories and family lore in proving Murrieta's existence. He referred to the book published by Manuel Rojas, a historian based in Sonora. Rojas found two documents that he claimed were proof that Murrieta began life in San Rafael del Alamito between 1824 and 1828. The first is a record of baptism of Joaquín's brother, Joseph Anselmo Murrieta, in 1823. The parents listed are Don Juan Murrieta and Doña Juana Orozco. The second document, dated December 1849, is another baptism, and the godparents listed are one Joaquín Murrieta and his wife, Carmen Feliz.[16] The latter shows that a Joaquín Murrieta lived in Sonora in the 1840s. If the Joaquín listed is the same man who went to California, then his name would've been Joaquín Murrieta Orozco, including both the paternal and maternal names, as is common in Spanish-language surnames. Carmen Feliz is often rendered as Rosa or Rosita, or Carmela, in the later stories. So, even here, with actual documents, we don't see clearly.

And that's where the documents end. Family lore and town memory has Joaquín traveling north when gold was discovered in Sutter's Mill. But there are no public documents confirming the existence of Joaquín Murrieta in California until 1852. It's then that a Joaquín Murrieta is listed as a potential murder suspect in the killing of a US military officer named General Joshua Bean.[17] One suspect, a Reyes Feliz, later said to be the brother of Rosa or Carmen, claimed that he heard that Joaquín Murrieta killed General Bean. Reyes Feliz, although exonerated on the charge of killing the general, was hanged nonetheless for other crimes. Another suspect, Ana Benítez, who was described as "the woman of Joaquín Murrieta," said Joaquín didn't do it—someone else killed General Bean.

Despite the potential leads directing suspicion at this Joaquín Murrieta, the man had vanished. Authorities couldn't find him. The surname Murrieta, or any of its derivatives, was not printed in the newspapers again until May 1853. But the news constantly reported about "the notorious robber Joaquín." It was "Joaquín" that made headlines—not Joaquín Murrieta. That fact is why so many historians have a hard time believing Joaquín Murrieta was real. Perhaps, as the documents show, a Joaquín Murrieta did come from Sonora, but to attribute everything done by "Joaquín" to one man fails to understand the context of the California gold rush, where Mexican argonauts were being criminalized en masse. In essence, it was easier to attribute all the violence and banditry being carried out in California to "Joaquín," the notorious robber.

And so, I decided, in that office with Rogelio Ruiz, to tell the story of Joaquín Murrieta as the legend that it is: the building blocks for other stories—in my case, the building blocks for Zorro. I realized that in leaving Rogelio's office, I was leaving the last secure thing in the story of Murrieta. There was a man named Joaquín Murrieta Orozco who was married to Carmen Feliz in Trincheras in 1849. People in Trincheras remember *that* Joaquín as the famous one in California history. But once the story crosses the border, it's just really hard to say.

7 | I AM JOAQUÍN

JOAQUÍN MURRIETA AND HIS LEGEND signify so many things, and have signified so many things, to so many people. Murrieta isn't just one man. But that's the point: legends are deep wells from which we draw up story elements to quench our thirst for meaning in the present. Even if the Joaquín Murrieta from Trincheras didn't cross into California in 1850, many, many Sonorans like him did. When gold was struck, Sonorans were some of the first to go north. Chileans, too, with Chinese, French, African Americans, Miwoks, Anglos, and others all rushing in. Some ten thousand Sonorans ventured north. Their destination was what was known then as the Southern Mines. The goldfields of California stretched to the north in the lower watershed of the Sacramento River, and then on to the south to the watershed of the San Joaquín River. The Southern Mines also went west to Stockton, a regional supply center, and then to the south, near what is today Merced, California.[1]

Family lore and the narrative formed about Murrieta in the United States present the story of Joaquín's journey in similar ways. Joaquín left Sonora to go north to the goldfields, taking his wife and others—a brother-in-law, cousins, etc.—in 1849 or 1850. That would've been a year or so after gold was discovered at Sutter's Mill in January 1849. Joaquín encountered trouble: his wife was raped—later stories include her murder as well—while his brother (sometimes half brother) was lynched and Joaquín was flogged for stealing a mule. Those events forced Joaquín into banditry, horse thieving primarily, with hopes to sell the horses for profit back in Mexico.[2] Joaquín became a wanted man. The governor placed a price on his head, and California Rangers hunted him down,

46

killed him, and cut off his head. On this last point, Murrieta's death, there are lots of disagreements. Sometimes Joaquín wasn't actually the unfortunate soul to lose his head—it was one of his lieutenants instead.

But of all the legends of Murrieta, virtually none of them tell what happened to Joaquín's wife after she was raped. The exception to that was in a version of the story where she was also murdered. But that was a later addition. In essence, she disappeared from the story, even though Murrieta's revenge hinged on male honor transgressed. And, in that era, when sexual violence was done to a woman, it was that woman's male relatives who were expected to avenge the wrong. Here, a female oral history fills in the gaps left out by the male-told popular legend. Frank Latta collected the story, told to him by a woman who claimed she was the widow of Joaquín Murrieta's nephew. It was then passed down to that woman's daughter, and Latta heard it told again in the 1970s.[3]

Murrieta, in this oral history, did not die after the California Rangers attacked. Instead, he and a companion escaped north, where Murrieta's wife was waiting for him. En route, the two were ambushed by Anglo-American vigilantes, and Murrieta was fatally wounded. He managed to make it home to his wife, but soon died from his injuries. Before he died, however, Joaquín told his wife, called Rosa in this telling, that she shouldn't tell anyone of his death or where he was buried. Rosa, according to Latta's female informant, said she "sold everything and went to San Francisco. She married the compañero who had brought Joaquín home and helped bury him. The newly married couple went to Mexico on a boat." After that, as the story goes, Rosa was never heard from again.

As one historian wrote of the tale, it's "no simple story of a helpless woman raped and then widowed as her husband seeks vengeance. This reinvented female tradition brings Joaquín home to a household and ranch managed by his womenfolk, and buries him in the safety of its foundations." And, "to frustrate any lingering sentimentality," the story allows Rosa to sell it all, to remarry, and to sail off into the sunset back in Mexico.[4]

The life, and especially the death, of Joaquín Murrieta has been a fertile legend from which generations of Mexican Americans in the borderlands have found meaningful stories to tell—both men and women. The legend of Joaquín reflected the real experience of Mexicans living in the region.

The period right before Joaquín supposedly journeyed to California—a period that saw thousands of Sonorans travel to California—was a momentous time in Mexico's history. From 1846 to 1848, the United States fought a war with Mexico.

The conflict radically altered the Sonoran sense of place. Before the war, Sonora had been in the middle of Mexico's northwest territory. After the war, the Sonorans found themselves sharing a border with a nation that had just claimed half of Mexico's land—New Mexico, a little chunk of Kansas, parts of Colorado and Wyoming, Utah, Nevada, and, of course, California. A little after that, there was Arizona. The Treaty of Guadalupe Hidalgo, which ceded these parts of Mexico to the United States, also gave up Arizona—but then, in 1853, the Gadsden Purchase gave a little more, slicing another sliver off Sonora and Chihuahua. Tucson went to the Yankees.[5]

It's not enough to say that these Mexican territories, which became American territories, were simply part of some ambiguous Manifest Destiny design of the United States. Territorial expansion was a distinct policy of US president James K. Polk (1845–1849). It wasn't an accident. Polk was a protégé of Andrew Jackson—Old Hickory, as he was known—of Trail of Tears infamy. Jackson removed the Cherokee and other "civilized" tribes from the American Southeast in order to make way for Anglo settlers. As Old Hickory lay dying, Polk, at the time called Young Hickory, ran for the presidency in 1844 on a platform of annexing Texas. But Polk had larger designs than that, and those stretched to California. Called in the press Jackson's "chief cook and bottlewasher"—a guy of little import, in sum—Polk surprised everyone, except himself and his politically ambitious wife, by winning the presidency and starting a war with Mexico over a boundary squabble. He didn't stop until Los Angeles had been invaded in the west and Mexico City in the south.

Even before the war began, Polk called one of his cabinet members into his office to describe his vision for the future. "Slapping his leg for emphasis," one historian wrote, "Polk told him that 'the acquisition of California and a large district on the coast' was one of the priorities of his administration. It was God's will that Mexico's richest lands, especially the fertile stretch by the Pacific, pass from its current shiftless residents to hardworking white people better able to husband their resources."[6] Manifest Destiny, the term coined by a nineteenth-century writer named John L. O'Sullivan, which held that the United States had been destined by God to stretch from sea to shining sea, was not one of history's accidents. It was a policy carried to completion through war.

And the Mexican-American War was the bloodiest and most costly the United States had fought up to that point. Some 16 percent of the seventy-nine thousand Americans who served in the war died. Probably twenty-five thousand Mexicans were killed. Disease dispatched most of the Americans, while combat accounted for most Mexican deaths—warfare was often directed at Mexican civilians. It was a "wicked war," according to future president Ulysses S. Grant.[7] It was a war concocted at the highest levels of American leadership. It's no wonder, then, that official policies of racism and exclusion followed Anglo-American settlers to California once gold was discovered.

On January 24, 1848, James W. Marshall found gold at Sutter's Mill on the American River, near Sacramento. Hundreds came, then thousands—as many as three hundred thousand during the next decade. The land that had been Alta California was still Mexican in every way but name. Miners wrote about what they ate, for instance—"the national dish of meat and chile pepper," one prospector wrote in a letter home, "wrapped within two tortillas."[8] Basically, the Anglo-American settlers ate tacos. The gold digging was done in the wash of river banks, and surface deposits were called "placers," which came from the Spanish word meaning "pleasure," because it was way easier to find gold in the wet rocks and silt than having to mine the ore out of rocks. So many Sonorans migrated north to the goldfields outside of Stockton that they called the boomtown Sonora. One encampment was known as Yackee—for the Yaqui tribe from Sonora. Soon, however, with more gringos settling in the region, the name was changed from Yackee to Yankee camp. It's a name shift that describes something of the coming ethnic and racial tensions in the goldfields.

To protect Anglo-American claims on the territory, which became the thirty-first state in the Union in September 1850, a tax was levied on all miners who were not US citizens. The goal of the Foreign Miners' Tax Act was to make gold mining too expensive for the Chileans, Chinese, French, and Sonorans. Twenty dollars a month was required from these populations for the right to do the same thing US citizens were doing without the tax. And the kicker was that the tax could be enforced by just about anyone with enough force behind him to terrorize the so-called foreign population.[9]

The Sonorans protested. On May 19, 1850, some four thousand Sonoran miners went to the plaza in Sonora Town in Tuolumne County to call for the repeal of the edict. By 1851, the tax was repealed, as so many Chinese and Mexicans had left the goldfields that complementary Anglo-American businesses suffered as a result—stores that sold supplies, and boardinghouses and landlords that lost rents because of it.[10] In 1852 a new tax went into force, but at a reduced three dollars per month. And yet, Anglo-American miners had preference and precedence in law.

Racial violence was tacitly endorsed. Posses were raised to deal with a rising incidence of "foreign banditry." The national policy of annexation and aggression was repeated on the state, regional, and local levels. Many Mexican miners protested. Legal protest gave way to an increasing number of reports of foreign bandits plaguing the countryside. In the 1920 silent film *The Mark of Zorro*, the first movie depiction of Zorro, the initial title sequence reads: "Oppression—by its very nature—creates the power that crushes it. A champion arises—a champion of the oppressed." The historical setting for Zorro, stated to take place before the US annexation of California, in reality looks a lot more like the era of the gold rush than it does California under Spanish rule.

Early in 1853, after the various foreign miners' taxes, after tensions between Anglo-American settlers and Mexican populations had increased, "Joaquín" appeared in the newspapers. Joaquín was the personification of the troubles that besieged the region. "It is well known," wrote one publication, "that during the winter months a band of Mexican marauders have infested Calaveras County, and weekly we received the details of dreadful murders and outrages, committed in the lonely gulches and solitary outposts of that region. . . . The band is led by a robber named Joaquín, a very desperate man, who was concerned in the murder of four Americans some time ago in Turnersville."

The efforts of the incensed miners to root out the robbers were foiled by the outlaws. "Joaquin," the account stated, "as we understand, committed other outrages on the same night." A "systematic search for Joaquín and his associates" was undertaken. "At the same time," the report frankly described, "they resolved to burn the habitations of the Mexicans, indiscriminately, deprive them of arms they might have in possession, and give them all notice to quit." The newspaper triumphantly claimed, "We are glad to hear that one of the gang has been caught at Yankee camp and another at Cherokee Ranch. Both were immediately strung up."[11]

Joaquín, not identified with a surname, became a pretext to unleash a race war on the Mexican inhabitants of the region. "The entire Mexican population," wrote the newspaper, "has been driven from San Andreas and the fork of the Calaveras." White settlers took it upon themselves to force Mexicans from the area. "If an American meets a Mexican," the newspaper recounted, "he takes his horse, his arms, and bids him to leave. The Americans engaged in the [vigilante] band are divided into gangs, and are stationed in every part of the country."

At the town of Double Springs, for instance, a large meeting of Anglo-American settlers gathered. They passed resolutions "making it the duty of every American citizen at all events to exterminate the Mexican race from the country. The foreigners should first receive notice to leave, and if they refused they were to be shot down and their property confiscated."[12] The national policy of annexation soon was replicated on the local level. All Mexicans were criminalized as the notorious robber "Joaquín" became the identifiable justification for racial violence.

"These turbulent times," says Don Diego Vega in *The Curse of Capistrano*. "Where can a man have peace to read the poets."[13] As turbulent as life was under the Spanish missions, California's real turbulence took place after annexation by the United States, in the days of the gold rush.

After initial reports in 1853, "Joaquín" and his band of outlaws became the culprits for every kind of misdeed in the Southern Mines. A legend began to form around Joaquín, each time embellished in the press. One report said he was born in Jalisco; that he had a regular chain of communication with a gang of confederates scattered throughout California; that he "entered capital cities disguised as a friar." He was six feet in height, reported the *San Francisco Whig*, and he had "immense muscular strength," was "well versed in the use of arms," and had a "cruel and sanguinary" disposition. He had a "dark, sallow complexion," in one report, but at times he was said to be fair skinned and blond, a regular phenotypical occurrence in Sonorans. "During the Mexican War," wrote the *San Francisco Whig*, "he was known to wear a coat of arms." He was even said, in the report, to be "almost superhuman."[14]

More reports followed. One unnamed rancher described a chance encounter with the bandit Joaquín. A young Mexican man and some of his group chanced across the rancher's land, asking for refreshments. One of them, according to the rancher, wore "a false beard and mustache." As the host complied with their requests for food and drink—the conversations were in English—the subject of Joaquín came up. Did they have news of the outlaw, asked the rancher, since they'd come from the placers? The disguised man replied, "I am that Joaquín, and no man takes me alive, or comes within one hundred yards of me with these good weapons."[15] Joaquín, the newspaper reported, told the rancher his story of injustice done to him at the hands of the Americans. The rancher was shocked that Joaquín was well educated and not from "criminal stock," but a good family. There was a justification for his crimes. He could blend in, disguised, and he could speak English. The governor of California, John Bigler, put out a reward for his capture, dead or alive, for $1,000.

By May 1853, Joaquín was being described as an avenger. "The real name of the bandit is Joaquín Muliati," reported the San Francisco Herald, garbling the Spanish surname. He "speaks English fluently, and in his foraging expeditions, has always a fresh horse at hand. He was heard to say that he would never kill a Spaniard."[16]

This Joaquín, whether Muliati or known by alternate surnames such as Carillo and others, was the perfect nightmare of the Anglo-American newspapers and the establishment: he had "almost superhuman" strength, he could be disguised and spoke fluent English, but at a moment's notice he could reveal himself as "Joaquín," an avenger who didn't molest the Spanish-speaking population but was the scourge of the gringos.

No story better encapsulated this than one report from the spring of 1853. It was said that Stockton posted wanted posters for the bandit, offering various rewards—some versions of the story said it was $1,000; others said $5,000. Allegedly, when Joaquín saw the reward, he thought it too little. He jumped off his horse, walked up to the poster, and wrote, "I will give $10,000 myself." He then signed it simply, "Joaquín."[17]

Here, then, in the newspaper accounts, we can already see some of the narrative elements of a disguised, dual-identity Zorro. Both Joaquín and Zorro are called outlaws, bandits, and highwaymen. "Caballero," says Sergeant Gonzales to Don Diego, unaware that the man is actually Zorro, "we have been regarding in conversation this fine Curse of Capistrano, as some nimble-witted fool has seen fit to term, pest of the highway."[18] The newspaper accounts about Joaquín referred to him as a plague, just like Zorro was the so-called curse of San Juan Capistrano. In both stories—in those about Joaquín and about Zorro—rumors attended them, grandiose deeds. Joaquín and Zorro were the thorn in the flesh of some, and the recognized heroes of others. Consider that Joaquín "always had a fresh horse"—the population was assisting him, aiding and abetting him. In one Los Angeles newspaper, the editor of the Spanish-language *La Estrella* went so far as to deny the rumors he'd heard about Joaquín. "Who is Joaquín?" the editor asked. He was not a devil or spirit, the editor wrote. But his denials showed that people did believe all sorts of things about Joaquín. "Nobody sees Joaquín," wrote the editor, "and yet he appears in three or four places at the same time." "There are others," the editor noted, "(and these are the silliest) for whom he represents a hero, an avenger of various personal grievances that we have received from the Americans."[19]

The narrative forming about Joaquín—avenger, scourge of some, hero to others—was the same mystique that surrounded the fictional Zorro in McCulley's stories. Joaquín, then, was a "shape-shifter," held by some to be almost supernatural, superhuman, and an avenger. To others, he was a highwayman, a bandit, a "notorious robber." That's the legend on which Zorro's story was formed.

And no one knew the identity of Joaquín—the same shtick always formed part of the Zorro novels. The California legislature, for instance, raised its bounty and its contingent of Rangers to bring down, dead or alive, "one or either of the five Joaquins, viz: Joaquin Muliati, Joaquin Ocomorenia, Joaquin Valenzuela, Joaquin Botellier, and Joaquin Corrillo."[20] Any Joaquín would do, it seemed, because the *idea* of Joaquín was what Governor Bigler and the Rangers were after, not any one man. A certain segment of the population supported "Joaquin"—and if every and any pretender to that title were cut down, went the government's logic, then perhaps the unruly Mexican problem would be stopped.

The corrupt Captain Ramón in *The Curse of Capistrano* thinks likewise. After Zorro has just humiliated him, made him apologize to Lolita Pulido for offending her honor, Ramón writes the governor: "I have the greater part of my force in pursuit of the fellow, with orders to get him in person or to fetch me his corpse. But this Señor Zorro does not fight alone. He is being given succor at certain places in the neighborhood, allowed to remain in hiding where necessary, given food and drink and, no doubt, fresh horses."[21]

Captain Ramón, as with the legislators of California in Joaquín's day, wanted to do damage to the base of support for their respective wily bandit. In Captain Ramón's case, it was a plot device so that Ramón could get revenge on the Pulido family for Lolita's rejection of his violent advances. But the narrative elements from Joaquín's story are firmly embedded in the Zorro mythology.

It was only after Captain Harry Love of the California Rangers returned with a Mexican head that Joaquín was definitively given the surname Murrieta. Until that time, Joaquín was associated with as many as five surnames. Love managed to secure affidavits of identification of the severed head, which always stated something specific like, "the said head of Joaquin Murieta"—or sometimes "Muriatta."[22] Regardless, the governor got his head and managed to silence his Whig Party opponents whose newspapers were the very same ones shouting so loudly about a rogue Mexican highwayman. Ultimately, the Mexican "problem" of banditry was a political one. The governor's opponents were supporting the embellished tales in the newspaper in order to undercut Governor Bigler's bid for reelection. Bigler, with the head of *the* Joaquín Murieta (the spelling with one *r* became the predominant one) in a jar, got elected to a second term in office.

———————

As I climbed into the Sprinter van and we pulled out of the Cerro de Trincheras archeological site, all of this began to take shape, in seed form. It made sense that the people of Trincheras would see Murrieta as a symbol of their own struggle on the border with the United States. Many of the sons of Trincheras ventured to the United States, never to return. And those who did return often bore the scars and traumas of America's xenophobia during the gold rush era.

The legend of Joaquín Murrieta grew even larger in successive years. In 1854 a half-Cherokee newspaperman named John Rollin Ridge, who'd migrated west after the Trail of Tears, and whose own family had been on the pro-integrationist side of the Cherokee tribe and suffered because of it, wrote *The Life and Adventures of Joaquín Murieta*. It was pitched as a history, but just scratch the surface and the novelized Joaquín appears. John Rollin Ridge quotes dialogue he would have had no way of knowing. But many of the embellished tales were rooted in the newspaper accounts. The Joaquín in the book passes easily as a gringo. In one famous section of the book, Joaquín sits playing cards at a popular gaming establishment. The men at his table boast about meeting Joaquín and what they'd do to him if they met him. The real Joaquín, until then unknown to his fellow cardplayers, jumps on the monte table and declares, "I am Joaquín." In one engraving of the scene, published in 1859, Joaquín is even depicted throwing his shirt open like some sort of proto-Superman.

It's a scene repeated again and again in many Zorro stories—in *The Curse of Capistrano*, but also in the film *The Mark of Zorro* (1920). The unveiling, "I am Joaquín," or "I am Zorro," is a central identifier of the link between the two stories. A man, physically masked, or just able to pass as a gringo, through voluntary self-revelation, identifies who he is. Joaquín, as with Zorro, draws on the trickster in Native American folklore. Joaquín, who handed down the ability to Zorro, is the master trickster. He's able to shape-shift to suit his audience. Both are adept at what we might today call code-switching. Joaquín can be a good English-speaking gringo one moment, and the next instant be revealed as the Mexican avenger. Don Diego, the foppish popinjay, can be the effete, harmless aristocrat, and then, under the mask of Zorro, an avenger of the oppressed.

Code-switching is a term taken from linguistics. It identifies how bilingual people switch from one language to another and drop certain mannerisms or words to converse in a second language. But, culturally speaking, racial minorities in America have always needed to switch between one culture and the dominant white normative culture. One language and diction in one context; another language and diction for another.

Code-switching is about survival. It's a tool of the oppressed. It's not that Joaquín's dual identity—gringo English speaker or Mexican avenger—is the first or only appearance of this phenomenon in America; it's that it is so pervasive in the experience of racial minorities in the United States.[23] To be Mexican and American, to be African and American, to be Asian and American, all come with the need to bear a dual identity to some extent. One can find it in W. E. B. Du Bois's *The Souls of Black Folk* (1903):

> It is a peculiar sensation, this double-consciousness, this sense of always looking at one's self through the eyes of others, of measuring one's soul by the tape of a world that looks on in amused contempt and pity. One ever feels his two-ness, an American, a Negro; two souls, two thoughts, two unreconciled strivings; two warring ideals in one dark body, whose dogged strength alone keeps it from being torn asunder.[24]

Du Bois's double-consciousness gets a whole new meaning if we see it at work even in the American superhero genre.

And one can find the dual identity of the immigrant—in a very different context—in the Jewish origins of Superman. For instance, not only were his creators, Joe Shuster and Jerry Siegel, Jews—along with a majority of early creators of the comic book superhero—but also the story material itself speaks of Jewish experience. Superman is an immigrant from an "old" dying planet. He comes to the "new" world and takes up residence in midwestern America.[25] He struggles to hide his true nature. He learns to hide in plain sight. He projects a goyish identity—Clark Kent—but really he's as strong as ten men and can leap tall buildings. (In the original stories, Superman was still learning to fly and his superstength had its limits.) He's a defender of the people, a kind of twentieth century Golem who protects the weak and serves truth and justice—with the American way added later.[26]

Joaquín Murrieta is part of the long story of race in America—a story that has been retold over and over. In this case, it became narrative material for Zorro, and Zorro helped infuse the American superhero with the dual identity, as did a host of the experiences of other minority and immigrant groups.

But I'm getting ahead of myself. That's the story I saw as I drove out of Trincheras toward the US-Mexico border. To become Zorro, Joaquín Murrieta had to cross the border. I could only follow, as all signs pointed to *el norte*.

8 | THE RETURN OF THE HEAD OF JOAQUÍN MURRIETA

I SET OUT FOR THE BORDER, but got tired. Neither I nor Jason, my traveling companion, felt much like enduring the hassle of crossing today. So it was a cheap motel for the night. I thought about Murrieta and the Mexicans who made this same journey 160 years ago—many of them did it on foot. I felt grateful for cars and barely working AC.

After settling into our room for the evening, I decided to e-mail someone who could help me understand more about Joaquín Murrieta. His name is John Valadez. He's an award-winning Chicano filmmaker. I recently saw his latest documentary, *The Head of Joaquín Murrieta*. The film follows his search for the famous decapitated head of Murrieta and his eventual "discovery" of the thing. Turns out, someone from California sent him the head in a package! Valadez decides, in the film, to take a road trip from his home in New York to California in order to bury the macabre package he was sent. His journey ends when he buries the jarred head—we get a brief glimpse of it—in the Arroyo de Cantúa, the place where Murrieta was allegedly killed by California State Rangers.

No joke. It's a crazy film.

I decided I had to talk to John Valadez. If there was anyone who could give me some perspective on Murrieta, and his link to Zorro, it was Valadez.

I sent off a pathos-laden e-mail. *Help!* was basically what it said. He wrote back almost immediately: "Are you free to speak today? Saludos, J.V."

When the call came I felt nervous and I couldn't explain why. Murrieta was an enigma. Was he even a real guy? Was he a criminal? A bandit? Or was he just a symbol—always a symbol—of the dark history of violence, hatred, and racism wedged between Mexicans and Anglo settlers in California? Maybe it was even deeper than that: Murrieta represents the historic trauma of Mexican Americans in the United States. It was complicated, in short. And I had this feeling that the head in a jar was really not what this story was about. *Whatever you do*, I thought, *don't start off by mentioning the head.*

I picked up after several rings.

"Stephen! Hello," John Valadez laughed his greeting. "So good to speak with you."

I was taken off guard. John enthusiastically offered to help in any way he could, which immediately put me at ease.

I told him about my book—about finding the Latinx roots to Zorro, describing how the American superhero owes its life, in part, to Mexican American history, experience, and culture. John was on board. I started by asking about his documentary of Murrieta.

"What struck me about the film is how personal it is," I told him. "It tells the story of Murrieta and America's storied past of racial violence . . . but it also tells your story."

John's film describes how, as a kid growing up in Washington State, his nickname at school was the racial slur "spic." His classmates addressed him as such even in his school yearbook. In the film, he makes the tale of Murrieta his own, drawing a line of connection between Murrieta's death and his own experience of racial prejudice. Murrieta, for him, is a mythic figure that tells a true story of the precarious position of Mexican Americans in the United States. He can relate to that.

"Murrieta," John told me, "is legend built on myth built on legend. I can't even begin to unravel the twisted tale of human memory he represents."

"What was the question?" he asked me.

In my mind, all I could think was: *Don't ask about the head!*

"So, John," I started to ask, "how in the world did you get sent a human head in the mail?" *I asked about the head. Why stop now?* "I mean, was this real, or am I missing something?"

John laughed again. It's infectious, his laugh. It once again put me at ease.

"It all started fifteen years ago," he said. "Well, actually, it started with Richard Rodriguez."

Richard Rodriguez is one the most celebrated Chicano writers in America. One of the most celebrated writers in America, *period*. He wrote an essay, John reminded me, called "The Head of Joaquin Murrieta."[1]

"You know the essay, right?

"Yes, of course," I told him. The essay is probably one of the most important things written on Murrieta and Mexican American memory. As John continued to talk, I remembered that Rodriguez describes how grandmothers would say things to small children about Murrieta that were incredibly Zorro-like:

> *Yes, he became a robber, but not a bad man maybe. He gave what he stole to poor people. . . . He kept the blackest horse for himself. They said his heart was as black as his chin. He wore a black hat with a black feather, and a big black cape. And you could only see his eyes.*[2]

I began to think that the legend of Murrieta increasingly took on elements—the black hat; you could only see his eyes (because of a mask?); his black horse; giving to the poor—that would inspire the creation of Zorro.

Rodriguez articulates the code-shifting, the disguises, and the intent to deceive Anglos—all of which are part of the dual identity of Zorro and many modern superheroes.

"*The gringos were afraid of him . . . for he spoke many disguises. They say he could talk like a gringo. They say he could talk Chinese. Sometimes he pretended he was a little old man. Sometimes he pretended he was a girl with golden curls and a little high voice.*"[3] The gringos, Rodriguez writes, would think they had him, but "*he always disappeared,*" or he had escaped to "*the other side of the hill, laughing at them.*" "*If Joaquín was a bad man,*" Rodriguez recounts the grandmothers saying to small children, "*those gringos made him bad.*"[4]

John Valadez was telling me the story of Murrieta. I knew this story, but somehow his telling of it was incredibly compelling. He stuck to the bare facts about Murrieta's supposed death. All we know, he said, is that one morning in 1853 a troop of California Rangers ambushed a group of Mexicans—allegedly a gang of horse thieves. In the encounter, four Mexicans were killed. One of those was taken to be—or purported to be—Joaquín Murrieta and another, Three-Fingered Jack. They cut the head off one of the Mexicans and chopped off the hand of the other. They put those grisly trophies in alcohol to preserve them. The Rangers took the head and the hand and traded them in for reward money.

"But what if this was just some random Mexican kid?" John asked me. He posed the same question in his documentary. And the way he talked about it was very convincing. *What if this Mexican kid was just in the wrong place at the wrong time?* No one had a photograph of Murrieta. Journalists at the time, John explained, scoffed at the idea that the human head in the jar was Murrieta's head, hence the need for affidavits and some sort of legal legitimacy. The official story was that it was Murrieta's head, but many people didn't believe it even at the time.

But then the head had an afterlife. John told me how Richard Rodriguez knew a priest named Alberto Huerta, a Jesuit from San Francisco, who wanted to find and bury the remains of Murrieta. "We're talking about a human being," Rodriguez quotes the priest in his essay, "and because the head symbolizes the struggle and suffering of the Mexican people in California."[5]

After Captain Harry Love and the other California Rangers got their $5,000 bounty, the head of Murrieta, or whoever's head was in the jar, toured mining camps, saloons, and brothels.

"For a dollar," John told me, "you could see the head of Murrieta."

Captain Love appeared with it, like some sort of macabre western sideshow. John explains how the former California Ranger would reach into the brine and hold the head up to the morbidly curious audiences.

Love eventually settled down and retired to Santa Cruz. Legend has it that Captain Love died in a shoot-out with his wife's lover. And the Ranger who decapitated the head, a guy named Bill Burns, wound up in an insane asylum in Stockton.

"A cowboy Macbeth," Richard Rodriguez writes of Bill Burns, who created the "dreadful pickle" in the first place.[6]

But there's more, John continued. The head was acquired by one Dr. Jordan of Dr. Jordan's Pacific Museum of Anatomy and Science, which was located at 1051 Market Street in San Francisco. "Kangaroo canisters," "Egyptian Mummies," and the "Amazing Cyclops Child" filled the shelves and display cases alongside the head of Joaquín Murrieta, the Mexican bandit on whose literal head was placed both the fears and the altruism of all Californians, once upon a time.

"There was a three-legged chicken next to the head," John added. "I'm telling the truth," he said seriously, "except for the parts that aren't true."

He laughed again, his infectious laugh.

I asked about Murrieta's dark side. He was feared, supposedly, by Mexicans as well as Chinese and Anglos.

John agreed that Murrieta's dark side is part of the legend, but he didn't have a good reason why Murrieta can be seen as both a hero and a villain at the same time. Later, after rereading Richard Rodriguez's essay, I realized Rodriguez gives as good an answer as any to my question. "Maybe," writes Rodriguez, "the Robin Hood part of the legend has persisted so long among Mexicans because Mexicans felt they had a share in Murrieta's victimization; thus perhaps a share in Murrieta's revenge."[7]

John continued with the saga of Murrieta's head: "The San Francisco earthquake of 1906 destroyed the museum." He chuckles. "The poor Cyclops child! The three-legged chicken! All gone." He paused. "And so, too, the head."

About fifteen years ago, John told me, he went to California to interview Richard Rodriguez. When John arrived, he found out that Father Huerta—the priest from the Rodriguez story—had died. But back in the 1980s it had been Rodriguez and Father Huerta who had tracked down the "dreadful pickle." They discovered an Old West museum—a shabby, two-bit museum—and found a head floating, "hair like sea grass," in a glass jar. The owner claimed it was *the head* of Murrieta. Father Huerta wanted to bury it. "Someone should bury the thing," Huerta tells Rodriguez in the story. "We can deal with the guilt history places on us," the priest continues, "only when we free ourselves from the ghosts."[8] Rodriguez's story ends there—he and Father Huerta leave the museum and there's no closure. They don't bury it. The end.

John Valadez, for his part, wanted to track down the head again—the one originally found by Rodriguez and the priest—and finish the job of burying it. Valadez desired to bring some closure to the long story of Murrieta's head, even if it wasn't the real McCoy, so to speak. But when John visited the same two-bit Old West museum, he discovered that the former owner had died, and the family said that the thing had been disposed of. John didn't totally believe them, so he left his card with the family. John told me that he even offered the family $1,000 for it. Yet, in the end, there was no head forthcoming and, John thought, no documentary.

"Until I received a package in the mail," John said cryptically.

"So, this family sent you the head?" I asked.

"It wasn't the same guy in the Richard Rodriguez story," John said. He guessed that someone found the card he'd left and sent him the jarhead in an effort to get rid of all the creepy Americana that the two-bit museum had on display. "It's weird," John admitted. "It's quirky. My wife was freaking out: 'Get rid of that thing!'"

I was absolutely enthralled at this point.

"I went to buy a plane ticket. I wanted to bury it in the Arroyo de Cantúa in California. Then I thought, *I can't bring a head on a plane!*" John paused for effect. "A Mexican carrying a head in a jar raises red flags with TSA!" He laughed. "So I got my cinematographer and we did what any respectable Chicano would do: we did a road trip."

I couldn't tell, because we were talking on the phone, but I suspected John was smiling.

John's movie is about more than the weird package. He visits Texas and the infamous Hanging Tree, where reportedly dozens of Mexicans were lynched. His film describes how there are 871 documented cases of Mexicans who were lynched in some thirteen states in the American West after the Civil War.[9] In proportion to their population, there were more Mexicans who died by lynching in the West than African Americans who were lynched in the American South. That fact checks out in the historical record.[10]

In the film, John buries the head. It's the only time in the movie when you actually see the thing. It looked fake, honestly, which John conceded.

"Is it a real head?" he asked. "Well, duct tape was holding the lid, and the glass didn't look wavy and warped like nineteenth-century glass. I was half expecting to see MADE IN CHINA somewhere on the floating thing." But then added, "I'll tell you what Richard Rodriguez told me: 'When you start to delve into the story of Joaquín Murrieta there is no steady ground. No easy answers.'"

John paused. He now seemed more somber.

"The legend of Joaquín Murrieta is a story that haunts America," he said. "It's like the story of the Donner Party. Nothing adds up."

What I admitted to myself after I said goodbye to John Valadez was that I hadn't asked him the most important question. *John, I wish I had asked, did you deal with the ghost? Did you lay it to rest?* Perhaps, I thought to myself, the ghost of Murrieta had taken other forms and was haunting us still, wearing other masks. I realized that the Head of Murrieta floating in a jar—even if it wasn't Murrieta's head, even if it was a fake head—is important for us to remember. It symbolizes the racial violence that characterized the Old West, but also the way in which this violent history has been cut off from the broader stories we tell of American history. In the same way the history of Murrieta has been cut off from the history of Zorro and popular culture, the history of Mexican Americans has been lopped off from the story of America.

Finding the origins to Zorro is about dealing with the ghosts, uncovering the painful history of the Old West, which might allow us to see American culture as a product of Latinx contribution. It's time to reclaim Zorro's lost head and tell better stories.

And to do that, I'd have to investigate Johnston McCulley and how Zorro laid the blueprint for the modern American superhero. I'd have to go to Southern California, where McCulley lived and worked and created the first Zorro story in 1919.

PART II

MASKS

But when you're gone, who remembers your name?
Who keeps your flame?
—Lin-Manuel Miranda,
Hamilton: An American Musical

9 | WRITER BEHIND THE MASK

Research Log #3
Glendale, California
1:47 PM

FOREST LAWN MEMORIAL PARK is so much grander than I'd imagined. It's got rolling hills, meandering lanes, Italian Renaissance–inspired white marble mausoleums, almost countless columbarium, and at least three different churches on the cemetery grounds. There are a whole lot of dead celebrities fit all in one place. Forest Lawn is often called the "Resting Place of the Stars," and it delivers on that moniker. Humphrey Bogart, Jean Harlow, Clark Gable, Errol Flynn, and Elizabeth Taylor are interred here. Bob Kane, cocreator of Batman, is at Forest Lawn—so are Clayton Moore, best known as the Lone Ranger, and Tom Mix, one of the original silver screen cowboys. Mary Pickford, the first Hollywood supercelebrity, is at the star-studded cemetery, while Douglas Fairbanks Sr., the first on-screen Zorro, and Pickford's husband, has his own memorialized burial in Beverly Hills.

There's a whole lot of Hollywood history buried in Glendale, and my traveling companion and I had come to see it firsthand. We arrived at Forest Lawn after lead-footing it from the border—a night in Phoenix, and finally we reached the Los Angeles metro area. I was a little tired.

We pulled up to the guardhouse at Forest Lawn's entrance.

"Name of deceased," the woman asked, not unkindly.

"Uh, Johnston McCulley," I said, leaning over from the passenger seat.

"Just a moment." The guard—or is it concierge?—looked to be searching in some sort of database. "Lot #24,516. That's in the Iris Columbarium." She gave us two handy photocopied maps. She'd thoughtfully drawn, in purple highlighter, a squiggly route from the entrance to the Iris Terrace complex, where McCulley's ashes are located. We said thank you and leisurely motored our way passed Whispering Pines in the direction of the Great Mausoleum. (Elizabeth Taylor is buried, of course, in the Great Mausoleum.) Other sections—or can I call them neighborhoods? I'm not sure how to describe them—dot the landscape. Vale of Memory stretches out behind us, right next to Rest Haven, and then Vesperland. (The so-sad-we-don't-visit-it Baby Land is somewhere on the other side of the dale by Vesperland.) My absolute favorite of the section-neighborhoods is the aptly named Slumber Land.

Forest Lawn Memorial Park—now a registered trademark with twelve locations in the Los Angeles metroplex—was the vision of a businessman named Dr. Hubert Eaton. After establishing the park in 1906, over the next decade Eaton added commissioned art, sculptures, and replicas of famous Italian masterworks in stained glass and marble. In 1917, Eaton erected a towering stone tablet at Forest Lawn called *Builder's Creed*. It's engraved with Eaton's own take on the Christian Apostles' Creed, a sort of article of faith for the modern American afterlife:

> I believe in a Happy Eternal Life. . . . I shall try to build at Forest Lawn
> a great park, devoid of misshapen monuments and other customary
> signs of earthly death, but filled with towering trees, sweeping lawns,
> splashing fountains, singing birds, beautiful statuary, cheerful flowers,
> noble memorial architecture with interiors full of light and color, and
> redolent of the world's best history and romances.[1]

Eaton built, in other words, a cemetery for Hollywood's rich and famous.

Honestly, it sounds a lot like Disneyland, what with all its themed "Lands." Walt Disney, I realized, is supposedly buried at Forest Lawn. But I couldn't remember if it was just his body that was buried here—or was the whole thing about Disney's body being placed on ice in some hyperbaric chamber, in case science progresses to the point where he (or just his head?) can be revived, just an urban legend? It made me think about Murrieta's head, and how perhaps there would be some odd affinity between Disney, the creator of the 1950s

Zorro TV show, and Murrieta, the original Zorro, if science did progress to the point where . . .

And then I snapped out of my macabre reverie when I saw we'd arrived at the Iris Terrace. Michael Jackson's cremated remains are interred in the other wing of the same Iris building. As I walked up Sunrise Slope, I saw little notes tied to the shrubs that skirt the stone complex—memorials to the King of Pop. There were "I Luv U"s tied on the branches, but also hearts and "RIP"s written in the dust of the church-like windows. You can't get into where MJ's ashes are entombed—it's off-limits. I thought about the life of Michael Jackson for a fleeting moment as I walked up the slope toward the other end of the Iris Terrace. He had a tragic life. He made amazing music. And, apparently, he also molested kids close to him. That's awful. Maybe, I thought as I arrived at the entrance to the terrace, it's fitting that both Michael and McCulley are laid to rest in the same complex. McCulley, I'd come to find out, was convicted of rape in 1909, about a decade before he created Zorro. What do we do with the art created by men who did such awful things?

"Yes," a voice crackled over the intercom at the doorway to the columbarium.

"Johnston McCulley . . . uh . . . lot 2-4-5-1-6," I said, trying to sound like I knew what I was doing.

"One minute," the voice said.

The wait seemed overly long. I wasn't even sure I could get access without being a relative.

"Wall elevation 1-4," the crackly voice said, then a long buzz followed as the door opened.

It took a minute to find it. There were hundreds of tiny niches, rows and rows, that ascended at least twenty feet up. Mercifully, McCulley's niche was toward the bottom. Under his surname was inscribed JOHNSTON 1883–1958 and the name of his third wife, LOURIS M. 1889–1956. Here lay the guy who created Zorro in 1919. He took tropes from nineteenth-century adventure novels, mixed in a bit of the Scarlet Pimpernel and the legend of Joaquín Murrieta. But it's Murrieta's story, and the history it stands for, that has been lost. And, I realized, some of Zorro's ghosts are of Johnston McCulley's making.

Before Johnston McCulley penned some 850 pulp fiction stories, before he created Zorro in 1919, before he was convicted of rape a decade before Zorro's creation, before he became a journalist just to pay the bills while working on his real dream, before all that, he was just a kid from Illinois who dreamed of becoming a famous playwright. History, as I've found with other dreamers in other stories, would not be so kind as to grant him that wish. No one remembers the plays of Johnston McCulley. Only the most serious pulp aficionados can name even one of the various and sundry dual-identity pulp characters McCulley created besides Zorro—Thubway Tham, the Mongoose, the Bat, the Crimson Clown, the Black Star, et al. And, as far as I can tell, no one knows much of McCulley's rape conviction. Yet it's all right there in the court records of Multnomah County in Portland, Oregon.[2]

But Zorro, people know. There was a time when only a ubiquitous *zft zft zft* air *Z* was all that was needed to denote the character. It's less so these days. Many young college students, as I've discovered while teaching my own university classes, have only a vague idea of who Zorro might be. Nevertheless, Zorro was the one eternal creation, in that art-will-live-on sort of way, that Johnston McCulley left behind. Very few indeed, know much about McCulley himself, his career, and his oeuvre, if we can call it that. There's a writer behind the mask of Zorro, and he lived, well, a rather haunted life. There's biographical grist for Zorro in McCulley's own history. But, interestingly enough, McCulley's early life looks a lot more like the ambitious, scheming, ladder-climbing Captain Ramón from *The Curse of Capistrano* than the upright fighter for justice Zorro. Johnston McCulley had a knack for alter egos.

And yet, the guy lived a pretty average midwestern childhood, although there was definitely some sadness. McCulley's mother died when he was a baby, and his father died before Johnston graduated high school. It was McCulley's grandparents, on his father's side, who basically raised him. John Wesley McCulley, his grandfather, was born in 1835. John Wesley was just five to ten years younger than Joaquín Murrieta.

Although John Wesley McCulley and Murrieta never met, in a way their life stories crossed. Both had a pioneer spirit, the audacity to move in search of new opportunities, wealth, and land. John Wesley moved west, from his birthplace in Virginia, to Ohio. From Ohio, John Wesley wound up in Chillicothe, Illinois, a town located on the Illinois River in Peoria County. Today,

Chillicothe doesn't seem much like a frontier, but in the early 1840s it was pretty far west. By 1860, Chillicothe boasted a population of 696 people. John Wesley was listed in the 1860 census as a grocer.[3] The document also lists John Wesley's wife, Emily McCulley. She was nineteen at the time. The couple had a son, Rolla Andrew McCulley, who later became the father of Johnston McCulley.

A pioneering spirit wasn't all John Wesley McCulley shared with Joaquín Murrieta. Their paths did cross briefly in terms of geography, although by the time John Wesley made it out to California, Joaquín had been dead for almost a decade. In 1861, while other men of his generation joined up to fight in the Civil War, John Wesley said no thanks. He struck out for California instead, leaving his wife and son behind. Emily, in fact, was pregnant with their second child at the time. Perhaps war provided John Wesley with an excuse, as well as a reason, to leave town.

Whatever the rationale, John Wesley settled in Sonoma County, not far from where, less than ten years before, the scenes of Joaquín's life and exploits had played out. Those exploits continued to play out in the haunted imaginations of Californians. The legend of Joaquín Murrieta was in formation. But the gold rush, which had given life to Murrieta's story, had ended. The game of surface mining, in the placers, was all but over by the 1860s. John Wesley bought fifty acres and planted tobacco and fruit trees.[4] It's no stretch of the imagination to think, as an Anglo-American planter, John Wesley heard stories of Murrieta from other settlers in the region.

After the business of planting and harvesting paid little dividends, John Wesley sojourned for a time in Portland, Oregon. He moved on to Idaho, where, as family lore has it, he found gold, then returned to Chillicothe and Emily with $3,000 in his pocket.[5] With the Civil War ended, John Wesley settled down in the small Illinois town. He farmed for a while, but then went back into the grocery business. Johnston McCulley worked with his grandfather in the small store.[6]

Perhaps Johnston's first introduction to Murrieta came through his grandfather's stories. One is tempted to think of John Wesley recounting the halcyon days of Old California to his grandson while the boy stocked shoes, dry goods, and produce. There were many routes of transmission Murrieta may have ridden on to make it into the mind of Johnston McCulley. It's an important point to make. The tale of William Lamport, in contrast, was confined to the

1872 novel of Riva Palacio in Mexico. The novel has never been translated into English and wasn't widely distributed in the United States.

In Chillicothe, John Wesley and Emily McCulley's family expanded. In 1881, their son Rolla married Clara Belle Raley. The two moved north to Ottawa, Illinois, where the Raley family owned land. It was there, in Ottawa, that Clara Belle gave birth to her first and only son, John William McCulley, on February 2, 1883.

"Johnston" was a name of McCulley's own choosing when he began to publish. The name, or nickname, by which he was known in early life was the slightly less flattering sobriquet "Little Willie."[7] It was given to differentiate him from the other Johns and Williams that populated the McCulley family tree—he also had an uncle named John. But "Little Willie" was also a reference to McCulley's diminutive size. He was a small child and, in adulthood, a thin man of sleight stature. The nickname was probably given by his grandmother, as his mother, Clara Belle, died when the boy was just an infant. Young Rolla, just twenty-four at the time, looked to his parents for support and soon moved back to Chillicothe. It seems from that time on, John Wesley and Emily played the main caregiving role in the life of their grandson. They adopted him, in fact, in 1884. Rolla moved away, married a new woman, and had a child they named Vida McCulley.[8] Tragedy struck again. Rolla died from complications after a construction accident. And Vida, Johnston's half sister, died at the age of thirteen. Young Johnston—"Little Willie"—had lost his mother, his father, and his half sister all before the age of fifteen.

John Wesley and Emily tried to fill in the missing pieces in young Johnston's family. In 1894 the *Chillicothe Bulletin* ran a story informing the public that "Little Willie" was being taken by his mother to visit relatives in Missouri and Texas. By all accounts, the newspaper was referring to his grandmother. His stepmother lived in another town. And so, Johnston McCulley's first appearance in print was as an eleven-year-old boy called "Little Willie" being handheld by his grandmother, off to see the relatives.[9]

Did all the death and diminutiveness in McCulley's early life produce in him a penchant for imaginative world-building? It's an alluring thought.

Maybe it provided him an escape from the losses he'd experienced in real life. "Why seek to depress folks," McCulley was once quoted in an interview, "who have enough depression in their ordinary routines of their lives?"[10] In fiction, he found a way to put right the wrongs he saw in his own world. "Express contentment and happiness and the might of right," he continued, "without going to extremes and writing stuff of the silly, happy type."[11]

Fiction allowed McCulley to become bigger and better than himself—to make something of his life. There's always something bordering between defensive rage and self-aggrandizement in McCulley's correspondence and published interviews. He was ever trying to play the big shot. When asked in one interview what was the best part of being a fiction writer, he answered: "Aside from the fact that there is money in it—that every novelette or four-parter or full-length novel means a fat check—and eliminating a certain amount of fame and self-satisfaction that is the author's, the best feature of the writing game is that your office is anywhere you choose to have it." Just when McCulley would have us believe that travel and freedom was the best part of being a fiction writer, hiding fame and money in a parenthetical clause, he showed his hand. "All you need is a post office where manuscripts may be mailed," he concluded, "[and] a bank where the checks can be cashed."[12] McCulley also added himself to the list of America's most important writers, when asked by an interviewer to name a list of three. "Those, of course, in addition to myself," he said after naming three others.[13]

McCulley's posturing, climbing, and boasting perhaps took root in the furtive soil of childhood loss and diminutive nicknaming. It's also plausible the guy was just a huge SOB by inclination and temperament. But given his background and life history, it's reasonable to think there was a more complex element in McCulley's psychological makeup. McCulley aspired to play the hero of his own story, to be like Zorro. Yet there's also something of Captain Ramón, and several others from the corrupt rogue's gallery of Zorro villains, in McCulley. There's a bit of impetuousness in the writer, a skosh of tantrum. Captain Ramón, like McCulley, is an outsider, a man not born with a silver spoon in his mouth, and one who begrudges those who were. One character-ization McCulley gave to Captain Valentino Rocha, the antagonist in *Zorro Rides Again* (1931), might equally be applied to McCulley himself. "Capitán Rocha," McCulley writes, "led his troopers on across the plaza and straight toward his destination. His head was up. His eyes were flashing. Inwardly he was seething. He sensed that the town was laughing at him and he was sensitive to ridicule."[14] Or, too, there's something of McCulley in Captain Ramón's disdain for Zorro's highborn advantage. Captain Ramón, after Lolita Pulido rebuffs him yet again, says to her: "I am sick of hearing so much of gentle blood. . . . Mine is gentle enough, but it also can be hot at times."[15]

The hotness of McCulley's blood didn't show indication of boiling over in the earliest paper trail of his life—not at the time, anyway. We do see "Little Willie," like Captain Ramón, reaching for something beyond his natural-born status. McCulley wanted out of tiny Chillicothe, Illinois. In April 1900, while still in high school, McCulley wrote a speech titled "The Best Thing in the World."[16] It won first prize in his school and qualified him to compete in the statewide Interscholastic Oratorical Contest held at the University of Illinois in Urbana-Champaign.

In early 1902, after graduation, McCulley had begun giving public lectures at the Apollo Opera House in Princeton, Illinois. "Mr. McCulley," the advertisement reads, "has placed the price of admission at 25 cents."[17] At the age of just nineteen, he set a cover charge for people to hear his lectures. By October of that same year, he had met and married his first wife, Zylpha Harper. Zylpha was a sixteen-year-old stenographer McCulley met in the office of a Peoria real estate agent. McCulley, now with a wife to support, gave up the lectures. He was hired on as a cub reporter for the *Peoria Star*, where he worked for a year or so. Restless, he then moved to the competition, the *Peoria Journal*. A few months after that, he went to Iowa to work on an ill-fated publication that folded shortly after he arrived in the state.[18]

Not content to return to Peoria's newspapers, McCulley needed a fresh atmosphere. He moved to Portland, Oregon, where John Wesley had lived briefly in the 1860s. Zylpha McCulley followed, as did John Wesley and Emily, his grandparents who had always been the stabilizing force to McCulley's peripatetic soul. No big fat checks had yet rolled in. McCulley began writing furiously in an effort to change that fact.

It was in Portland that McCulley first started using the byline "Johnston McCulley." He got a job as a crime and police reporter for the *Oregonian*, and as a culture and drama critic for the *Oregon Journal*. Portland, at the time, was the third-fastest-growing city in America. It went from a lumber and dock town of 46,000 in 1890 to a hustling and bustling city of 210,000 in 1910.[19]

Portland had its haute couture. A burgeoning theater district boasted the Marquam Grand, the Belasco, the Empire, the Star, and the Baker. New, smaller theaters like the Lyric, appeared on SW Seventh Avenue and Morrison Street. Traveling companies and vaudeville troupes passed through the city, but stock companies, the permanent players at the theaters, established a popular following. Moving pictures popped up first in nickelodeons and arcades, but by 1905, intermissions at dramatic theaters would play shorts on projection systems called Vitascopes or the "wonderful Veriscope" or the Viclorama.[20] Johnston McCulley nightly watched and then reviewed the latest plays and productions.

Portland had its vice, too, which McCulley became acquainted with as a crime and police reporter. Vice, in its various forms, whether gambling, drinking, opium, or prostitution, had long been established in Portland's North End, along Burnside Street near the banks of the Willamette River. Crimps, as the middlemen who waylaid sailors and sent them out to sea (often drunk and/or against their will), worked mainly from the North End. The practice of shanghaiing men, the forcible kidnapping of workers for unwanted oceangoing adventures, was on the wane by 1905, but it still happened.[21] Even today, bars and other establishments along Burnside showcase "knockout drops"—essentially trapdoors—in the floor where unruly or inebriated patrons fell to subterranean tunnels and from there were frog-marched to the river. When the so-called shanghai tunnels, a network of underground passages connecting North End establishments to the docks, were excavated in the 1970s researchers found artifacts—a nineteenth-century woman's shoe, parts of opium pipes, and a horrifying human-sized cage.

By the time McCulley started following the crime beat, reform was in the air. A new mayor, Harry Lane, vowed to clean up and clear out vice in the city. But vice is hard to get out of the carpet. At the end of 1904, a bribery scandal erupted in the press. The chief of police, no less, Charles H. Hunt, was implicated in taking hush money from an East Coast gambling syndicate. Chief Hunt received several hundred dollars with the promise that he would "throw the town open" to all kinds of illegal gaming, including slot machines. A grand jury formed to investigate the case toured the North End on a fact-finding mission. While the grand jurors condescended to view for themselves, in the words of the newspaper, "such brazen flaunting of sin and degradation," it was noted that among those witnesses called to testify was one "Johnston W. McCulley, police reporter on a morning paper."[22] McCulley, it seems, was so intimately involved in affairs of Portland crime and vice and police corruption that his testimony in the grand jury investigation was considered expert.

Here, then, was McCulley's training ground as a pulp writer. By day, he trolled through the muck of human tragedy and prodigal living. By night, he put on tie and frock coat to observe the pleasant, the heartbreaking, the only sometimes whimsical, and the (quite often) terrible productions put on by Portland's growing number of stock companies. Everywhere he went he looked for potential story ideas. He sought out plots in his police reporting, while fishing—one of his favorite pastimes—and later, while motoring in automobiles, which became a passion for McCulley. "There's a plot in the peculiar facial expression of the man he meets on the street," one newspaper feature wrote of McCulley. An unusual twist of a bird's song or the act of digging in the garden might trigger a story idea. "Love, hate, greed, revenge, self-sacrifice," the feature quoted McCulley, "have a million angles each." McCulley's story recipes supplied a dash or a dollop of all these ingredients, often in similar ways. "Combine two or three," he said, "mix with a few characters and you have a plot."[23]

Many Zorro stories work that way. Zorro, a man with a dual identity, battles a corrupt official—motivation varies—while wooing a pretty young senorita, usually saving her from said corrupt official, but in the meantime, modeling heroic virtue and thwarting any schemes to interrupt idyllic Spanish fantasy. Rinse. Repeat.

McCulley began to write short stories seriously in 1904. He later wrote advice to aspiring authors, which revealed much of his own early writing experience. "The beginner," he said, "is going to have many of his manuscripts returned, but that is no reason why he should quit."[24] McCulley struggled to find the right mix—adventure, action, character, theme, plot. His first success was a play he wrote called *The Heir Apparent*, produced by the Empire Theater's stock company in 1905.

The theater as art seems to have been McCulley's first love. He was a drama critic. He knew of the latest playwrights and actors in New York and Chicago. He followed their careers. McCulley was something of a snob when it came to the theater. Throughout his life he continued to pester editors with new plays he'd written, many of them unproduced. Writing pulp stories, on the other hand, was about a check and about fan service. "Give the public action," he told one interviewer, "that's what it wants—lots of it. Give them romance, the downfall of ulterior motives and the triumph of right. This can be done just as easily in a murder mystery tale the same as in a story of Biblical times, and in an entertaining manner instead of like a sermon."[25]

The Heir Apparent had some success. There were positive reviews; McCulley's chest swelled a little more with pride. And he was already toying with elements that would later make it into Zorro. The play had a case of mistaken identity, as in many of his stories. But there was also, according to one review at the time, "a delicious vein of comedy . . . supplied by the intrigues of a Sergeant."[26] Even then, McCulley was forming the boasting comic relief of Sergeant Pedro Gonzales, the big, blubbering, Falstaffian character who provided the main humor in almost every Zorro tale.

———

If McCulley's time in two social worlds—Portland's theater district and skid row North End—taught him some of his plots, characters, and themes, it also developed his racial consciousness. Zorro's status as a wealthy Spaniard, a hero with whom white audiences could identify, was not an accident. The writer had clear ideas about race. McCulley wrote about race as a reporter on the crime beat, and he wrote about it as a drama critic.[27] Wearing his mask as a drama critic, McCulley reviewed a production put on at a Japanese theater in Portland. Under the headline QUEER SCENES IN JAP THEATER, McCulley, as a seasoned dramaturge, detailed the many ways the Japanese production reversed the commonplaces of Western theater. In other words, he wrote about how they were doing it wrong. The back row of the theater was best in the Japanese theater, he wrote. No one laughed but to ridicule bad actors. "The leading man," he noted, "is not the hero, but the villain." He offhandedly mentioned "Jap hieroglyphics" appearing on a stage scrim. "Ever heard a Jap woman acterine wail?" he posed to his readers. "If you haven't, don't do it. It won't pay." "You can't even recognize your old-friend jokes," McCulley continued, "when they are dished up in Jap talk." A friendly Japanese American man, McCulley told his readers, helped translate the action on stage for him. He quoted the man in dialect, leaving out definite articles, making the man's speaking voice sound like a fortune cookie. Overall, McCulley presented himself as a head-scratching, incredulous Anglo-American drama critic bewildered and befuddled by the Japanese American culture he encountered. "The audience," he concluded, "which was not small, seemed to enjoy the show. Many nodded their heads and declared it was good. And perhaps it was. You can search me."[28]

All the more revealing of McCulley's view of race is a 1906 review he wrote of a play called *Strongheart*, staged at Portland's Heilig Theater. The story follows the journey of a young Native American man who goes to college among white men. It's a star-crossed love story. Strongheart, the eponymous lead character, falls in love with his best friend's sister, a white woman. When Strongheart reveals his intentions to his friend and his other school chums, they upbraid him for the very idea. Strongheart is an Indian; he can't possibly believe he could marry a white woman. It turns out the best friend's sister loves Strongheart after all—conventions be damned! Yet, we learn, the prejudice goes both ways. Because Strongheart's love interest is white, the couple discovers that Strongheart's tribe won't allow her to come live with them, especially since Strongheart has now been appointed the new chief.

McCulley agreed that racial lines couldn't be crossed. "It has put the Indian," McCulley wrote of the play, "in the walks of life frequented by the white man and drawn the invisible but invincible race line without being illogi-cal, melodramatic, or conventional." McCulley summed it up: "The call of race has been stronger than the call of love." For McCulley, it was not as though there was nothing of value in art that depicted the problems of race relations. But *Strongheart* was valued by McCulley—where the Japanese theater was not—because the Native lead character of the play, Strongheart, was played by a white actor, Robert Edeson. Edeson was "little less than wonderful," accord-ing to McCulley. "He gives the Indian temperament exactly."[29] Nonwhites could be heroes, in other words, but the actor who portrayed that minority character needed to be white. Any drama, or later any Hollywood films, had to deal with minority cultures and issues of race relations in an environment told by white voices.

All this—the depiction of a very real-world Japanese culture that McCulley didn't like, in contrast to the play McCulley loved, *Strongheart*, with its white lead actor—sheds light on the creation of Zorro. Zorro's self-professed "blue blood," the self-conscious designation of Zorro as white, Zorro's aristocratic status—these were not accidents of McCulley's characterization. McCulley knew that a drama like *Strongheart* worked—the play had "few equals on the stage today," according to McCulley—because it told a thorny racial story in safe, white language.

So, too, with Zorro. McCulley had to differentiate Zorro from the Mexican peasants and Indians in his story. The problem was that Spaniards, at the time, held a suspect white identity in America.[30] But if a blue-blooded Spaniard was cast as the hero of the story, then that character stood in for whiteness. Many writers and moviemakers believed at the time that middle-class audiences—white audiences—could only identify with a character, like Zorro, as a hero if he was white in story terms. Zorro became the white proxy in McCulley's tales. His breeding, blood, and wealth stood in for whiteness in comparison to the poor Mexican peons, the workaday soldiers, and the Native Americans who were cast in supporting roles or as villains. Zorro was not a carbon copy of Joaquín Murrieta. Murrieta's Mexican identity told a story uncomfortable for white audiences. Joaquín Murrieta had to be whitened, lifted in social status, and cleansed of his story that told of American racial violence.

And that's what happened. Zorro had to be made white to be palatable to American audiences in 1919. Even if Zorro's "Spanish-ness" was suspect at the time, he was the whitest character in the story. The pattern of whitewashing became even more apparent when Hollywood superstar Douglas Fairbanks played Zorro on the silver screen for the first time.

But before that story is told, we have to inhabit McCulley's drama a bit longer. In 1906, McCulley's first short story was accepted for publication. It was called "The Rotting Log," and it appeared in the *Pacific Monthly*. He'd submitted many manuscripts, some returned only with printed rejection slips, but others with detailed notes. "It pays to dig into it," McCulley said regarding learning from editorial feedback, "and discover for one's self wherein the trouble lies. After that discovery is made it is quite an easy matter to correct one's faults." He learned that "any proper story has three parts—problem, conflict and solution." He read voraciously. "The novice can gain much by reading much," McCulley noted. "He must get some idea of how others do it—don't copy them, but get into the swing of telling a story the way the public likes it to be told."[31]

McCulley managed the swing of it. He sold three stories in 1906, eight in 1907, seventeen in 1908, and twelve in 1909. A decade later, he sold forty-six stories in both 1919 and 1920. He published in some of the best-known pulps of the era, as well as other magazines. There was the *All-Story, Blue Book, Railroad Man's Magazine, Cosmopolitan, Top-Notch Magazine, Detective Story Magazine, Western Story Magazine,* and the *Evening World,* among others. The publications owned by the Frank A. Munsey Company of New York featured a good number of McCulley's stories—mainly westerns, detective stories, and adventure tales. Robert H. Davis, managing editor for many of the Munsey publications in that era, became McCulley's main conduit to the pulp pages. McCulley received his first big fat check as an author from the Munsey company. "Little Willie" was making a new name for himself as Johnston McCulley, magazine writer.

10 | THE BLOOD OF LOLITA PULIDO

BUT THEN IT ALMOST FELL APART—McCulley's marriage, his writing career, and, it would seem to him, most importantly, his reputation. In fact, McCulley's first marriage did fall apart, while his writing career remained intact, albeit a bit teetering. What happened?

In 1907, while McCulley began churning out short stories—and he actually seems to have received enough fat checks at that point to quit his job as a reporter—McCulley's grandfather, John Wesley, died. McCulley traveled with his grandmother by train back to Chillicothe, Illinois.[1] John Wesley's remains rode with them. They laid him to rest. Soon after the funeral, Johnston returned to Portland.

For McCulley, as the only father he'd ever really known, John Wesley's death was shattering. John Wesley was something of a world buffer for McCulley. Like any good parent, he was that stabilizing force that could steady the shaking legs of a child embarking on endeavors *out there* in the cruel world. Johnston McCulley was twenty-four years old—not so young as to be just a kid in the world, but perhaps young enough to have felt himself adrift.

At this point in McCulley's story, it would be easy to attribute the next series of events—dark as they turn—to McCulley's history of loss, John Wesley's being the most recent and, perhaps, the most deeply felt. Chalking up the, frankly, despicable actions of McCulley in this period of his life to the grief, rage, and ennui he may have felt after his grandfather's death is too easy. It's a generous interpretation, to put it lightly. It's the "Don Draper defense": in the TV show *Mad Men*, the lead character's philandering, lies, and general despicable behavior are linked to childhood trauma and also to the violence he experienced in the Korean War. In pointing out McCulley's loss, then, I don't want to let McCulley off the hook.

An equally acceptable explanation is that McCulley, perhaps, by temperament and background, had always taken a certain license with his behavior, believing himself to be above rules that governed others because of his literary talents. He took value in playing a big shot. That big-shot belief about himself was confirmed by big checks, adoring readers, and editors who wanted to print his work. Maybe John Wesley's death represented the lifting of an important impediment to his unsavory inclinations—like a lid taken off a boiling pot. With John Wesley dead, perhaps he no longer cared what people thought, at least to an extent. And it's also reasonable to skip the psychobabble altogether and admit that perhaps the timeline is a mere coincidence. The fact that John Wesley's death was followed by a series of awful events is simply correlation, not causation. Maybe McCulley was always up to awfulness—he just didn't get caught before (or after).

Hemingway's longtime girlfriend Martha Gellhorn liked to say, "A man must be a very great genius to make up for being such a loathsome human being." ("Well, I guess she would know," essayist Claire Dederer sharply commented.[2]) The jury's still out on whether Johnston McCulley's artful compensation was enough.

———————

"I am the wife of Johnston McCulley," began Zylpha McCulley in a letter to Munsey editor Robert H. Davis, "from whom you, and others of the Munsey Co., have purchased numerous short stories, serials, etc., for the magazines."[3] This is the first appearance of Zylpha McCulley's voice in the record about what life was like with her husband. Her voice seems full of sadness.

"I am in very deep trouble," Zylpha wrote. She didn't know where her husband was. She arrived in Illinois to visit Johnston only to receive a report from a Peoria journalist that McCulley had eloped with a cloak model named Olga Patterson. Zylpha McCulley asked Robert Davis for help in finding her husband. Mrs. McCulley enclosed a news clipping with her letter. REPORTER ELOPES WITH HIS AFFINITY, the headline read.[4]

Why Johnston left Portland is unclear. But in the fall of 1908, he showed up in Peoria, without his wife, and was hired on as a special correspondent by his old paper, the *Peoria Journal*. It was the *Peoria Journal*, in fact, that published the first news of McCulley's departure with his "affinity." "He had achieved some success as a magazine writer of short stories," wrote the *Journal*, "and filled the management of the paper with dreams of glory he was about to impart to its columns."

Whatever the truth or untruth of what McCulley said or didn't say to his fellow *Journal* reporters, it's worth noting here that the editorial staff of the paper, who wrote the article, seemingly couldn't stand McCulley. "He carried some more or less flattering letters," the article continued—an article appearing in the very paper McCulley worked for, remember—"from various publishers which seemed to bear out his statements and he was regarded with some awe and a good deal of respectful attention by his fellow-scribblers in this city who have not yet arisen to the dizzy heights to which he had apparently attained." McCulley, according to the *Journal*, "talked glibly" of making $300 to $400 every month. The "fat check" was a point of conversation in the newsroom. McCulley told his newsroom colleagues that he was doing *reportage* for the paper "more for exercise than anything else."[5] One imagines the news reporters pretending to gag into their fedoras behind McCulley's back.

McCulley, according to the paper, met Olga Patterson, "a stylish girl, with dark hair and eyes and a vivacious manner," not long after his arrival in Peoria.[6] The paper even described a kind of meet-cute in which both McCulley and Patterson were reaching to use the same phone at the same time. Apparently flush with a new $300 check from the Frank A. Munsey Company, McCulley cashed it and ran off with Patterson. He left a note for Zylpha, reported another newspaper, "telling her that he had left Peoria to start life anew, that she was a good woman but not suited to his genius, and that she could return to her friends in Portland."[7] Zylpha didn't return to Portland, but she did go to the local courthouse and wept before the judge. Since wife abandonment was a punishable offense at the time, a warrant for McCulley's arrest was issued.[8] It was at that point that Zylpha wrote her letter to Robert Davis, Johnston's editor, asking for any news of her husband.

"I was married to Mr. McCulley when I was but sixteen," she wrote to Davis. "I am 22 years old now, but our married life has been happy until this woman, whom Mr. McCulley met only one month ago, came into his life. I hear very dreadful things about her."

Zylpha McCulley's assertion that married life with Johnston had always been happy shouldn't be taken at face value. She was probably protecting herself and her own reputation by claiming as much. In the divorce proceeding from September 1909, which I obtained from the Clackamas County Court archives, Zylpha McCulley described a history of abuse:

> That from a time shortly after the said marriage, until the present time, defendant [Johnston McCulley] has treated plaintiff [Zylpha McCulley] in a cruel and inhuman manner, and has heaped upon plaintiff personal indignities, rendering her life burdensome in various manners, and more particularly as follows, to-wit: That at various times during the year 1908, while plaintiff and defendant were living together at Portland, Oregon, the defendant struck and assaulted the plaintiff, and cursed plaintiff, and applied to plaintiff vile and opprobrious epithets; that on account of the said cruel acts of defendant, plaintiff has been obliged to live separate and apart from defendant ever since the 13th day of January, 1909, and has been obliged to support herself, and defendant has failed, neglected and refused to contribute anything to plaintiff's support.[9]

Whatever Zylpha McCulley penned to Robert Davis about a happy marriage, it was written in desperation. "I am heartbroken, Mr. Davis," she wrote, "but you cannot possibly understand how dreadful it is, and how dreadful I feel." She was a wife in a trauma spiral, of which the abandonment was only the most recent. "I have always helped my husband in his literary work," she explained to Davis, "and he, himself, has often given me credit for his success, but now that this dreadful thing has happened I fear his life will be ruined." Put in an awkward position, Robert Davis replied, "I sincerely hope he will repent, and that he will find it within his nature to do the just and manly thing by his wife."[10]

A week later, from Savannah, Georgia, Johnston repented—sort of. He finally wired his wife news: "Regained senses here today. Remember nothing. Don't know how I got here. What happened? Letter follows. Feel well now accept [sic] headache. Advise immediately if you get this—Johnstone [sic] McCulley."

And on the same day: "Have seen papers. All wrong. Demand retraction. See letter coming—Johnstone McCulley."

And a third, again, on the same day: "Answer immediately if you have received my two former messages—Johnstone McCulley."[11]

The wireless communications read like a string of panicked text messages. *What happened? It's not my fault! Oh shit!!!* When McCulley saw the papers, he instantly went into defensive mode. He hired a lawyer and threatened to sue the *Peoria Journal* for libel.[12] The father of Olga Patterson, the cloak model with whom McCulley had his *cinq à sept*, lawyered up as well. McCulley later claimed the *Peoria Journal* printed a retraction. I have found no record of it.

Zylpha McCulley's letter did cause problems for her husband. Robert Davis, editor of the Frank A. Munsey Company, was concerned, to say the least.[13] The Peoria article named Munsey in its exposé of McCulley. Davis had no intention of allowing McCulley's scandal to cast a cloud on the Munsey Company's reputation, pristine as it certainly was, given that they published such high-brow stuff as pulp fiction. That said, Munsey put out other, more reputable periodicals, and Davis wanted to protect their already fraught image. McCulley had no idea his wife had written Davis, so it most likely came as a surprise to Davis when a letter from McCulley showed up on his desk shortly after. In typical McCulley fashion, the letter began: "I am sending you today, by express under separate cover, a serial entitled 'WHEN THE WORLD STOOD STILL.' I trust it will create a sensation in your office of the sort that makes you rush for a check book. If it is not available, of course—well, you know!" McCulley alluded to "serious domestic trouble" but not the kind described by Zylpha McCulley in her letter to Davis. Johnston noted trouble, not with his wife but with his wife's family, relating to "the settlement of an estate." McCulley didn't let on his more serious domestic trouble. "I feel more like working than I have for some time," he confided to Robert Davis.

Davis, once again in an awkward position, replied that McCulley needed to explain his affairs because the Munsey Company had been named in the *Peoria Journal* article. "We would like to have a little light on the subject before resuming our business relations."[14] McCulley once again went on the defensive. He sent Davis a long, dense, two-page letter in reply. He denied the story in the papers. "Some of my wife's relatives circulated the story of my elopement," he wrote, "with the intention, I believe, of making the break between my wife and myself final." He told Davis he "scarcely knew the young lady mentioned in the newspaper story."[15] The culprits, according to McCulley, "were his wife's family" and "the professional jealousy of a reporter." McCulley cited the fact that Zylpha had found out about the affair only after a *Peoria Journal* reporter informed her of it. McCulley assured Davis that "Mrs. McCulley and I have again joined forces, since she is now convinced of my innocence."

The case was settled for Robert Davis: "I am glad you have adjusted your affairs to your satisfaction and that you and Mrs. McCulley are reunited." Davis bought "When the World Stood Still" and promised to look at two more he had on his desk before sending McCulley his next check.[16]

The picture McCulley painted for Davis was like a modestly well-done forgery. From twenty feet, it looked like the real thing—like the truth. But close up, not so much. Zylpha and Johnston McCulley had not reunited, as the divorce suit later in 1909 made clear: "Plaintiff has been obliged to live separate and apart from defendant," the affidavit reads, "ever since the 13th day of January, 1909." McCulley's insistence that all had been mended with his wife was a lie.

What's more difficult to verify is the truth of the elopement. McCulley flatly denied it, as did Olga Patterson's father. Yet that's not so strange. Both men had a vested interest in claiming innocence—both their reputations were on the line. Zylpha McCulley certainly believed it. The *Peoria Journal* believed it too, and the details squared with the kind of man they took McCulley to be. "He was always an erratic individual," wrote the *Journal*, "and his recent escapade is no surprise to those who knew him intimately."[17]

McCulley's faltering messages from Savannah provide the biggest clue to the truth of the affair. We may not be able to know exactly what happened— but something did happen. "Regained senses here today. Remember nothing. Don't know how I got here. What happened?" It sounds like McCulley waking up after being under the influence of some power he couldn't, or wouldn't, control—rage or lust or booze or maybe all three. It sounds, in fact, like Dr. Jekyll waking up after having been taken captive, once again, by his Mr. Hyde alter ego. *What sort of monstrous things have I done under the influence of my other self?* It's no wonder writing alter egos in his fictional characters was easy for McCulley. He'd experienced the phenomenon himself.

———

It got worse. McCulley returned to Portland after a stint in Georgia and Illinois. Zylpha McCulley did as well, but there's little evidence she accepted him back or that they lived under the same roof.

McCulley continued writing. He sold an average of a story a month in 1909. He worked as a press agent for the Lyric Theater, which had produced a subsequent run of his play *The Heir Apparent* in 1907. In June 1909, McCulley produced a new play he'd written called *The Love Ranch*, a romantic western drama, which was staged at the Lyric.[18]

In the fragmentary paper trail of his life, Johnston McCulley next appears in September 1909. The Portland newspapers ran a story that McCulley had been charged with wife abandonment and cruelty, which related to the divorce suit then pending in the Clackamas County court. And worse still, on the morning of September 25, 1909, there appeared this report in the *Oregonian*: "Johnston McCulley, a magazine writer, was arraigned under the name John Doe McLaren, and charged with a statutory offense involving Lena Boyd."[19]

I remember the first time I read that bit of news. I uttered an expletive somewhat loudly to the otherwise empty room I was sitting in. At least a solid baker's dozen of new questions were being cooked in my mind at that moment, and the temperature was rising. There were procedural questions, like what was the "statutory offense"? And there were questions about identity, like who was Lena Boyd? But also a whole other species of thought, not a question, really, but a general sense of horror. What if Johnston McCulley, the creator of Zorro, was also a rapist?

I had to be sure, and delved further. Another report, from September 30: "Johnston McCully [*sic*], who is held in the County Jail on $5000 bail for a statutory offense against Lena Boyd, pleaded not guilty yesterday afternoon, as did William Churchill, accused of a similar offense."[20] Each newspaper article leaked out new information. Newspapers at the time didn't use words like *rape*. I found out that the age of consent in Oregon at the time was sixteen. Lena Boyd was fifteen. On October 2, 1909, the *Oregonian* reported that McCulley had yet to provide bond, and he had been held in the county jail for a week. He entered a plea of not guilty. According to the paper, "William Churchill is accused of a similar offense against the same girl at the same time."[21] *At the same time* rang in my ears. It only added to the grimness of the alleged offense. William Churchill, as it turned out, was an usher at the Lyric Theater. The two men apparently knew each other via their relationship to the Lyric.

But what about Lena Boyd? How McCulley and Churchill came in contact with her was a mystery.

I needed to find some nonnewspaper sources to corroborate the charges. I found them in the Multnomah County Circuit Court archives, which hold inconsistent records for a case that happened one hundred years ago, but the court proceedings and the ruling of the judge were there: "Judgment No. 41497, In the Circuit Court of the State of Oregon for Multnomah County, Nov. Term, 1909 . . . The State of Oregon vs. John Doe McLaren or Johnston McCulley."[22] New details emerged in a mixture of handwritten notes and type-written bureaucratic procedures. I learned that the assault had taken place on August 7, 1909; that Lena Boyd and her mother, Isabelle J. Boyd, had been the two witnesses who testified before the grand jury; that the grand jury found sufficient evidence to indict Johnston McCulley "of the crime of rape," and that McCulley, according to the indictment, "did then and there unlawfully and feloniously carnally know one Lena Boyd, a female child under the age of sixteen years." The charge "statutory offense" was no longer vague. The charge was rape. I tried and failed to get access to the records of the grand jury investigation. Even one hundred years later, grand jury records remain sealed to the public.

The full account of what took place on August 7 remains blurry, but what I'd found was enough to put a rough sketch together. After the indictment, a warrant was signed and Johnston McCulley was arrested. He first gave his name as John Doe McLaren, likely to keep his name out of the papers. William Churchill was also arrested at that time. The judge, Earl C. Bronaugh, ruled that McCulley had to give his real name. He said it was John McCulley. He entered a plea of not guilty, as did Churchill.

While McCulley sat in jail trying to raise bail, the divorce proceeding issued by his then wife, Zylpha McCulley, was finalized. Zylpha was allowed to resume her maiden name, as the marriage had produced no offspring.

McCulley told reporters that there were at least a half dozen individuals he was pursuing to help him pay the $5,000 bond. The judge lowered it to $2,000, and whoever agreed to help him with the money did so, and McCulley left county lockup.

A trial was set for November. Yet, when November rolled around, the trial was put in continuance because, all of a sudden, no one could find Lena Boyd, the deputy district attorney's main witness. "Where is Lena Boyd?" the

Oregonian asked on November 12. "The District Attorney's office," reported the paper, "received information that the girl had left the city a week before. This was supplemented with the report that she and her mother, Mrs. Isabella [*sic*] Boyd, had gone to Indiana, their former home."[23] The deputy district attorney told the *Oregonian* he feared she had been intimidated, or that someone had tried to pay her off to leave the state. It was his belief, he told reporters, that "someone has induced the girl to leave the state." One article reported that "the girl and her mother agreed to leave Portland any time they were given $200."[24] Was this hush money? Did McCulley or one of his friends or his lawyer interfere? Was there intimidation?

Many of these questions don't have definitive answers.

Whether Lena Boyd returned, and why she apparently left, is unclear in the record. But by the end of November, both McCulley and Churchill changed their pleas from not guilty to guilty "of the crime of rape as charged in the indictment filed herein."[25] The case didn't go to trial. Did Lena Boyd and her mother show up after all? Perhaps the threat of Lena Boyd showing up to testify influenced the decision of McCulley and Churchill to change their plea. It's quite likely both were told if they pled guilty they'd probably get a more lenient verdict. And that's what happened: "It is therefore considered and ordered by the Court," reads the verdict, "that the defendant John McCulley, be imprisoned in the Oregon State penitentiary for a period of four (4) years, and it appearing to the Court that the defendant has not previously been convicted of a crime, and if he be permitted to go at large, he will not again violate the law. It is therefore ordered that the judgment of imprisonment in the cause be, and the same is hereby suspended, and the defendant is allowed to go on parole, on condition."[26] Johnston McCulley, as well as William Churchill, got off on parole and probation. They served no further jail time.

At the sentencing, Judge Bronaugh sermonized to the two defendants. The judge "said he had investigated the case carefully and was satisfied that the girl in the case was not above reproach." In slapping the wrists of the two convicted rapists, he also threw aspersions on the virtue of young Lena Boyd. She was somehow to blame, according to the judge. I imagine Judge Bronaugh looking at McCulley from his seat on the court bench, offering his lecture in misogynist morality. Whatever the truth of the judge's facial expression, the *Oregonian* quoted his comments to McCulley and Churchill: "The fact that a girl has started on the wrong path does not excuse a man. Especially when the girl is lacking in years of discretion." The judge proceeded to render his final pronouncement. "I am extending the parole," he said to the court, "in the hope that the young men will avail themselves of the leniency of the court, conduct themselves as men should, and respect womanhood, whether that womanhood is worthy of respect or not."[27] In other words, according to the judge, Lena Boyd was not worthy of respect but, as manly men, they shouldn't have raped her because they needed to respect the Office of Womanhood.

Who is Lena Boyd? That was the question asked by the *Oregonian*, and it's a question I kept coming back to. The newspapers called her a fifteen-, and sometimes, a sixteen-year-old girl. According to Judge Bronaugh, she "was not above reproach," meaning she shared in the blame for the rape—a not uncommon, although wrong, assertion in rape cases, then as now. She was supposedly a girl that had started down the wrong path and, although she lacked years of discretion, she was not considered a woman worthy of respect. The newspapers and the judge were talking *about* Lena Boyd. We never got to hear *from* Lena Boyd, to hear her voice.

But there are clues as to what her voice sounded like. For instance, she accused McCulley and Churchill of the crime. The two men knew each other through the Lyric Theater—McCulley was a press agent and playwright, Churchill an usher.[28] It's unclear what happened and how it happened.

I first thought that the August 7 incident may have happened at the Lyric Theater—a young, overawed Lena Boyd was seduced and then raped by McCulley or Churchill after a production. I discovered that that probably wasn't the case. The Lyric Theater was closed on the night of August 7, a Saturday, and didn't reopen for the next season until the following weekend.[29] I checked the Portland City Directory from 1909. It turns out that McCulley's apartment was less than a mile from where Lena Boyd boarded at a rooming house with her mother.[30] There may have been a chance meeting or, perhaps, an acquaintance made first at the Lyric, and then later renewed in a subsequent engagement, which ended in the traumatic rape by both McCulley and Churchill "at the same time."

However it happened—the introductions, the interactions, the rape—Lena Boyd, with her mother, reported it to the police. Lena Boyd testified before the grand jury. Lena Boyd had a voice. Although it hasn't been preserved in its entirety, and not in quotable words, her voice is there in her decision to come forward in a day and time when, in the end, she was made to share the blame for the incident. But it was her reputation that was ultimately ruined.

Lena Boyd was a ghost after appearing in just a pair of newspaper articles and in the court documents from 1909. I scoured the newspapers of the era for any information on her. Genealogical websites provided listings for "Lena Boyd" in a variety of states—Illinois, California, Indiana, and others.

Finally, I found a match. A woman on a genealogical site posted a brief life story of a "Lena Opel Boyd." Her mother was Isabelle. The dates matched up—Lena O. Boyd was born in Indiana but lived in Portland at the time of the McCulley assault. And Lena O. Boyd matched the siblings in a 1910 census. The woman who posted it, Janet Boyd, is the granddaughter of one of Lena's brothers; that makes her Lena's grandniece. Janet Boyd told me what she knew of her great-aunt. "When Lena Opel Boyd was born in September 1893," she wrote me, "in Adams, Indiana, her father, William, was 40, and her mother, Isabelle, was 33. [Lena] had four brothers and one sister. Isabelle was pregnant with baby #6 when her husband Wm. Boyd died. [Lena] died in Hillsboro, Oregon, at the age of 33."[31]

I wrote Janet back. I told her everything I knew about Lena Boyd and Johnston McCulley, the rape, the case—all of it. It was a pretty weird e-mail to send, I've got to admit. *Ah, yeah, so your relative knew the guy who created Zorro and that guy was also convicted of raping her.*

Janet was really kind. She thanked me for the information. "I now wonder why [Lena] died at such an early age," she wrote me. "She was only 32 or 33 meaning she was raped at 15 or 16. How awful." Janet and I wrote back and forth furiously. Every e-mail seemed a plea that perhaps if we continued to talk about it, some new detail would occur to her, or I would've found some new document to share. "Poor Lena's mom died just 3 years after the rape," she wrote in one e-mail, "on December 9, 1912 in Portland, Oregon, at the age of 53, and was buried there. . . . [Lena's] dad died when she was only one-and-a-half. [Isabelle] was a widow with six children. Rough life."[32]

Janet's intimate family memories are only partial. "I wish now I had talked more about family with my grandparents," she wrote me. Though partial, her memories fill in some gaps, both factual and emotional. Isabelle, a widow with six children, moved to Oregon for new opportunities after the death of her husband. The 1900 and 1910 censuses list her as boarding in a rooming house. Lena O. Boyd was there too. It seems they struggled to make ends meet. Isabelle was listed as a domestic maid; Lena, as a clerk in one document and a "feeder" in another, which meant she worked for a printing company feeding paper into a press.

Somehow Lena's path crossed with McCulley and Churchill. It needn't have been connected with the Lyric Theater, but that's a possibility. When the rape happened it probably took place in a familiar location. Why? One newspaper report said that "there were a young married woman and her husband concerned in the case."[33] That report is both illuminating and vexing. Was it a case of mutual acquaintance in a familiar apartment? Were there flirtations between Lena and McCulley or Churchill? Was there some sort of romantic potential in the meeting? Or was it an incident without preliminaries?

Even in our own day, we seem at a loss to understand a full accounting of how and why rape occurs. The data, however, show that in a majority of cases women who are raped know their assailants.[34] That probably held true in Lena Boyd's experience. Men and women had tighter strictures on male-female interactions in 1909 than today. Perhaps the anonymous young married woman and her husband were two of the intermediaries introducing the parties involved.

Whatever the exact details, we need to listen to and believe Lena Boyd. She went to the police. She testified. And, although one newspaper reported that "the girl and her mother agreed to leave Portland any time they were given $200," the statement reveals more about the state of Lena and her mother's desperation—a survival strategy, perhaps—than evidence that she was somehow lying about the rape. In 1909, in an era when women were victim-shamed constantly, Lena Boyd had everything to lose by pushing the legal issue, by reporting it, by testifying before the grand jury. She had really only to gain the truth in telling her story.

McCulley's life was only momentarily upended. He left Portland under a cloud and moved to Seattle. Apparently, the terms of his parole were loose enough for him not to have to remain in Portland. He worked as a journalist again, but there are no bylines for him in this period. He shows up in Denver, Colorado, in 1913, and in Kansas City, Missouri. City directories list him for both Denver and Kansas City in the same year.[35] He lived a peripatetic life. All he needed was a mailbox for manuscripts and a bank to cash his fat checks.

By 1915, McCulley was in Los Angeles. He worked for the *Los Angeles Times* and the *Los Angeles Herald*. Sometime before 1918 he married again, a woman named Ruth McKinnie.[36] McCulley wrote stories, read into the history of California, and continued to sell copy to the pulps. He sold sixteen stories in 1916, twenty in 1917, and thirty-two in 1918. He moved to Colorado Springs and began writing stories about Old California. Zorro, based in Murrieta lore, was just one of many.

There's a passage in *The Curse of Capistrano* that, once I learned about Lena Boyd and the rape, started to rattle me quite a bit. It's the scene in the novel where Captain Ramón enters Lolita Pulido's house without the proper chaperones present. Only a few servants are at the hacienda. Her parents aren't there. Ramón makes romantic advances and proposes marriage, even though Don Diego is courting Lolita. (Lolita can't stand Diego because he's a fop and doesn't seem very manly.) She also doesn't know Diego is Zorro, even though she's falling in love with Zorro. To Lolita, Ramón lacks propriety in entering her house with no thought to honor and discretion.

"Pretty words from the daughter of a man who is about ruined," Captain Ramón tells Lolita after she flatly refuses his marriage proposal.

"Ruin would not change the blood of the Pulidos, Señor," Lolita rejoins. "I doubt whether you understand that, evidently having ill blood yourself. Don Diego shall hear of this. He is my father's friend—"

Ramón cuts her off midsentence. "And you would wed the rich Don Diego, eh, and straighten out your father's affairs? You would not wed an honorable soldier, but you would sell yourself—"

"Señor!" This time Lolita cuts Ramón off. She's unable to handle the insult, that she would simply give herself to a man in order to put her father in better financial and social standing. She slaps Ramón.

At this point, the scene becomes pretty excruciating to read. An encounter reminiscent of it quite probably played out in McCulley's own life.

After Lolita's slap, Ramón returns the insult by trying to force Lolita to give him a kiss. "I shall take a kiss to pay for that. . . . Such a tiny bit of womanhood can be handled with one arm, thank the saints." Lolita "fought him," writes McCulley, "striking and scratching at his breast." Ramón laughs at her. Lolita is "spent and breathless" because of the struggle and for her fear of what

Ramón proposes to do. She calls for the aid of the saints, while Ramón resumes laughing at her. "He threw back her head and looked down into her eyes."[37]

Zorro intervenes at this point. He saves the day and makes Ramón apologize on his knees. Lolita freely decides to give Zorro "the kiss he would've taken." The whole scene, complete with its sexual assault, is really strange to read knowing the history of Johnston McCulley. Was the guy conscious of how oddly similar his fiction was to an occurrence in his own life?

It got me thinking about a larger question posed by many writers and journalists in the wake of the #MeToo movement. Author Claire Dederer, for instance, distilled the essence of many of my questions about McCulley and his work in an essay she wrote for the *Paris Review*: "What do we do with the art of monstrous men?"[38] Her essay explores her own complicated relationship to the films of Woody Allen. Allen is a genius filmmaker. He also left his life partner Mia Farrow for his wife's stepdaughter, Soon-Yi Previn. By all accounts, Allen's sexual relationship with Soon-Yi began when she was a *very* young adult. Do we boycott Allen's work? Do we decide not to pay to consume Allen's art, to support the work with our wallets, or do we decide it's OK to watch it if someone else paid with their wallets? There's a whole set of ethics and morals involved. And, perhaps most importantly, Dederer dispenses with the "we"—she asks, what do *I* do with it? On that level, the individual choice, Dederer is left with her own ambivalence. Some of Allen's films she can watch and separate the art from the artist; other films, she can't.

And, of course, Woody Allen is just the tip of the iceberg. There are the films of Roman Polanski, a director accused of raping an underage girl. There are a slew of sexual improprieties in Hollywood and in the entertainment industry. There are also, say, the rampant anti-Semitism of Wagner or the misogyny of Hemingway. The list goes on. "I sort of teeter back and forth," Dederer said in an interview with National Public Radio, "almost on a balance beam between the rage at what has been done and the gratitude to the women who've come forward, and then this feeling that I'm unwilling to give up the art. Kind of where I end up is thinking that every audience member is responsible."[39]

Responsibility is a subject I brought up in a college course I taught on the history of Zorro. What do we do with Zorro, I asked my class, now that we know what we know about McCulley? Some students, many of them male, wanted to see McCulley's fictional description of the sexual assault scene of

Lolita Pulido as McCulley's veiled mea culpa for his real-life actions. Didn't Zorro punish Ramón in the novel? asked these students. "Fight, insulter of girls," Zorro goads Captain Ramón at the end of the novel. And when Zorro finally kills Captain Ramón in a duel, Zorro says, "He will never insult a señorita again."[40] I saw several female students give sidelong glances at one another, and not a few eye rolls. Hands shot up around the room. One female student adroitly pointed out that McCulley might have simply been diverting attention, not unlike a minister who preaches virtue on Sundays while engaged in reprehensible behavior outside the church.

We read into literature what we want to see, I told my class. The reality is that we don't know. McCulley never commented on the incident explicitly, which in itself speaks loudly to McCulley's character. And just because it all happened in 1909 doesn't begin to excuse it. In the end, Zorro, whether we like it or not, carries the ghost of sexual violence. At the end of the term, one of my students, a woman, wrote this on her final exam: "Johnston McCulley is the author of *The Curse of Capistrano* (1919). He created the 'vigilante Zorro.' This is the basis for modern American superheroes. Side note: He is a convicted rapist."

All this got me thinking of Lolita Pulido in the first Zorro novel. McCulley, in *The Curse of Capistrano*, titled one of his chapters "The Blood of the Pulidos." The title refers to the strength of character Lolita showed in the midst of a cruel imprisonment by Captain Ramón. Lolita Pulido rejected Captain Ramón's forced amorous advances. Imprisoning Lolita and her family was Captain Ramón's revenge. It's ironic, I suppose. McCulley, the culprit in the case, penned a story with a strong female character. That got me thinking of the strength of character of Lena Boyd, McCulley's own victim. But the characterization of Lolita Pulido in one passage made me see Lena Boyd clearly, if only for a moment.

> But there was Pulido blood in the señorita's veins, and Gonzalez had not taken that into account. . . . One hand came from behind her back, and in it she held a long, keen knife such as sheep skinners used. She put the point of the knife against her breast and regarded them bravely. "Señorita Lolita Pulido does not return to the foul cárcel now or at any time, señores," she said. "Rather would she plunge this knife into her heart, and so die as a woman of good blood should. If his excellency wishes for a dead prisoner, he may have one."[41]

And then, later in the chapter, after Lolita escapes, she mounts a horse while the soldiers try madly to capture her: "She wheeled the horse's head, kicked at his sides as a trooper rushed around the corner of the house. A pistol ball whistled past her head. She bent lower over the horse's neck and rode."[42]

The fire. The courage. She could handle herself. She did what she had to do. Lolita Pulido had been sexually attacked and put in prison. But Lolita Pulido was no victim. Lena Boyd did no less. Lena Boyd was not content to remain a victim. She spoke up. She testified before the grand jury even when, in the end, her reputation was shattered because if it.

By all accounts, when Johnston McCulley arrived in Los Angeles in 1915 the rape of Lena Boyd was not foremost in the writer's thoughts. What was on McCulley's mind was writing a story about Old California.

11 | BECOMING ZORRO

WHEN MCCULLEY ARRIVED IN LOS ANGELES, the people of California were in the middle of constructing a myth about themselves and their region. The gold rush, what with all its racial violence, greed, and strife, just would not do as a founding story. Politicians, novelists, and businessmen, but also chambers of commerce, architects, and early movie stars were all busy creating what social critic Carey McWilliams would later call California's "Fantasy Heritage." Murrieta's journey to becoming Zorro could not have happened without the Spanish fantasy heritage.

What was it, this fantasy? Carey McWilliams defined it, with the purpose of exposing it as a fraud, in a passage in his now famous book *North from Mexico* (1949). "Long, long ago," writes McWilliams, "the borderlands were settled by Spanish grandees and caballeros, a gentle people, accustomed to the luxurious softness of fine clothes, to well-trained servants, to all the amenities of civilized European living." The region was inhabited by "kindly mission padres," he continues, who won their Indian converts through their "saintly example." It was hard work, but any Indian hostility fell prostrate at the feet of these industrious, meek friars who shepherded their flocks with gentle hands. "Life was incomparably easy, and indolent in those days," McWilliams adds. One needed only cast a seed here or there, and lo and behold, the fertile soils gave forth a bounty wholly out of proportion to the work put into it. There were siestas during long afternoons, which were only interrupted out of the sheer pleasure one took "to open an eye and lazily watch the corn stalks shooting up in the garden light." The Spanish dons gathered by night in romantic

97

patios and plazas. "Gentle wines," McWilliams notes, were sipped between conversations of the day's events. There were "memories of castles in Spain." Young people raced horses "over the green-rolling hills and mustard fields of Southern California"; at night, they did their "contradanzas and jotas to the click of castanets." And "as the moon rose," McWilliams closes his portrait of the Spanish fantasy, one "could find a young love-struck ranchero chancing under the window of his beloved's room. He would sing the old love songs of Spain. . . . All in all, this life of Spain-away-from-Spain in the borderlands was very romantic, idyllic, very beautiful."[1]

After painting such a fine portrait, in terms, in fact, that sound a lot like the setting for Zorro, McWilliams stands back from his creation, pauses a moment to smirk at the reader who's leaning forward all warm with romantic ardor . . . and then proceeds to take out a large club and annihilate the word picture—and with it, the Spanish fantasy heritage of Southern California. "Indeed," McWilliams takes his first swing, "it's really a shame that it never existed." "Los Angeles," he swings again, "is merely one of many cities in the borderlands which has fed itself on a false mythology for so long that it has become a well-fattened paradox." Take, for instance, McWilliams argues, the idea that the original inhabitants of the city were blue-blooded Spaniards. Nope, not so much, McWilliams writes. Most of the founding group of Angelenos were Indians, married to Indians; many were mulattos or mestizos, and there was even a man simply listed in the first town census as "Chino"—or a man from China. "None of this would really matter," McWilliams takes his third and most important demolishing swipe at the fantasy heritage, "except that the churches in Los Angeles hold fiestas rather than bazaars and that Mexicans are still not accepted as part of the community."[2]

Los Angeles, in other words, and many other cities in Southern California, mythologized having a Spanish heritage—one that never existed—and rejected the very real Mexican American history that built the region. Anglo-American women dressed up in full Spanish costume for balls, but referred to the population of Mexican Angelenos as "greasers." Hollywood filmed romantic Spanish films with heroes called Ramona or Zorro, but everywhere in Los Angeles Mexicans were excluded from "restaurants, dance halls, swimming pools, and theaters."[3] It was a corpulent, immense, distended belly of a paradox indeed. McWilliams was the first scholar to bring attention to it, the first to take a strong swipe at its foundations.

Like the Spanish fantasy heritage, Zorro is an American paradox. It's not the only one, to be sure. Take, for example, the creation of jazz. It's one of the only cultural forms entirely particular to the United States and has become emblematic of American identity—and yet, African American musicians who created jazz suffered under Jim Crow and segregation in the era when jazz came to life. Or consider how the generation of early comics creators felt they needed to change their names from, for instance, Stanley Lieber and Jacob Kurtzberg to Stan Lee and Jack Kirby in order to seem non-Jewish enough for a WASPy American readership. Zorro, then, as with jazz and comics in their own contexts, was birthed in a specific historical moment in Southern California. The culture for which California became known belonged to Mexican Americans, but Mexican Americans were everywhere derided and excluded. That's a pretty crazy paradox, but it's part of Zorro's origins.

McCulley, when he moved to Los Angeles in 1915, was everywhere confronted with the Spanish fantasy. "He studied the Old California mission empire for years," one feature profile of McCulley states. "Zorro was intended to express the spirit of the caballero of the times," the feature adds.[4] The paradox at the center of Zorro was the Spanish fantasy heritage. Although McCulley wrote his character to be Spanish, to evoke soft guitars and romantic adventure, Zorro bears the mark of Joaquín Murrieta. The history and experience of Latinx people in California are part of Zorro. That history and experience have been covered up by layers of black silk, velvet, and satin—with a nifty mask, to boot.

The Joaquín Murrieta whom Johnston McCulley encountered was not the newspaper Joaquín from the early 1850s. And although there's good reason to believe that McCulley did read John Rollin Ridge's *Life and Adventures*, the figure of Murrieta had been further mythologized since Ridge's 1854 novel. The construction of the Spanish fantasy and the development of the legend of Joaquín grew together in the sixty-odd years between the gold rush and the creation of Zorro. The Spanish fantasy and the legend of Murrieta were like two trees that could only bear fruit by cross-pollination. It was from the splicing of these two stories—the Spanish fantasy and the bandit Murrieta—

that Zorro sprang to life. And, we should add, nineteenth-century adventure novels helped, like a nearby industrious beehive, providing a constant sprinkle of swashbuckling, devil-may-care derring-do.

The Spanish fantasy heritage of Southern California developed as a consequence of the expansion of the United States across the American continent. At first, the newly formed United States—just thirteen colonies in the eighteenth century—painted Spain with the same black brush as had the British, their former colonial master. The British created a "Black Legend" about Spanish colonization—that all the pillaging, raping, and marauding of the Spanish was, at any rate, far more monstrous than the British project of colonization had been in North America.

Many of the early leaders of the United States were quick to read Spanish failure into the quest for Latin American sovereignty. While Mexican insurgents sought to throw off Spain's yoke in 1813, Thomas Jefferson quipped: "A priest-ridden people" were beyond "maintaining a free civil government."[5] In 1821, John Quincy Adams, then secretary of state, noted that the Latin American republics "have not the first elements of good or free government. . . . Arbitrary power, military and ecclesiastical, was stamped upon their education, upon their habits, and upon all their institutions."[6] The Black Legend, created about Spain by the British, was easily transferred to early American leaders, who applied it to their fellow Latin American republics in the western hemisphere.

And yet, as the United States expanded across the continent, as it gained territory that had once belonged to Spain in Florida, in Texas, and in California, as well as other states in the west, the Black Legend about Spain softened, while condescension remained for former Spanish colonies like Mexico. Consider, again, President James Polk's statement to his cabinet member on the eve of war with Mexico in 1846: "It was God's will that Mexico's richest lands, especially the fertile stretch by the Pacific, pass from its current shiftless residents to hard-working white people better able to husband their resources."[7] The lands originally colonized by Spain, then badly maintained by Mexico, had naturally—even providentially—passed into the hands of "hard-working white people"—in other words, white Anglo-Saxon Protestant citizens of the United States. Spain was no longer painted so black in the popular imagination, but Mexico was. The Spanish fantasy heritage allowed the Anglo-American settlers to tell the story of the providential process by which they got the land, but also to conveniently leave out Mexico.[8]

Johnston McCulley's Zorro stories are redolent of Spanish California fantasy. In *The Curse of Capistrano*, McCulley's first sentence mentions "the roof of red Spanish tile," an aspect of Spanish architecture that only in the 1910s became a common building material.[9] Despite McCulley's insistence that *The Curse of Capistrano* was set in the days of Spanish rule, "he wove elements of the Spanish-Mexican Period of early California into his Zorro stories," writes one historian, "setting them in a novelistic genre."[10] McCulley blended the Spanish and Mexican periods together, taking elements of the Murrieta gold rush era and painting them with the Spanish fantasy brush. All of Old California was Spanish, in other words, even the parts that were actually Mexican.

The Spanish fantasy heritage solidified in the 1880s, some forty years before McCulley wrote his first Zorro novel.[11] At California statehood, the vast majority of Mexicans were employed in agricultural pursuits or mining. But a small population of wealthy Mexican ranch owners claimed direct heredity from the Spanish colonial era. The wealthy Mexican rancheros called themselves *Californios*. Californios presented their racial status as blue-blooded Spaniards, inheritors of aristocratic status. It was a fiction, by and large, the same fiction that Carey McWilliams would point to in articulating the Spanish fantasy heritage of the region almost one hundred years later. But when California became a state, that fiction—that Spanish dons and senoritas had passed through the Mexican era untainted by intermixing with Indians and other peoples of color—allowed Californios leverage with Anglo-Americans. It afforded Californios a heightened status over the poorer, immigrant population of Mexicans. The myth of Californio nobility became part of the Zorro narrative.[12]

Californios and Anglo-Americans looked to Franciscan friar Junípero Serra as the founding father of their new state. Novelist and writer Helen Hunt Jackson (1830–1885) did much to popularize Father Serra. She brought the Franciscan's accomplishments to a national audience. Her two-part essay "Father Junípero and His Work" (1883) pitched Serra as a Catholic palatable to American Protestants. Jackson followed on her successful essay with a novel, *Ramona* (1884). It was read widely and presented California's missions in a wholly sympathetic light. Although set in Mexican California, the heroes of the book are Spanish friars who look completely different from the rapacious characters who had inhabited tales of the Black Legend. In the same year *Ramona* was published, Junípero Serra was given a legal holiday in California. Three monuments dedicated to Serra came to dot the state from south to north.

Even the hostilities of 1898, which led to war between the United States and Spain, could not wipe out the fantasy heritage of Old California. The US invasion of the Caribbean, with future president Theodore Roosevelt's Rough Riders leading the charge, didn't manage to permanently dampen America's "Spanish craze," as one historian has termed it. In 1912, President William Howard Taft dedicated a monument to Christopher Columbus in Washington, DC, in celebration of the Spanish explorer's "discovery" of America. He told the crowd assembled to forgive and forget any lingering hostility toward Spain. Among the speakers at the ceremony was the director of the Los Angeles Chamber of Commerce, Joseph Scott. As one orator from New England endlessly eulogized about how the English Pilgrims had brought civilization to North America, Scott calculated his response. "Long before the so-called Anglo-Saxon had set foot as a colonist upon American soil," Scott told the audience, "the followers of Columbus had penetrated the heart of Kansas and gone down as far as Buenos Aires. . . . The Spanish race, with its indomitable faith, pursued almost alone its mission of civilization and evangelization of the aborigines of America."[13] Upholding the "fortitude of the Spanish race," in the words of Scott, the California business community had a clear economic rationale in upholding the Spanish fantasy heritage. Scott and other promoters where even then trying to attract tourists to the region. One early destination was El Camino Real, the old king's highway, which would figure so prominently in McCulley's early Zorro stories. In reality, the royal road was just a dusty network of roads that only sort of connected the twenty-one Spanish missions in the colonial era.[14] But it had a mystique about it, largely due to entrepreneurs who *said* it had a mystique, and who created it as a tourist attraction.

Hollywood, in its infancy, got in on the game of picturing the Spanish fantasy in early silent films. Famed director D. W. Griffith, later known for *The Birth of a Nation* (1915), adapted Helen Hunt Jackson's novel *Ramona* into a film of the same name in 1910. The film, like the novel before it, highlighted California as a place of sun, ease, and romance. Mary Pickford portrays the title character, a virtuous mestiza girl, whose chastity and virtue is protected by saintly Spanish friars against swarthy, villainous Mexican abusers. It was an early example of white actors playing Latinx characters in Hollywood films. One film historian notes that "in order for American middle-class audiences to sympathize with, identify with, or even desire" nonwhite characters, the class status and racial status of the character had to be changed.[15] Often that could be done by having a white actor or actress, such as Pickford, play the nonwhite character. But it was also done, as with a figure like Joaquín Murrieta, by lifting the social status of the fictional character and by making the character "whiter" relative to other characters in the story. For instance, one character, the hero, would be presented as Spanish, or Californio, the heir of aristocratic privilege and having blue blood, while other Mexican characters were peons, all speaking with thick accents or exhibiting various stereotypical traits. That was the journey by which Murrieta traveled from notorious Mexican outlaw to romantic masked avenger.

The Joaquín Murrieta encountered by Johnston McCulley had had a makeover. He underwent the Spanish fantasy treatment. Between Ridge's *Life and Adventures* and McCulley's Zorro, Murrieta's class status was raised and his ethnic identity was whitened. With each new incarnation of Murrieta, the legend edged closer and closer to the character we know as Zorro.

The connection between Murrieta and Zorro becomes clear only within the context of the Spanish fantasy heritage of California. Without the Spanish fantasy heritage, it's easy to miss the evolution from Murrieta to Zorro. Murrieta was a Mexican bandit—Zorro, a Spanish don. The link is lost. Without the context of California history, Zorro's likeness to Orczy's Scarlet Pimpernel or to Dumas's Count of Monte Cristo or to other pulp heroes like John Carter, Tarzan, or even the little-known Jimmie Dale / the Gray Seal seem to be better bets. McCulley no doubt read these other tales. He no doubt drew on them in creating Zorro.

But if we look again at what McCulley actually said about the creation of Zorro, none of these literary or pulp predecessors is named. "He studied the old California mission empire for years, and has written several stories dealing with mission times," wrote reporter Seth Bailey in a 1923 interview with McCulley. "Zorro was intended to express the spirit of the caballero of the times," McCulley told the interviewer.[16] McCulley stated that his inspiration for Zorro was found in Old California history, which often blended the period of the Spanish missions with the era of the gold rush in its setting. If we look for a hero from that era of Old California, the guy we have to acknowledge is

Joaquín Murrieta. But when McCulley encountered Murrieta, he was a whole lot more aristocratic, and a whole lot whiter, than the original legend.

Plenty of people in California continued to think of Murrieta as a criminal, or a cutthroat Mexican bandit. But the legend was changing. Ridge's 1854 novel was plagiarized, shortened, tightened up, and made gorier in an 1859 *California Police Gazette* publication. Ridge had presented his Joaquín as having "more noble impulses," often doing violence only when he had to. The villain of Ridge's novel is Three-Fingered Jack (*Tres Dedos*), who delights in killing—especially in cutting the throats of Chinese immigrants. The *Police Gazette* version, in contrast, ups the violence, "lingering over dripping blood, severed heads, and other body parts."[17] It's no wonder the *Police Gazette* plagiarism was far more popular, and more widely read, than Ridge's *Life and Adventures* original.

But the versions didn't stop. Soon, it was translated into French and Spanish. In 1862, Robert Hyenne used the *Police Gazette* version as the basis of a French-language publication, which listed Hyenne as author. In 1867, Carlos Morla Vicuña produced a Spanish translation based off the French pirated version, taken from the *Police Gazette*, which, of course, had its basis in Ridge's novel. Vicuña's Spanish version casts his "Murieta" as Chilean, as Vicuña himself was from Chile. It was the first time that Murrieta was said to hail from South America. But it made sense, as many Chilean gold miners experienced the same prejudices as Mexicans in 1850s California. Other plagiarisms continued—so much so that John Rollin Ridge, before his death, took suit against those who had stolen his work.[18] And yet, Murrieta's story was unleashed. There was no containing just where his legend would lead.

While California newspapers continued to write about Murrieta as "the famous bandit," "a renowned bandit," or even, by 1910, as one of "our own picturesque cutthroats," a certain nostalgia crept in for the old pioneer days, the days when Old California was "infested with a desperate band."[19] Murrieta was becoming, if not a hero plain and simple, certainly a kind of noble antihero. Many Anglo-Americans, ordinary folks, some who had lived in the goldfields in the 1850s, didn't back away from stating that a fair bit of mob violence was justified in dealing with unruly Mexicans. But the rancor of the past diminished over time. One woman, a Mrs. Lee Whipple-Haslan, for instance, reminisced that vigilance committees had cause "to put the fear of the Lord . . . into the hearts of Mexicans," but she also had to admit that Murrieta "was painted blacker than he deserved."[20]

For every newspaper article that clamored to set the record straight on the real Murrieta, just as many plays, books, and, later, films presented a different version of Murrieta—usually with aristocratic lineage and noble parentage. In 1858—a year before the *Police Gazette* plagiarism appeared—Charles E. B. Howe wrote a five-act play called *Joaquin Murieta de Castillo*. It's hard to know how widely read the script was, or how many people saw it produced, but the play cast "Murieta" as a Cuban-born Spanish nobleman. He had aristocratic heritage and manners. In the drama, he has very little to do with the notorious bandits of whom he is the supposed leader. A noble cause induces him to seek justice. "Revenge, with its unholy light, takes possession of my soul," Joaquín cries after his wife is raped and murdered—the murder not being part of Ridge's original 1854 novel. The California Rangers still kill Murrieta in the play, but he comes off as a protector of the weak. One female character exudes gratitude: "How can we thank you, our noble preserver, and how can I repay you for your timely protection of my family? I know you are good as you are wildly beautiful."[21] One path to Murrieta's redemption, as with all masked avengers, including Zorro, was through his sex appeal.

Soon Joaquín Murrieta had a habit of switching sides. The Anglo-Americans weren't always the bad guys in some stories. Joseph Badger's 1881 novel *Joaquín, the Saddle King* paints Murrieta as a "blonde Spaniard who fought on the U.S. side in the war with Mexico, thereby becoming 'a hero to all North Americans.'"[22] It was Murrieta's ethnic fluidity, one of his characteristic traits from the beginning, that aided his evolution into Zorro. By introducing a Spanish, or partially Spanish, heritage into Murrieta's pedigree he could become the hero of so many vastly different tales. Yet, from the start, Murrieta had been a trickster, a shape-shifter, a bandit who was fluent in English and—because of his manners, his good looks, and his charisma—could pass himself off as gringo and masquerade incognito wherever he wished. He was, from the start, a code-switcher. Still, books like *The Saddle King* did something new. Murrieta wasn't a Mexican bandit pretending to be a gringo in the novel—in *The Saddle King* he was fighting for the United States. That was a genuine evolution with direct links to the creation of Zorro. For Murrieta to become Zorro, he had to no longer be the enemy of the United States.

The high-born, whiter fictions about Murrieta had a wider audience than did newspaper reports in California. The public's memory was short. In 1911 the *San Francisco Call* ran a column of "answers to queries" from readers. One individual wrote the paper asking: "Who was Joaquín Murrieta?" The paper replied: "Joaquín Carrillo, alias Murieta" was the "son of a respectable Mexican family, born in this state."[23] In other words, according to the newspaper, Murrieta was a high-born Californio, not a Mexican immigrant. Even the newspapers, supposedly holding a longer public memory than ordinary citizens, had begun to soften their descriptions of Murrieta. One could read stories about the "enchanted cave of Cantua Canyon," the "former headquarters of Joaquín Murrieta." "Here," one article claimed, "the treasure of the renowned bandit was supposed to be buried."[24] Murrieta was a legend growing in romance in tandem with the Spanish fantasy heritage of the region.

A well-nigh mythical novel of Murrieta's life appeared in 1912. Author Carl Gray, the nom de plume of Charles Caldwell Park, published *A Plaything of the Gods*. In the novel, Murrieta is raised in Old California by a kindly friar in the shadow of an idyllic mission. Note here that when McCulley says he studied Old California under the Spanish missions, he could also be referring to a time that included Murrieta. In Gray's version, Murrieta has aristocratic heritage but doesn't know it. Two mission priests talk about the young Murrieta:

"What a wonder of strength and quickness," one friar says to the other. "Tell me something about the child, amigo mío."

"I am glad thou hast seen him thyself, else hadst thou not believed it possible," the friend replies. "He is the son of Doña Catalina Murrieta, and, it is claimed, has royal blood from both sides of his house; his mother is a descendant of Don Fedro de la Cuesta of Spain and his father is said to be the grandson of Maxixca, the old chief of the Tlascalans."[25]

Although Gray's novel was panned in one California newspaper for its incorrect portrayal of Murrieta, it didn't really matter. Gray's novel reached a national audience. *Publishers Weekly* wrote its own synopsis of the book: "Joaquín Murieta, a Spanish Californian living in the middle of the last century, when Americans cheated and robbed many of his countrymen, determined to avenge them. His story is here told in the form of fiction, closely following fact."[26] By the time Johnston McCulley encountered Murrieta, then, Joaquín looked more aristocratic, of blue blood, and whiter than he had back in the 1850s. Old California could mean 1820, in the days of Spanish control, or it could mean the era of the gold rush, in the 1840s and 1850s. Murrieta's legend rode across it all. And only sometimes was he cast as a monster. Mostly, he just looked a lot like Robin Hood. But, even here, Californians didn't need to look to Europe for their models. As one news editorial claimed at the time, "One does not need to look back six centuries to find the human foundation for the character of Robin Hood."[27] Murrieta was the native Robin Hood, right there in California.

The Spanish fantasy heritage created the conditions for Murrieta's evolution into Zorro. But how do we know that McCulley absorbed Murrieta into his stories of Old California? It was a question I had to ask myself as I surveyed the evidence. I wanted to make sure the Latinx origins to Zorro were really plain—not that Murrieta and the history his legend pointed to just hovered around Zorro, but that there was some clear line of evolution. I found no direct statements by McCulley naming Murrieta or any other potential bandit from the era—Salomon Pico, for example, or Tiburcio Vásquez, two Mexican desperados sometimes named in association with Zorro.[28] I looked back at what McCulley wrote before *The Curse of Capistrano*. I began to see the clear evolution of Murrieta into Zorro.

Take a novel, written in 1906, not by McCulley but by Edward Childs Carpenter. It's called *Captain Courtesy*, and it was reviewed in periodicals across the United States at the time. The novel's main character is not called Murrieta, but the story looks a lot like Murrieta and, at the same time, a lot like Zorro. Does *Captain Courtesy* follow the exploits of a young, handsome hero, like Murrieta's legend, who is the victim of a heinous crime, for which he seeks revenge? It does. Does *Captain Courtesy* have a side plot, like the Zorro novels, involving a pretty woman who is torn over her feelings for the main character, given that he is a bandit? It does. Does *Captain Courtesy* involve, like Zorro, a man in a black mask who goes by a sobriquet and has an alter ego? Indeed it does. He was called Captain Courtesy "since he spared his fellow countrymen and was gallant to all women—no matter what their caste or nationality."[29]

But here's the thing: Captain Courtesy in the novel is an American, with a Spanish mother and an Anglo-American father. His parents are killed by

Mexicans in the story, and he therefore embarks on his revenge against the corrupt *Mexican* authorities. Like *The Saddle King*, the novel *Captain Courtesy* flips the script on the Murrieta legend. The Americans are just "rugged, iron-nerved pioneers," while the Mexicans are described as having "a character primarily of rascality and greed."[30] Leonardo Davis, the alter ego of Captain Courtesy, vows vengeance:

> He took savage delight in waylaying Mexicans. But, at the same time, an innate chivalry, even upon the highway, asserted itself. His robberies were ceremonies, conducted with whimsy, with diabolical politeness. His formula was not, "Your money or your life!"—he began with profuse apologies, regretting that he should be obliged to interrupt the journeying horseman, and concluded by stripping his victim of purse and every ornament to his very spurs.[31]

Captain Courtesy, in the novel, soon gives up his need for deep-seeded vengeance and throws his lot behind the cause of California statehood. The Anglo-Americans in California "could no longer protect their homes against Mexican depredation," Carpenter writes in the book.[32] A revolution began in response. Captain Courtesy, "through agents, placed his spoils in the hands of the patriot leaders, rejoicing that he might aid in the overthrow of the Mexican government."[33] In *Captain Courtesy*, in other words, Joaquín Murrieta becomes an American fighting for California statehood, while the Mexicans are described as the villains running a corrupt government.

But how do we know Captain Courtesy is actually Murrieta? The novel calls the character Leonard Davis, after all. The answer is that readers interpreted the story as depicting Murrieta. In 1917, for instance, a senior class drama club in California put on a dramatic production they titled "El Capitán" in order not to completely plagiarize the novel by Carpenter. The newspaper review of the play glows with fawning descriptions of Old California dress, even congratulating one actor who "walked and moved in Indian fashion," while another actor "conveyed much of Spanish fire and dash with an underlying sincerity that increased his Latin charm." "It was," noted the press critic, "first of all, a dramatization of the story of our local Robin Hood, Joaquín Murieta, under the sobriquet of 'Captain Courtesy.'"[34] A senior class drama club, and the press critic who reviewed the play, understood that, despite the different name, the story was really about Joaquín Murrieta—though certainly white-washed. Apparently no one noticed, or really cared, about the contradiction. Murrieta had always been a character who fought against Anglo-American racial violence, while Captain Courtesy battled on the other side—fighting corrupt Mexican troops and for the United States' annexation of California. And yet, the two characters were now interchangeable. Murrieta was Captain Courtesy, and Captain Courtesy fed directly into one of Johnston McCulley's earliest novels about Old California.

In 1915, when McCulley moved to Los Angeles, he would've encountered Murrieta under the disguise of Captain Courtesy. Hollywood made a silent film version of the novel, which played nationwide. It starred Dustin Farnum. One reviewer of the movie noted, "In the latter part of the picture there is a beautiful love scene"—and love scenes in 1915 were far different than they are today—"between 'Captain Courtesy,' who throws off the highwayman's mask and appears as Captain of the Riflemen, and Eleanor, the orphan rescued by the padre."[35] Throwing off his mask is a very Zorro thing to do. The film had the story elements of Murrieta and Zorro—the mask, the dual identity, the tale of revenge.

And so, Johnston McCulley wrote in October 1915 and published in May 1916 a serialized novel called, of all things, *Captain Fly-by-Night*. "A charming and thrilling romance of California of the early days," reads a press synopsis.[36] McCulley's *Fly-by-Night*, like *Captain Courtesy*, and like the Zorro stories, is set in a nebulous Old California. The missions are still in place. Spanish or Mexican soldiers are in charge. In *Fly-by-Night* there's even a blustering comic relief character, named Sergeant Cassara, who in the Zorro stories would be named Sergeant Gonzales. The trick with McCulley's novel is that the Spanish are in charge. The Americans are nowhere in the novel. But the plot elements are very similar to both Murrieta and Zorro. Captain Fly-by-Night is the sobriquet of a famous rogue of the highway, as with Murrieta and Zorro. Sergeant Cassara says to one of his subordinates, reminiscent of both the Murrieta legend and Zorro: "Here—I have written orders for you! . . . Here is the hotbed of mutiny at present—and here one of their leaders! . . . Get him, dead or alive, sparing no effort, and promotion is yours! . . . Get him—Captain Fly-By-Night!"[37]

As with the novel *Captain Courtesy* written by Carpenter, then, McCulley's *Captain Fly-by-Night* flips the Murrieta script. While Captain Courtesy fights against the Mexicans for the statehood of California, Fly-by-Night fights against an Indian uprising for the Spanish colonial government. In both stories, there's an unmasking of true identity at the end. The main character has to lead a double life; he is often mistaken by the love interest as a weakling or a rogue, but at the same time she is attracted to the masked vigilante. *Captain Courtesy* is a more straightforward Americanization of the Murrieta legend. *Captain Fly-by-Night* takes the Americans out of the equation all together, allowing the Spanish hero to stand in for the Americans relative to Native Americans and poor Mexicans in the story.

And here's the point—Murrieta was clearly understood to be Captain Courtesy, and Captain Courtesy looks a lot like McCulley's *Captain Fly-by-Night*, which is, in literary terms, a dry run for Zorro. *Captain Courtesy* and *Captain Fly-by-Night* are romantic adventures with a whitened and socially ennobled version of the Murrieta legend. Yet a masked Murrieta now plays for the white team, whether American, in the case of Captain Courtesy, or Spanish, in the case of Captain Fly-by-Night. Zorro was simply the next articulation of the whitewashed Murrieta tale. Zorro, the fox, has always been something of a trickster.

12 | THE MARK OF DOUGLAS FAIRBANKS

IF JOHNSTON MCCULLEY created Zorro out of the rough material of the legend of Joaquín Murrieta, it was Douglas Fairbanks who made Zorro famous. Fairbanks also gave Zorro his bold sense of humor. Zorro in McCulley's first tale has courtly manners with a degree of dry humor, but Fairbanks knew how to make the humor pop. Zorro bears the mark of Douglas Fairbanks, the first movie star to play the character on screen, in 1920. Without Fairbanks, perhaps Zorro would've gone the way of McCulley's other dual-identity characters, like the Crimson Clown or the Thunderbolt—that is, just a footnote to bygone and forgotten pulp fiction oblivion. Fairbanks helped make Zorro, well, Zorro.

Zorro, however, would outlive them all—the original Murrieta legend, the pulp fiction author of the character, as well as Zorro's first film popularizer—in the American psyche. And yet, each had a hand in making Zorro an American icon. I imagine all three—Murrieta, McCulley, and Fairbanks—standing over a crib where an infant Zorro lays not quite asleep. Like some weird adaptation of the 1980s comedy *Three Men and a Baby*, the trio endeavors, with yet another musical number, to lull Zorrito to slumber. Each "father," if we can call them that, left a mark on the little cooing Zorro, only just born in 1919. And, like the central tension of the 1980s movie, it's hard to say who the *real* father actually is. But that needn't worry us. As in *Three Men and a Baby*, all three dads are necessary in bringing up *el zorro bebé*.

In Zorro are traces of all his parents. We see the traces of a Latinx immigrant story, and a history of racial violence and American annexation. Also, a pulp fiction hero that blends the Latinx story with other characters, like the Scarlet Pimpernel and the Count of Monte Cristo, but who, in the process, transforms Murrieta into a story about a white hero with whom many white, middle-class audiences could identify. And, in Zorro, there is also the likeness of a movie star's smile and charisma, his impossible athletic agility, a personality that perfectly embodies American visions of optimism, courage, youth, and can-do-ness—a hero, bigger, stronger, faster, than any one of Zorro's models. A hero, almost super.

Zorro, in other words, is a product of American culture. He's a product of diversity, both in terms of his Latinx origins and in the formative process that bought him to life. Zorro bears the marks of many hands and many stories mixed together until one story dissolves into the other, making them almost inseparable from each other. Latinx culture and experience, to change the metaphor, was stirred in with other stories to make something new. But that's basically how most all of America's popular culture was created: a spritz of this, a shot of that—shake, shake, shake—pour. And so, whatever Latinx origins Zorro may have had—and as we've seen, those origins are truly a part of the character—Zorro was created for American consumption.

It's no surprise, then, that American consumer tastes, which favored Douglas Fairbanks in 1920, helped to shape Zorro's character. When Fairbanks played Zorro on screen for the first time that year, audiences absolutely drank it up. Fairbanks became Zorro and Zorro became Fairbanks. Ever after, all other parentage, all other flavor—insert whatever metaphor you like—seemed muted by the sheer force of Fairbanks's hearty laugh.

————————

"I like to laugh," wrote Douglas Fairbanks in his 1917 juvenile self-help book, *Laugh and Live*. "It is a tonic. It braces me up—makes me feel fine!—and keeps me in prime mental condition." The book, an early example of cross-marketing, as film exhibitors got a break on showing a Fairbanks film if they agreed to sell his prescriptions for life right there in the theaters, is filled with adages, best practices, and Fairbanksian patter. ("Whistle and Hoe—Sing as We Go" is probably my favorite chapter title.) Laughter is the fundamental building block for a happy, successful life, according to Fairbanks. And it's a habit you have to form. All other bodily disciplines, physically keeping "in fit," he writes, or in intellectual or moral progress, proceeds from a constant practice of a good belly laugh.

> Laugh and live long—if you had a thought of dying—laugh and grow well—if you're sick and despondent—laugh and grow fat—if your tendency is towards the lean and cadaverous—laugh and succeed—if you're glum and "unlucky"—laugh and nothing can faze you—not even the Grim Reaper—for the man who has laughed his way through life has nothing to fear of the future. His conscience is clear.[1]

Laughter, a smile, an upturned chin, a straight posture, good physical exertion, a body "in fit"—all these were part of Fairbank's persona both on and off the screen. When people went to a "flicker," as films were known, they wanted to see Fairbanks be Fairbanks. He smiled. He laughed. He had no fear. Americans, after the end of the First World War and the devastating Spanish influenza, needed a guy like Fairbanks. He was the man everyone wanted—and wanted to be.

Fairbanks's persona wasn't so much a product of a cynical public relations campaign as it was a strategic, though deeply felt, creation of Fairbanks himself. Only later, after the actor had become famous, did the Hollywood star machine, then only in its infancy, cynically manage his public image. Fairbanks really believed in the power of laughter to project—and even to force—happiness into the world.

There's something unalloyed in Fairbanks's earnestness. He never gave an ironic wink. You can see his ingenuousness on screen in his portrayal as Zorro—the broad smile, the sincerity, the guileless glee. The theatrical poster of *The Mark of Zorro* pictures a masked and costumed Zorro leaning on a barrel of wine, which at the time was illegal due to prohibition, while a circular portrait of Douglas Fairbanks smiling, wearing a modern suite and tie, hovers on the side of the barrel. It's as if the advertisement says: *Hey, this is just Doug being Doug . . . the guy in the mask is Fairbanks!* In fact, the genuine, authentic manner in which Fairbanks portrays Zorro is actually a reason why many audiences in our own day don't prefer the Fairbanks Zorro to, say,

Tyrone Power in the 1940 remake, or even Antonio Banderas from the 1998 and 2005 films. Fairbanks's authenticity was a hallmark of the silent film era. One Fairbanks biographer aptly notes:

> It is harder to get modern viewers, with their postmodern, postironic eye, to see earlier films through the lens of their original audiences. The same is true of the early silent Pickfords [films starring Fairbanks's wife, the most famous silent-era ingenue]: before you can be postironic, you need to be ironic; before you can be ironic, you have to see things as purely and with a whole heart as a child seeing a film such as The Wizard of Oz for the first time. That is the mental state that is hard to return to, but it was closer to how the earliest audiences greeted the pure heroics and twinkling charm of Fairbanks's characters.[2]

Fairbanks really believed in his laugh, and audiences believed in it too.

The Douglas Fairbanks persona started before he was even on film. Take an early description of the young actor, while he was still on Broadway. Author and playwright Edna Ferber wrote a story in 1914 in which the protagonist's younger brother exclaims to his mother: "They call it the juvenile jump, and all our best leading men have it. I trailed Douglas Fairbanks for days before I really got it."[3] Fairbanks was a devoted disciple of President Teddy Roosevelt, who championed strenuous living as the foundation of heroic virtue. "Weasel words from mollycoddles will never do when the day demands prophetic clarity from greathearts," Roosevelt famously said. "Manly men must emerge for this hour of trial."[4]

Fairbanks briefly met his hero when Roosevelt visited a Broadway play Fairbanks was cast in. "I'm for him to the end," Fairbanks said of Roosevelt after the meeting. "He's got them all beat. He's a wonder." The actor even later paid $5,000 to use Roosevelt's favorite epithet for a wimp—"mollycoddle"—as the title of a 1920 Fairbanks feature film. In The Mollycoddle, Fairbanks's character transforms from "weasel words" to "prophetic clarity" and shows the valor of a "greatheart." In one of Fairbanks's last roles on Broadway before moving to Hollywood, the New York Times described the actor as bringing a "whole-souled sunniness" to the play, "an infectious affability . . . a great deal of spirit and a lively sense of comedy."[5]

Fairbanks seemed made for the movies. Harry Aitken, film producer and founder of the brand-new Triangle Film Corporation, signed Fairbanks to a ten-week, $2,000 per week contract. Fairbanks, with then wife Anna Beth Sully and his son Doug Jr., moved to Hollywood in July 1915.

Hollywood, as a place where movies were made, was really only five years old in 1915. In 1910 director and failed stage actor D. W. Griffith took forty members of the cast and crew of the American Mutoscope and Biograph Company from their snowy East Coast headquarters to the sunnier climes of Los Angeles to aid Griffith's fast-paced production schedule. Hollywood started more from exasperation over how to make movies in bad weather than from any innate Hollywood glow. Film techniques and camera technology at the time were in their relative infancy. Snow in the winter months in New York and New Jersey, two initial capitals of early filmmaking, meant a halt to production. Griffith, a consummate experimenter, couldn't let the weather stand in the way of his vision. When the Biograph Company's cast and crew arrived in Los Angeles, they raised the total population of Hollywood to approximately two hundred people.[6] The Hollywood we've come to know didn't really exist in 1910.

Among those who traveled with Griffith was an up-and-coming star, Mary Pickford, age seventeen. With her blonde curls and large, tremulous eyes, she had been christened the new "Biograph Girl," the company's lead actress. Mary's younger brother, Jack Pickford, traveled with his sister out west. They stayed for four months in a hotel, sharing a communal bathroom with two other actresses. They put on their costumes before leaving the hotel in the morning and trudged down dirt roads in their crinolines and togas, or in feathers and paint. They had to learn to ride horses, not so much for western films, but as the only mode of transportation. Griffith's shooting location was an empty lot where sets could be erected quickly and torn down just as fast. But the director also filmed on location, using the hills, rivers, and valleys of Southern California as picturesque backdrops.[7] During that first trip, Griffith filmed *In Old California* (1910), the first movie shot entirely in Hollywood. That same year, Pickford starred as an innocent Native girl in *Ramona*, adapted from

Helen Hunt Jackson's 1884 novel. From the beginning, then, Hollywood put on film the Spanish fantasy heritage of the region. Zorro fit within an already established vision of California's past, created first by California writers, and then filmed and distributed by Hollywood.

The power of film to project, as well as reflect, visions of US history was already established by 1915 when both Douglas Fairbanks and Johnston McCulley arrived in Los Angeles. Just as D. W. Griffith had an early hand in putting the Spanish fantasy heritage on screen, the director played a key role in telling the white Southern fantasy heritage, an incredibly racist one at that, through the medium of film.

D. W. Griffith set up a permanent Fine Arts Studio in Los Angeles and produced, in 1915, *The Birth of a Nation*. The film is today considered one of the most important early features of the silent era. Yet, to many contemporaries at the time, as well as to modern viewers, the film is deeply problematic, though perhaps *disturbing* might be a better word. Its depiction of the Ku Klux Klan as heroes, and its portrayal of black characters as rapacious villains—black characters were played by white actors in blackface—is not only an unsettling reminder of American racism but also an example of the way film can, and does, forward racist ideas.

In 1915 nativism was rising in the United States. Defined as "the intense opposition to internal minorities on the ground of their presumed 'foreign' connections," nativism was barely distinguishable from racial prejudice.[8] Many in the United States, with millions of new European immigrants arriving every year, touted America as a melting pot—that these once-foreign peoples could assimilate and become citizens, each group blending into the others to form a united people. That dream was dying by the outbreak of World War I in 1914. Fear of foreign enemies within US borders caused a backlash against immigrants, African Americans, Latinx people, as well as Catholics and Jews.

Douglas Fairbanks's hero, former US president Teddy Roosevelt, gave a speech in 1916 proclaiming "America for Americans." Although Roosevelt's speech admitted that all could become US citizens as long as they checked their foreign heritage at the door, many more radical groups seconded the sentiment and used it as fodder for a campaign of hate. Organizations such as the American Protective League, the American Legion, the American Defense Society, and the Ku Klux Klan became active antiforeign proponents. The Klan had originally been started by ex-Confederate soldiers as a way to strike fear into the newly emancipated African American population of the South. It was revived in the 1910s with a broader platform, adding a nativist bent that targeted all non-Anglo-Saxon-Protestant peoples in the United States.

The Birth of a Nation was the first film to be screened at the White House. President Woodrow Wilson commented: "It is like writing history with lightning. And my only regret is that it is all so terribly true." By 1924, the US government, in thrall to nativism, passed the Johnson-Reed Act, which established the first quota system on foreign immigration, favoring new arrivals from Northern Europe. D. W. Griffith's film became a fantastic recruitment tool for the Ku Klux Klan.[9]

What makes *The Birth of a Nation* all the more problematic is that it was so technically artful. Even if Griffith didn't establish the basic grammar of filmmaking, he honed it. He was the first US director to use new film techniques—fades, dissolves, close-ups, flashbacks, crosscutting—to startling effect.[10] "*The Birth of a Nation*," wrote the late film critic Roger Ebert, "is not a bad film because it argues for evil . . . it is a great film that argues for evil."[11] It tells a compelling story through technical achievements without equal at the time—and it's racist as hell. It was abnormally long, especially for that era, at 190 minutes, but audiences readily plunked down their two dollars to see it, which was an exorbitant rate in 1915. Griffith presents a view of history whereby the bucolic, idyllic antebellum South was ground underfoot by the North, and then terrorized by a newly energized African American population of ex-slaves who threatened white supremacy and the sexual virtue of the South's white women. The film's second act follows the growing alliance of Reconstruction-era carpetbaggers and black freedmen in a cabal of corruption. Because a white man just can't take it anymore—and after the hero sees some white children scare black children by dressing up like ghosts in white sheets—the white protagonist establishes, in secret, the Ku Klux Klan. The founder has to hide his KKK identity from his family, as well as from the woman he loves. He wears a mask, an identifiable costume, and masquerades by night as an avenger-vigilante. The Klan's first mission is to avenge the rape of a white woman and set right the wrong done by corrupt Northern authorities, as well perpetrated by racially impure pretenders, to the Southern way of life.

If it sounds at all familiar, it's because the plot is not far off from Johnston McCulley's basic Zorro plot. The two visions, the Spanish fantasy and the white Southern fantasy, share more in common than one might expect. Griffith based his movie on Thomas Dixon Jr.'s 1905 novel *The Clansman*. The similarities between McCulley's *Curse of Capistrano* and Dixon's novel are even more striking than between Griffith's movie and *The Clansman*. Take, for instance, the bevvy of KKK code names Dixon lifted off the real-life Klan for his novel, which read like a list of superhero alter egos: Night Hawk, Grand Dragon, Grand Turk, Grand Cyclops, and Grand Titan. The Klansmen's lair, Zorro-style as well as Batman-style, is a hollowed-out cave where they hold their secret meetings. "Your lover's men," the hero says, "will be riding to-night—these young dare-devil Knights of the South, with their life in their hands, a song on their lips, and the scorn of death in their souls!"[12] Like Zorro, and like Batman and other later superheroes, the Klansmen are costumed, masked vigilantes.

Dixon's novel, and Griffith's movie, emphasizes—again, like Zorro—blue blood, hierarchy, and virtue. There are chivalric elements in Dixon's novel, where an oath must be taken "to protect the weak, the innocent, and the defenseless from the indignities, wrongs and outrages of the lawless, the violent, and the brutal; to relieve the injured and the oppressed: to succor the suffering and unfortunate, and especially the widows and the orphans of Confederate Soldiers."[13] Consider McCulley's statement that Zorro was written to channel the "spirit of the caballero of the times." *Caballero* is a word that can mean both "gentleman" and "knight."

In Zorro, as well as in Dixon's novel and Griffith's movie, the plot centers on a masked hero who must protect aristocratic women from poor, mixed-race people. Zorro saves Lolita Pulido from the unwanted sexual advances of the mixed-race Captain Ramón, while in *The Birth of a Nation* the Klansmen avenge the sullied virtue of a white Southern woman from the unwanted sexual advances of Gus, a black freedman. "Under their clan-leadership," Dixon writes in the novel, "the Southern people had suddenly developed the courage of the lion, the cunning of the fox, and the deathless faith

Statue of William Lamport, Angel of Independence Monument, Mexico City. *Author's photo*

Historical plaque commemorating the birthplace of Joaquín Murrieta, Trincheras, Sonora, Mexico. *Author's photo*

One of the earliest depictions of Joaquín Murrieta (notice the Superman-esque pose). *California Police Gazette*, "Joaquin Murieta, the Brigand Chief of California. A Complete History of His Life from the Age of Sixteen to the Time of His Capture and Death in 1853" (San Francisco, 1859). *The Bancroft Library, UC Berkeley*

Zorro's debut in *The Curse of Capistrano*. Cover illustration by P. J. Monaghan. *All-Story Weekly*, August 8, 1919. *Archives and Special Collections, University of Louisville*

ABOVE LEFT: Douglas Fairbanks in *The Mark of Zorro* (1920). Fairbanks's stunts and swashbuckling derring-do became an important inspiration for later comic book superheroes. ABOVE RIGHT: Republic Pictures' second serial with the masked character, *Zorro's Fighting Legion* (1939). Carleton Young (as Mexican president Benito Juárez) and Reed Hadley (as Zorro).
BELOW: Lobby poster of *The Mark of Zorro* (1940), starring Tyrone Power and Linda Darnell. *Photofest*

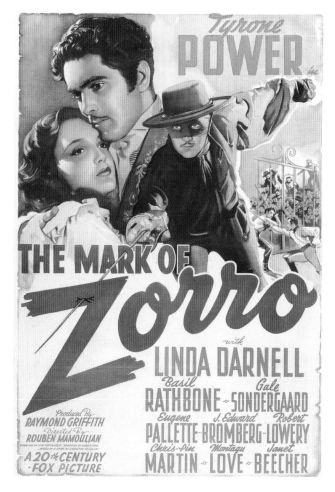

ABOVE: Republic Pictures' *Zorro's Black Whip* (1944), starring Linda Stirling and George J. Lewis. The film serial marked the second time a female character donned the black mask and the first time a Mexican American actor portrayed a Zorro-like figure. BELOW: Republic Pictures' *Ghost of Zorro* (1949), starring Clayton Moore (as Zorro) and George J. Lewis (as Moccasin, Zorro's sidekick). Moore went on to become the first actor to play the Lone Ranger on television. *Photofest*

Above Left: Publicity photo of Guy Williams (as Zorro) and Britt Lomond (as Captain Monastario). Disney's *Zorro* created a huge sensation even though it ran for only two seasons (1957–1959). Above Right: Lobby poster of *Zorro: The Gay Blade* (1981). George Hamilton portrayed twin Zorros, Don Diego Vega and Bunny Wigglesworth. Zorro had become the stuff of satire and nostalgia. *Photofest*

Right: *Dracula Versus Zorro* #2 (Topps, 1993). Don McGregor revived Zorro in the comics in the 1990s. Cover art by Tom Yeates. Interior art by Rick Magyar. *Author's collection*

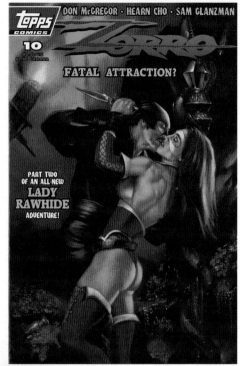

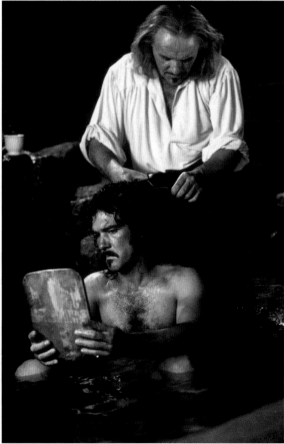

ABOVE LEFT: Preview issue for *Zorro* #1 (Topps, 1993). Frank Miller's landmark Batman graphic novel *The Dark Knight Returns* (1986) influenced Zorro's darker mood in the 1990s. Written by Don McGregor. Cover art by Frank Miller. Interior art by Mike Mayhew and John Nyberg.

ABOVE RIGHT: *Zorro* #10 (Topps, 1994). The 1990s' sexy comic aesthetic made its way to Zorro. Written by Don McGregor. Art by Hearn Cho and Sam Glanzman. *Author's collection*

LEFT: Antonio Banderas (as Zorro / Alejandro Murrieta) and Anthony Hopkins (as Zorro / Diego de la Vega) in *The Mask of Zorro* (1998). The literal transformation of Murrieta into Zorro. *Photofest*

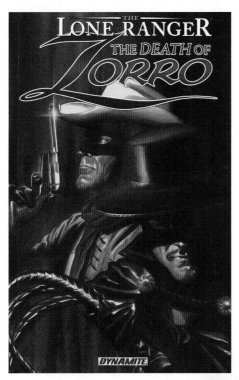

ABOVE LEFT: *The Lone Ranger: The Death of Zorro* (Dynamite, 2011). Taking a page from Superman's death, Dynamite Entertainment killed off the masked man. Written by Ande Parks. Art by Esteve Polls. ABOVE RIGHT: *Django/Zorro* #5 (Dynamite, 2015). Zorro was revived and teamed with Django. Alternate cover art by Butch Guice and Alex Guimarães. Written by Matt Wagner and Quentin Tarantino. Interior art by Esteve Polls. RIGHT: *Zorro: Swords of Hell* #1 (American Mythology, 2019). Zorro faced the undead as well as his own whitewashed past. Written by David Avallone. Art by Roy Allan Martinez. *Author's collection*

El Muerto "Angel" by Javier Hernández. A generation of Latinx comics artists took inspiration from Zorro. Hernández's character was named Diego de la Muerte (after Zorro's other identity, Diego de la Vega) before being turned into El Muerto by a pair of Aztec gods. *Javier Hernández*

of religious enthusiasts."[14] Thomas Dixon's "homicidal Klansmen," writes comics historian Chris Gavaler, "are the first twentieth-century dual-identity costumed heroes in American lit."[15] Gavaler argues that "most likely McCulley borrowed from Griffith, and [Bill] Finger borrowed from McCulley" in cocreating Batman.[16]

To what extent Griffith's movie, or Dixon's novel, influenced McCulley is unclear. Obviously, there are literary parallels in the basic plot triad of corrupt government, victimized population, and masked hero with an alter ego. I've found no evidence, outside of internal literary evidence, that McCulley was especially drawn to the novel or the movie. It's not that McCulley's Zorro bears a one-to-one relationship to *The Birth of a Nation*, but the success of Griffith's film reveals why McCulley's story became so popular once it was produced as a film in 1920. Audiences clamored for a story where a hero, played by a white actor, defended fantasy versions of US history. That fantasy could be set in the South of the Reconstruction era, or it could be set in Old Spanish California. Although used for very distinct purposes, both Zorro and *The Birth of a Nation* confirmed American notions about itself—that America was benevolent either in defending white Southern honor or in annexing California as a state. Zorro, though characterized as Spanish, exemplified virtues esteemed in the United States at the time. And if Zorro's California was suffering under corrupt rule by the Spanish, his heroics represented a kind of justification for the real-life US annexation of California.[17] Zorro becomes a kind of proto-American character, who fights European corruption in the New World, just as Americans had fought European corruption in the form of British and French claims to US soil. And as for *The Birth of a Nation*, some Americans saw that same corruption in Northern-led Reconstruction after the Civil War.

The link between the KKK, Zorro, Batman, and later superheroes is a dark one. It shows the truly odd mix inherent in the creation of Zorro, as well as a disturbing inheritance to the American superhero genre. And while not discounting the potential influence Dixon's novel may have had on McCulley, KKK code names, racial hierarchy, and white terror were not a product of fiction but were real features of American life. Masked vigilantes can also be race warriors crusading for hate. The difference, of course, is that Dixon's and Griffith's Klansmen didn't inspire their own group of serialized, fictional costumed heroes like Zorro or Batman.[18] (The real-life

Klan was frightening enough! So, too, at this writing, are the legions of white nationalists strengthening their organizations.) And Zorro, like Batman, emerged as a vigilante who often had to fight the violence of other, misguided vigilantes.

Both McCulley and Fairbanks arrived in Los Angeles in 1915, and no doubt both saw *The Birth of a Nation*. It's a galling facet of US pop culture that figures like Joaquín Murrieta, a hero who embodies resistance to racial violence, and like the Klansmen, who campaign for racial violence, can both hide behind the mask of Zorro.

———————

While D. W. Griffith did his auteur racist cinema in one corner of Hollywood, other studios multiplied around town. In Edendale, the Keystone Kops did their comedy. Thomas Ince directed films in Culver City. Universal established a studio. The Hollywood Hotel housed newly arrived actors. A social life developed in restaurants, bars, and cafés. New housing went up for production crews as well as for film talent. Stars such as Wallace Reid, Roscoe "Fatty" Arbuckle, Charlie Chaplin, Lillian Gish, and Mary Pickford became permanent fixtures in Hollywood. Douglas Fairbanks quickly joined their number.

In 1915, Fairbanks starred in his first feature, *The Lamb*, a film about a milquetoast wimp named Gerald.[19] In *The Lamb*, Fairbanks fumbles, trips, and coughs meekly—he's a coward. But his character, Gerald, transforms after lessons in boxing and jujitsu. He follows the woman he loves out west and there finds his true self—a hero who, because of his gallantry (and his pummeling of an Indian who has robbed his beloved), wins the girl at the end of the movie. As one Fairbanks biographer notes, the film established the leitmotif of many of his films, representing "the physical journey from east to west paralleling the spiritual journey from fop to hero."[20] Zorro, in other words, would not be an entirely new character for Fairbanks. It was the perfect culmination of the fop-hero dichotomy Fairbanks was already known for.

But *The Mark of Zorro* was different than the earlier Fairbanks fop-hero films. For one, the other films were modern suit-and-tie affairs. *Zorro* was a period romantic drama. The character of Zorro was mythic, almost archetypal, whereas the other films were particular, single instances of transformation. Zorro wasn't just *a* hero, like wimpy Gerald in *The Lamb*. Zorro was *the* hero— a hero symbolized with a black mask and costume. He was escapist fantasy. Anyone could imagine being the one behind the empty mask, or the one in the heroic embrace of the anonymous masked avenger. Zorro was a blank canvas for the fulfillment of fantasy revelries. That's what made Zorro so alluring to the average audience member. It's why Zorro had staying power as a way to tell stories of heroism, and, ultimately, it's the kind of chutzpah the character lent to later superheroes. That sort of vicarious hero cosplay was inscribed in McCulley's novel. Just the act of putting on the mask could change a person. "It is a peculiar thing to explain, señores," Don Diego says after his unmasking in *The Curse of Capistrano*. "The moment I donned cloak and mask, the Don Diego part of me fell away. My body straightened, new blood seemed to course through my veins, my voice grew strong and firm, fire came to me! And the moment I removed cloak and mask I was the languid Don Diego again. Is it not a peculiar thing?"[21]

But it was a role perfectly enacted by Fairbanks, the imaginary fantasy projected on screen for the first time. "Doug has never leaped so high, moved so quickly or kept in such constant motion so long before," one reviewer wrote of Fairbanks's Zorro at the time. "The man isn't human, that's what he isn't. He's perpetual youth, a three-ringed circus, the personification of all juvenile heroes, all rolled into one."[22]

How Douglas Fairbanks's screen version of Zorro came about is a meet-cute of happy accident and calculated risk. In other words, it began with a love story. Fairbanks met Mary Pickford in the fall of 1915. Both were married to other people at the time—Fairbanks to a New York socialite, the daughter of a magnate of industry dubbed "the Cotton King"; and Pickford, to actor Owen Moore, an alcoholic who could turn mean, especially when triggered by the enormous sums of money Mary was paid each year compared to his own relatively meager star salary. Pickford was the first actress to sign a two year, $1 million contract. That works out to around $43 million in today's dollars.[23]

Fairbanks and Pickford's romance began in secret and, both knew, should the affair be discovered, they risked ruining their careers. Both had worked hard to exude squeaky-clean public images, in keeping with their screen personas.[24] Fairbanks, the zealous go-getter that he was, was far more reckless in the relationship. He sent countless letters and telegrams, which Pickford kept in a small keepsake box, which was only discovered by a historian long after Pickford's death. "A mere thought of you stimulates as nothing else can," Fairbanks wrote Pickford in the midst of their affair. "You have grown sweeter-lovelier-bigger. . . . I can't tell you how thrilled I am at all times—your intelligence, your beauty—your kindness, your sense of justice—oh I am simply wild about you. I feel positively sure that no man *could* love a woman *more* than I love you my beautiful."[25]

Fairbanks, with shades of his not-yet-birthed Zorro character, wore disguises, false beards, and floppy hats—all in order to meet Pickford secretly and not alert the press to their amorous "friendship." To mitigate a potential scandal, Pickford's mother, always the consummate handler of her daughter's public image, hired a fixer to pay off various news outlets so they wouldn't print rumors of the affair.

When the United States entered World War I in 1917, Fairbanks, Pickford, and Charlie Chaplin (Fairbanks's best friend) went on tour to advertise Liberty Bonds. The close quarters only heated up the romance. By 1919, the three actors, along with director D. W. Griffith, went into business together. They formed United Artists Corporation, in a bid to gain more freedom in the production and distribution of their films. Both Fairbanks and Pickford divorced their spouses. They married each other in March 1920, becoming the first Hollywood power couple. The press and audiences alike called them "Doug and Mary." They bought a huge Beverley Hills mansion they dubbed "Pickfair," heralding all the "Bennifers," "Brangelinas," and other various star portmanteaus to come.

But would American audiences, as well as filmgoers worldwide, accept them? They were divorcées, after all, still a potentially scandalous thing to be in 1920. It certainly wasn't behavior keeping with their virtue-soaked on-screen personas. There was real doubt about their future. Had they traded in their careers for love? It was a risk, and there were a lot of fans to please. Hollywood silent films were also worldwide films. All one had to do was to translate the intertitles into whichever language the audience spoke for the films of Pickford and Fairbanks to be almost universally seen and talked about.

Pickford especially, but Fairbanks as well, was a global celebrity in 1920. Fortunately for the two stars, their romance was framed sympathetically in the press.[26] Many newspapers used Pickford's and Fairbanks's on-screen personae as a basis for how their off-screen romance was understood. Divorce and remarriage aside, Pickford was the innocent but fiery girl next door, who was simply—like so many of her screen roles—the victim of a bad marriage. And Fairbanks, too . . . well, the guy could smile, after all. He seemed so eminently likable. *Don't you want this couple to have their real-life happily ever after?* seemed to be the guiding story about Doug and Mary after they were married. And the answer from a war-weary population was mainly a resounding *yes*. For instance, *Photoplay* magazine published a mock Western Union telegram in its pages a month into Doug and Mary's European honeymoon: "Mr. and Mrs. Douglas Fairbanks—Honeymoon Lane—Happiness Always—Come Home—All Is Forgiven."[27] *The sanctity of marriage and all that*, seemed to be the general sentiment, but no one wanted to lose their favorite movie stars over the whole thing.

While in Europe to celebrate their nuptials, Fairbanks and Pickford were greeted by mobs of people, which confirmed their star status had only increased with the new marriage, not diminished. Doug had to "rugby rush" Mary in his arms through a crowd of Londoners when the pressing multitude threatened the small-in-stature young bride. Only in Germany, where their films weren't shown to any large degree because of the recent war, did the two actors meet with anonymity.

"Frankly, Mary, how do you feel about it?" Fairbanks asked his new wife while in Germany. "Do you like being left alone?"

"I definitely do not, Douglas," was Mary's reply. "Let's go some place where we are known. I've had enough of obscurity for a lifetime."[28]

It was only on the steamship back to New York that Doug finally leafed through a short serialized novel Mary had read to pass the time on their initial voyage to Europe, several months before. Pickford, always a woman with an eye and a talent for business, had liked the story, which had first been recommended by Fairbanks's creative team in Hollywood. They felt it could be Fairbanks's next film project. But it was Pickford who actually read it and prodded her husband to buy it. Without reading it, trusting Pickford completely,

Fairbanks had wired instructions to purchase the film rights to the story—*The Curse of Capistrano* by Johnston McCulley. Only on the return trip, then, when Doug's mind finally turned for a moment away from his I-only-have-eyes-for-you bride, did the star think about his new film project. Just what had he bought? As one Fairbanks biographer notes, he only really gave McCulley's novel a close read on the train from New York to Los Angeles. Pickford had to bait the always-restless Fairbanks into reading the thing by promising to play two games of hearts with him first. "Douglas was a man who never read *anything*," one acquaintance later said of the actor. He was smart and curious about the world, but "Douglas would do *anything* to get out of reading the printed word."[29]

In the end, he liked the story after all. Fairbanks saw in McCulley's Zorro a chance to showcase his heroics. "I would show them what I really could do," he later wrote. After the newlyweds arrived in Hollywood, Fairbanks set about writing a screen adaptation of the novel with cowriter Eugene Mullin. (Fairbanks usually went by a pseudonym created from his middle names, "Elton Thomas," when he wrote scenarios.) Fred Niblo, later famous for the original silent version of *Ben-Hur* (1925), was tapped to direct the still-to-be named Zorro film. It was called *The Curse of Capistrano* for a while and, briefly, *The Black Fox*. But it was Fairbanks who chose the final title, *The Mark of Zorro*. The phrase appears near the end of McCulley's novel: "Like the tongue of a serpent, Señor Zorro's blade shot in. Thrice it darted forward, and upon the fair brow of Ramón, just between the eyes, there flamed suddenly a red, bloody letter Z. 'The Mark of Zorro!' the highwayman cried. 'You wear it forever now, comandante!'"[30] The final title and the film, *The Mark of Zorro*, became so famous that, when McCulley's novel was reprinted in 1924, it adopted the movie title.

Fairbanks had his own production company, so he decided on his supporting cast. For the role of Lolita Pulido, he chose a young actress, Marguerite De La Motte, just eighteen at the time. Fairbanks had discovered her dancing in the show at Sid Grauman's theater in downtown Los Angeles. (The Chinese and Egyptian theaters didn't yet exist.)[31] De La Motte's first role had been in Fairbanks's own 1918 film *Arizona*, but that had been a supporting role. For *Zorro*, she was to play the masked avenger's love interest. She would go on to appear opposite Fairbanks in three subsequent films, more than any other leading lady.

THE MARK OF DOUGLAS FAIRBANKS | 125

Robert McKim would play Captain Juan Ramón, while character actor Noah Beery Sr. would portray the blustering, boasting Sergeant Pedro Gonzales. The other cast included Snitz Edwards (Barkeep), Sydney De Grey (Don Alejandro), George Periolat (Governor Alvarado), and Walt Whitman as Fray Felipe (the actor, of course, not the famous American author). None of them were Spanish, nor were they of Latinx origin.

Playing Bernardo, Zorro / Don Diego's trusted mute (and sometimes deaf) servant, was Tote Du Crow, a Native American silent film actor. Du Crow was the first nonwhite actor to receive billing in a Zorro feature film. In Zorro's manservant, not quite his sidekick—that would come later—one sees shades of the scores of Native American *aides du héro* that flickered across swashbucklers and westerns for decades to come.

Shooting began in the summer of 1920. Indoor set work was done at Clune Studios, with location filming in the San Fernando Valley. Fairbanks hired fencing master M. Harry Uttenhover to train him, Robert McKim, and Noah Beery Sr.

Excitement in the press grew as the November premier approached. One Brooklyn newspaper enthused:

> In *The Mark of Zorro*, coming to the Capitol Theatre next week, the one and original "Doug" Fairbanks surpasses anything which that combination comedian-acrobat-entertainer-extraordinary has ever done. The story itself, which is laid in the early Southern California of nearly a century ago settled by the romance-loving Spaniards, is so chuck full of surprises and action that the thrills literally trip on each others heels.[32]

There were even rumors—not true, as it turned out—that Mary Pickford would star as the "little señorita" in the film. Many of the prerelease articles on the film focused on Fairbanks's dual role in the film. But while there was general enthusiasm for the movie, no one knew exactly what to expect. And neither did Douglas Fairbanks.

The exact reason why Fairbanks chose to do *The Mark of Zorro* has been a question puzzled over by historians, as well as by Fairbanks's biographers. From the perspective of hindsight, it's clear the choice marked a clear shift in Fairbanks's career. Zorro became the film between his suit-and-tie modern movies, films like *The Lamb*, *Mr. Fix-it*, and *The Mollycoddle*, and his swashbuckling adventure features: *The Three Musketeers*; *Robin Hood*; *Don Q, Son of Zorro*; *The Thief of Bagdad*; *The Gaucho*; *The Black Pirate*; and *The Iron Mask*. But at the time he chose to make *Zorro*, Fairbanks was hedging his bets. His next film was *The Nut*, a return to form in a romantic comedy with a contemporary setting. And because of how long it took to know the full extent of box office returns in 1920 (a film went from exclusive runs in New York theaters and only then reached a general audience, sometimes six months to a year after the initial release), Fairbanks wasn't able to judge whether *Zorro* had been a success before making his next picture. He knew it was a departure from what had made his career. Period costume adventures had flopped at the box office in the past. The question, then, is why he took that risk.

One biographer notes that Fairbanks may have been influenced by his female fans, who wanted more love interest—and love scenes—in his films.[33] The actor may have been a silent era sex symbol to fans, but he himself was a bit of a cold fish when it came to looking lovingly into the eyes of his on-screen leading lady, much less giving her a tender or passionate kiss. Director Fred Niblo had to coax Fairbanks into his love scenes with Marguerite De La Motte. And the star told one scenario writer not to put any of the mushy stuff into her next script for him. At any rate, the rationale that Fairbanks gambled on *Zorro* to please female fans takes us only so far. He could've increased the mushy stuff in one of the bread-and-butter suit-and-tie films he'd become famous for. He didn't have to do a period drama. More romance (as in love) didn't necessarily mean a film with a romantic setting (as in Old California).

It also wasn't the case that Fairbanks did *Zorro* because he was using different source material for the film, as in pulp fiction. He'd mined that vein before. Although not a household name in 1920, Johnston McCulley was still pretty well known at the time as a guy who was selling stories for the movies.[34] The gamble wasn't on Johnston McCulley's story. Fairbanks liked the novel, once he actually read it.

But therein lies, perhaps, a partial answer to our enigma of why Fairbanks gambled on *The Mark of Zorro*. Mary Pickford read it too, and before Fairbanks. *Mary* liked the story—she told him to buy it. Fairbanks, in 1920, was in the midst of a far bigger risk than making *Zorro*—his career, his new marriage, the potential that his career could falter because of his off-screen love life. He was in a risk-it-all moment in his life. He rolled the dice, got divorced, remarried—and he won.[35]

The choice to make *Zorro*, a film different than his previous thirty-two movies, was a decision made on instinct and intuition—that his dogged will to laugh and to live would pay off in a new kind of action movie that audiences weren't expecting. Mary Pickford, the woman he'd risked it all for, told him to take another, far smaller risk on *Zorro*. In that sense, compared to the risk of marrying Mary, the choice for Zorro was an afterthought. If he could pull off marrying the most famous actress in the world, what was a little trajectory change in his movie career?

———————

Bets in love and movies were paying off for Douglas Fairbanks. *The Mark of Zorro* opened at the Capitol Theatre in New York City on November 29, 1920. The movie blew audiences away. They loved it, as historians suggest, because it provided fantasy and escapism at a time when many Americans were sorely in need of lighthearted diversion. Its success depended on a lucky cultural moment, as well as a calculated risk.

On opening day, the Capitol Theatre sold a record-setting twenty thousand tickets—that number climbed to ninety-four thousand by the time the movie completed its run at the theater.[36] It cost $266,204.28 to make, which was less than many of his other films. But *Zorro* returned a net profit of $458,825.74, a huge win at the box office for the fledgling United Artists Corporation.[37]

While audiences cheered, film critics gave it mixed reviews, a not unusual occurrence in the history of Hollywood motion pictures. But comments by the critics bring into focus just how much Fairbanks's star persona loomed over the whole production. Harriette Underhill, for instance, writing for the *New York Tribune*, seemed puzzled by *Zorro*. On the one hand, she wrote, "The picture is entertaining and amusing but not in the least convincing."[38] Underhill, with disbelief not unlike many critics of superhero films in our own day, sniped at a scene in the film: "When Zorro is backed up against a wall with 100 men waiting to shoot at him the only surprise lies in wondering which one of them he is going to pick up by the heels and hurl at the others." Underhill guffawed a bit at Zorro's so-called secret identity. "We knew all the time that Zorro was only Don Diego with a mask and a false mustache," she drolled, "and indeed it requires no great amount of movie sense to know this, for the only ones who are kept in the dark are the people about him." Harriette Underhill would be quite at home with a legion of nonnerd normals who just can't get into superheroes because *can't everyone plainly see that Clark Kent is Superman?* Even in 1920, Zorro, like later action-adventure heroes and superheroes, could be a bit passé for the film critics.

And yet, Underhill tapped into the wonder of a hero—a moving-pictures hero—bigger and better than other heroes heretofore. She applauded the name change—*Capistrano* was simply not as "euphonious" as *Zorro*— but also expressed awe at how the movie did something the book never could. "All the time we were watching" *The Mark of Zorro*, she wrote, "we couldn't help wondering what the original story was like. It couldn't have been anything like the screen version, for there couldn't be another hero like Fairbanks."

The movie, in fact, actually follows the narrative of McCulley's novel quite closely. Dialogue from the novel even appears as intertitles. The difference, the X factor, was Fairbanks. What Underhill searched for in her review was a way to describe how Fairbanks's persona, mixed with the immediacy, the immersiveness, and the affectivity of the movie medium, created a wholly different response in audiences than did a novel—even an adventure novel. The whole idea of a superhero—a figure more powerful than regular heroes—was birthed partially in Fairbanks's larger-than-life film portrayal of Zorro. For example, Underhill wrote,

> if an author had narrated that Zorro climbed the side of the church, slid in the window, changed clothes with a monk, walked out again, broke open jails, jumped from the floor to the first balcony and escaped on foot carrying a señorita in his arms with fifty armed soldiers after him no one would bother to read any further. He would say there ain't no such hero. But seeing is believing, as Dulcinea sagely remarked, and on the screen Zorro does do it, or at least Douglas Fairbanks does, for never once do you think he is Zorro.

Douglas Fairbanks became Zorro and Zorro became Douglas Fairbanks. But what's more, the actor's Zorro was a hero, because of the power of cinema, who surpassed earlier heroes in terms of athletic feats of derring-do. Beyond all the talk of which costumed, masked, dual-identity hero came first, Zorro's preeminent superhero status owes its best evidence to Fairbanks's film portrayal. Fairbanks's Zorro was a hero unlike any that had been seen before, all thanks to the magic of the silver screen and the actor's athletic, almost superhuman stunts.

For audiences and New York reviewers alike, no one but Fairbanks was behind the mask. The movie "is of California 100 years ago," Underhill wrote, "and Zorro is the handsome masked avenger who goes about putting a 'Z' on the cheek of the oppressors." Zorro was just a vehicle for Douglas Fairbanks's stunts, jumps, and athleticism. Fairbanks seemingly overshadowed any trace of Joaquín Murrieta in the story. But traces did remain, even if contemporary audiences and reviewers missed those traces entirely.

Many did notice that there were no Spanish or Mexican actors in *The Mark of Zorro*. But in 1920, that hardly seemed newsworthy. "The settings of the picture are picturesquely, and in some of them magnificently, Spanish," wrote one film critic at the time, "and they often contrast amusingly with the emphatically non-Spanish appearance of some of the players, including, of course, Fairbanks himself." Yet, was Spanish authenticity the point? Absolutely not. "The cast does what is expected of it," the reviewer continued, "and, as no one cares whether the story is consistently Spanish or just outlandish, there's no fault to find."[39] Newspaper reviews of the era didn't mention Joaquín Murrieta in connection to Zorro.

That wasn't the case with other films. Take one of D. W. Griffith's movies, for instance, a film called *Scarlet Days*, released in 1919 a few months before *The Mark of Zorro*. Set in the gold rush era (always a key Murrieta giveaway), *Scarlet Days* is about a roguish outlaw named Alvarez (Richard Barthelmess) who comes to the aid of the mother-daughter female protagonists, who have been wrongly accused of murder. Of the film, one reviewer in Philadelphia wrote, "The central figure, called Alvarez in the film, is based upon one of the most thrillingly interesting figures in the early history of the West—Joachin Murieta [*sic*]."[40] An important question to ask is *why* the reviewer made the assumption that Alvarez was Murrieta, since the lead character was never referred to as Murrieta. The gold rush setting is definitely part of the answer.

But, more importantly, narrative elements in *Scarlet Days* were key indicators of Murrieta inspiration.

Scarlet Days opens with an introduction of the Alvarez character: "The Wandering Knight—Don Maria Alvarez—blue-blood of old Spain—a frontier Robin Hood, who masquerades as a rich cattle buyer from Mexico." One intertitle reads: "This gentle-appearing youth was the most famous desperado and gunman in all California." The film proceeds to a tavern scene, which replays one of Joaquín Murrieta's most legendary actions—his self-declaration, "I am Joaquín." The version in *Scarlet Days* riffs on that legend. Alvarez enters a tavern, where the sheriff of Angel's Camp sits drinking at a gambling table. And like in the Murrieta legend it was based on, the sheriff (George Fawcett) exclaims with a clenched fist, "I'd give five hundred dollars to meet that outlaw Alvarez face-to-face." Alvarez, disguised as a peon in a colorful serape, overhears the sheriff's boast, just as Murrieta did in his legend. And like Murrieta, Alvarez takes the opportunity to reveal himself as the outlaw in question. Alvarez, reads the intertitle, "accommodates the Sheriff, without even asking for the five hundred."

Griffith's film, echoing the Murrieta legend as it developed, uses chivalric metaphors for the story. As far back as the late 1850s, in plays such as *Joaquín Murrieta de Castillo*, the use of chivalric language to describe the outlaw was common. In Griffith's version, Alvarez is called "the Wandering Knight," while the love interest is called "Lady Flameheart." Narrative elements in the film, not just its temporal setting, recommended to viewers evidence that Murrieta and his legend were the inspiration for the Alvarez character in *Scarlet Days*.

Many of the same narrative elements in *Scarlet Days*—the tavern scene and chivalric metaphors—are also used in *The Mark of Zorro*. While reviewers made the connection to Murrieta in *Scarlet Days*, they didn't in *Zorro*. Yet, that seems to be because of just how luminous Fairbanks was as Zorro. "There's too much Fairbanks in it," one reviewer noted at the time, and the movie was "spiced and speeded up to suit the taste of Douglas Fairbanks and the many who enjoy his gay and lively style of playing."[41] The viewer of *The Mark of Zorro*, in other words, was taken in by the actor and the story receded into the background. But the Murrieta narrative building blocks remained, nonetheless.

Scarlet Days provides a kind of cypher for understanding how traces of Murrieta can be seen in *The Mark of Zorro*. Lo and behold, Fairbanks's *Zorro*, like McCulley's novel, opens in a tavern scene. A boasting Sergeant Gonzales exclaims, "It's a good thing for that carver of Z's that he keeps out of reach of *my* sword. I'll carve Gonzales all over his body." Fairbanks, disguised as the sleepy fop Don Diego Vega, listens amused to Sergeant Gonzales. After Don Diego exits the tavern, the soldiers exchange ghost stories about Zorro. "This Zorro comes upon you like a graveyard ghost and like a ghost he disappears," one patron whispers. And another: "Zorro knows the deeds you do before you think them—takes any shape he wills—appears through keyholes!"

The comparison of Zorro to a ghost was a similar comparison made of Joaquín in the 1850s. Some reasoned, wrote one newspaperman in the early 1850s, "that Joaquín is a spirit," because "his spirit has made him invisible to people, for nobody sees Joaquín and yet he appears in three or four places at the same time, and always as the scourge of humanity." Or, too, continued the 1850s report, "others believe Joaquín is a demon who dines on the flesh and blood of his victims and satisfies his insatiable thirst by wringing the blood from their hearts."[42]

After the sergeant's boast and the ghost stories, the influence of Joaquín on Zorro's narrative actions continues in *The Mark of Zorro*. A Spanish private enters the tavern and posts a WANTED sign on the wall—a 10,000 peso reward for the capture of Zorro, dead or alive. The next to enter is Zorro himself, no longer dressed as Don Diego, but now with his familiar black costume. But he holds his cape up and obscures his masked face with his low-brimmed hat. Zorro, like Joaquín, scoffs at the poster. Whereas, in the Murrieta legend, Joaquín dismounts from his horse and writes on the poster that he will give a double reward for his capture and signs it with his mark (simply "Joaquín"), in *The Mark of Zorro*, Fairbanks draws his sword and cuts down the poster leaving a carved letter *Z* as his signature on the wall where the poster was hung moments before.

In the Murrieta legend, Joaquín could masquerade as a handsome gringo, and his proclamation "I am Joaquín" was the way the famous bandit revealed himself to his otherwise ignorant onlookers. In the film, Zorro's self-proclamation comes only after he carves his mark on the wall. When Zorro turns to face Sergeant Gonzales and the other soldiers, all swords are drawn only at that point, even though when the caped avenger entered, Gonzales and the rest had no idea who the mysterious stranger really was. Zorro, like Joaquín, reveals his identity through an act of self-revelation.

The traces of Murrieta in *The Mark of Zorro*, in other words, are plot-based actions, narrative elements. In *Zorro*, those actions—the tavern, the self-revelation, the reward poster, the signature, the whipping of an innocent monk—have been emptied of their original Latinx California context of racial violence. In the place of Murrieta, then, Fairbanks slips into the now-vacated story costume. *Zorro* mimics Murrieta's legend, but now the role—the hero—is no longer a folk legend who carried the memory of real Mexican American experience, but has become a famous white actor playing those actions for a different audience entirely. Such was the sublimation of the Latinx origins into Zorro. While Murrieta helped give birth to Zorro, Fairbanks made the character his own.

Fairbanks superseded McCulley's novel, as well. McCulley's use of Zorro carving Zs, for example, is limited to a few instances. Fairbanks, however, goes crazy with it.[43] He carves Zs like a dog marking its territory with a lift of its back leg and the wag of its tail. Fairbanks's Zorro carves Zs on the wall, on his opponents' flesh, but also in the breeches of Sergeant Gonzales, a gag played again and again in Disney's TV version in the 1950s. Fairbanks, too, as reviewers noted at the time, flew, jumped, and strutted his way through the film in ways wholly unforeseen in McCulley's *The Curse of Capistrano*.

But the legend of Joaquín hinted at the bandit's almost superhuman abilities—his strength, height, and spectacular skill. Fairbanks, however, was the one who brought his acrobatics to the screen, and any debt to Zorro's Latinx origins were lost in the process. In one iconic chase sequence, Fairbanks climbs the side of a church, leaps into a window, and precedes to take a meal break— "Never do anything on an empty stomach," he tells the frightened woman whose window he has just leaped into. Wiping his mouth after eating, he continues the game of cat and mouse with the soldiers, leading them where he wills. So notable is the scene to film history, in fact, that in 2011's Oscar-winning film *The Artist*, footage of the Zorro chase scene was reused, with close-ups of actor Jean Dujardin substituted in place of shots of Fairbanks.[44] Perhaps no one recognized Murrieta in Zorro because Fairbanks just wouldn't sit still long enough.

Murrieta and McCulley didn't disappear entirely from Zorro, despite Fairbanks's larger-than-life portrayal. We might say that Fairbanks, as with Tom Selleck's character in *Three Men and a Baby*, was reputed to be the biological father. But one should never count out the irrepressible Steve Gutenberg, nor the ever-emerging Ted Danson—the other "fathers" in the 1980s comedy. So, too, with Murrieta and McCulley. Their relative mark on Zorro appears throughout the next one hundred years. And, like the 1980s comedy, there's always a sequel.

13 | ZORRO IN LA LA LAND

Research Log #4
Beverly Hills, California
9:13 AM

IT REALLY IS A LAND OF SUNSHINE, BEVERLY HILLS—sunshine, and Spanish revival architecture. *The Mark of Zorro* helped build Beverly Hills, and the rest of Los Angeles for that matter, into a particular Spanish mission architectural style. The movie provided an aesthetic that home builders and home buyers loved. Mary Pickford even lectured at the American Institute of Architects on the subject. American colonial or English styles of architecture were inappropriate for Southern California, she told the crowd. Style-mixing was in bad taste. Movies, like *The Mark of Zorro*, as well as movie stars, told audiences and architects what was interesting and beautiful.[1]

I walked from my Beverly Hills Airbnb—yes, it, too, was done up in Spanish period style, although surprisingly reasonably priced—to the Margaret Herrick Library, the main archive of the Academy of Motion Picture Arts and Sciences. Douglas Fairbanks was the Academy's first president in 1927. The building where the Academy library is housed is named the Fairbanks Center for Motion Picture Study. And, of course, the Fairbanks Center is designed in faux Spanish mission style as well. It looks like a colonial Spanish church—white adobe, red-tile slanted roof, even a little steeple and belfry. A sanctuary for some of film's most sacred documents, is the aesthetic the Academy seems to have gone for.

The Fairbanks Center holds eighty thousand screenplays, three hundred thousand clipping files, ten million photographs, and countless production materials, manuscripts, and publicity folders documenting Hollywood's film history from its beginnings to the present. The Fairbanks Center, as a place that exudes the Spanish fantasy heritage, is no different from surrounding areas of Los Angeles. "Any average 1920s moviegoer," writes architectural historian Merry Ovnick, "associated particular settings with feelings of fear, playfulness, despair, romantic passion, family bonds, contentment, and other sentiments. A serenade balcony or a window in a corner tower triggered memories of vicariously experienced movie moments."[2] As the movies told audiences what was interesting and beautiful, those standards of beauty were then re-created in the real-world landscapes of Los Angeles.

And yet, the Spanish style hadn't really existed before to any large degree in the region, especially as Los Angeles had grown from a one-horse town to a motorized city between 1910 and 1920. Model Ts brought 420 carloads of tourists a day in 1922—that figure climbed to 500 the next year, while the railroads daily brought thirty-two hundred people to the city. From 1920 to 1925, L.A.'s population doubled. Three in ten visitors stayed at least five months; one in ten stayed permanently. There were six thousand home building permits in 1918; that number exploded to sixty-two thousand in 1923.

People, and not even just the filthy rich, wanted to live in movie sets. "Film audiences," writes Ovnick, were "educated in certain distinct aesthetic standards by silent film set design, lighting, and other cinematic techniques. . . . The streets of Los Angeles blossomed with reflections of that education."[3] Red-tile rooves multiplied, as did wrought-iron serenade balconies, hanging lanterns, and ornamental bougainvillea vines, bushes, and trees. With every walled courtyard and elaborate fountain, passersby could engage "in the drama of the house" and "reference them to film stories set in faraway times and places." "Like Rosebud lips," Ovnick writes, "these features became the decade's standards of beauty."[4]

Audiences loved *Zorro* because the movie allowed them to make the Spanish fantasy come true, if only in their home design. The Spanish architectural style became further proof that the history of the region was to be found in Old *Spanish* California, without reference to the very real Mexican American population who lived primarily in their own, largely segregated, enclave in East Los Angeles.

It seemed I'd come to the right place to study Zorro's impact on Holly-wood after the premier of *The Mark of Zorro*. Beverly Hills was a whole lot less tranquil than Forest Lawn Memorial Cemetery, but it was nice to be in the land of the living again.

Spanish revival architecture aside, I still couldn't get Johnston McCulley off my mind. Perhaps it was not so odd—I'd pondered the guy's life for quite some time, all while standing just three feet from his ashes. McCulley, as I'd come to find out, absolutely basked in the glow of *The Mark of Zorro*. His name became associated with the Fairbanks star persona.

The actor invited McCulley to join him and his creative team in Los Ange-les to pitch ideas for Fairbanks's next swashbuckler. McCulley, who frequently flitted about from New York to Los Angeles, with his home base in Colorado Springs, traveled at Fairbanks's request "as fast as the train will carry him," one newspaper account noted.[5] Fairbanks, Allan Dwan (one of Doug's frequent directors), Lotta Woods (chief of the scenario department), and Kenneth Dav-enport (writer of *The Nut*) all sat down in a big conference to hash out the new film. McCulley had in mind a couple of ideas, one of which was a sequel to *The Mark of Zorro*.

The sequel was developed with a clear swashbuckling flavor—pirate raiders, walking the plank, buxom "wenches"—and published in 1922 as McCulley's second Zorro novel, *The Further Adventures of Zorro*. McCulley's editor at *Argosy All-Story*, Robert H. Davis, wrote enthusiastically at the prospect of buying the pulp writer's stories. "I will be glad," Davis assured McCulley, "to get a crack at anything you have got to offer; not only now but hereafter, and to the merry end of time."[6] Little Willie was a hot commodity in both Hol-lywood and the pulps.

But Douglas Fairbanks didn't want to do a Zorro sequel, at least not yet. Fairbanks went for McCulley's other idea for a story, tentatively titled "The Spirit of Chivalry." *Photoplay* magazine reported it was a "tale of the medieval age, when knighthood was in flower, in which Doug will buckle on his armor and his ideals and fight an army of extras to save his lady's honor. It will not be a vegetarian picture."[7] So while McCulley wrote *The Further Adventures of Zorro*, Doug finished production on *The Three Musketeers* and worked with his scenario team on what would actually be his next picture, *Robin Hood* (1922). McCulley wasn't credited on the film. It's unclear from the record whether McCulley took offense. One imagines that he wasn't happy about the outcome—McCulley's treatment of "The Spirit of Chivalry" was remarkably similar to *Robin Hood*. Fairbanks didn't forget McCulley completely, however. He used elements of *The Further Adventures of Zorro* in his 1926 film, *The Black Pirate*.[8]

Nevertheless, McCulley gained notoriety as the hot writer for Hollywood films. "Old Spanish California stuff," reported the *Oakland Tribune*, "is coming to have a vogue in the movies."[9] And McCulley was the writer named as the Old Spanish California guy, first for *The Mark of Zorro*, and in 1922 for a film adaptation of *Captain Fly-by-Night* based on McCulley's 1916 novel. The writer took out an ad in *Film Daily*—"He never had a fizzle!" reads the page.[10] McCulley certainly had a high opinion of the power of his writing to bolster the careers of Hollywood stars. "He wrote 'The Mark of Zorro,'" the ad proclaims, "and put Douglas Fairbanks definitely on the film map."

McCulley was receiving not a few fat checks. His second marriage, however, had soured. He divorced his wife, Ruth McCulley, and, in Doug-and-Mary style, remarried shortly after. His new wife was Daisy Louris Munsey, who, although some historians have claimed otherwise, bore no relation to Frank A. Munsey, who owned many of the pulps McCulley wrote for. McCulley and Munsey met in New York, where the writer churned out many of his short stories in a small eleventh-floor apartment. Daisy Munsey was then managing the silent film career of her daughter, the actress Maurine Powers. The three quit New York and Colorado Springs and moved full time to Los Angeles. Daisy and Maurine took Johnston's last name—Maurine eventually changed her name to Beatrix Maurine McCulley, while Daisy started going by Louris—and they settled into a Spanish mission revival mansion in Glendale.[11]

All of this was on my mind as I made my way to the Fairbanks Center, because for most of the 1920s Zorro existed only as two films and two serialized novels. In the mind of the public, Fairbanks was Zorro. He couldn't resist reprising his role. In 1925 the actor decided to do a Zorro sequel after all. He didn't use McCulley's sequel, but instead adapted a novel called *Don Q's Love Story* (1909), by mother-son duo Kate and Hesketh Prichard, for the film. Zorro was an add-on to the Prichard novel.

The movie, *Don Q, Son of Zorro*, cemented Zorro's origins in Spain. Except for a brief vignette where we see an aged Don Diego, played by Fairbanks in makeup, the action all takes place in Spain. The elder Zorro takes down the sword he'd hurled at the wall at the end of the last film—"Till I need you again!"

he'd proclaimed in *The Mark of Zorro*'s closing scene—and says heroically in *Don Q*, the sequel, "I need you again!" He's off to Spain to aid his son, Don Cesar. The junior Vega, also played by Fairbanks—and how lithe and trim he looks in the film—has gone off to follow the family tradition of being educated in the finest Spanish schools. The film offers him as the best of the New World in the Old. He represents the best of the American character—honesty, directness, and vigor—whereas the elder Don Diego / Zorro had stood for the best of the Old World in the New—honor, courage, courtly manners, and a heroic style. His father is "the finest man in America," Don Cesar tells his fellows on several occasions.[12]

As in the first film, Fairbanks introduces elements to Zorro in *Don Q* that would become identifying features of the character in years to come. The film showcases the first use of Zorro's bullwhip, for example. Costar Mary Astor (playing Don Cesar's love interest, Dolores de Muro) remembered Australian bullwhip master Snowy Baker giving Fairbanks six weeks of unceasing training on the weapon. "While I was making up in my dressing room," Astor wrote in her memoir, "I could hear the repeated *swishshshsh-SMACK* of the whip. . . . He could soon do all the tricks with the bullwhip, and he was boyishly proud of his accomplishment."[13]

Fairbanks always wanted to do his own stunts—and to one-up the action from *The Mark of Zorro*. Donald Crisp, who played the film's heavy and also directed the movie, began to loathe Fairbanks's unending acrobatics. "He was always striving to be something he was not," Crisp later wrote through a fair bit of jaundice. "He would've killed himself showing off."[14] And perhaps Crisp's later unkind appraisal of Fairbanks was due, in part, to the fact that he was on the losing end of some of the actor's stunting. Crisp broke a foot while shooting the film and also received a nasty rope burn around the neck from one of Fairbanks's errant *swish-smacks* of the bullwhip.

Fairbanks was showing his age a bit, off screen at least—even as his on-screen silhouette was more svelte than ever. Mary Astor, a woman later known for off-screen hanky-panky with her male costars—she was even then, while filming *Don Q*, in a love affair with actor John Barrymore—found Doug to be, well, tepid. "I looked forward to meeting this man who was something of a legend around Hollywood," Astor later wrote. "But I found the man himself to be less exciting than the legends. For one thing, I was put out by his attitude toward me. He was nice to me, in the way a sophisticated man about town would be nice to a small and reasonably well-behaved child. I felt I merited more attention than that!"[15]

Even in 1925, with a half dozen more years of swashbuckling films ahead of him, Douglas Fairbanks was growing a little tired of the Zorro persona. "I found," he wrote later, "that I had once more started something I couldn't stop. If the public wanted acrobatics, I decided that I would give them what they wanted. . . . I quite forgot, myself, why I had started all these tricks. They began to possess me, almost as completely as the smile. . . . I romped, jumped and skylarked through one play after another."[16]

Fortunately, in 1925, those acrobatics paid off in *Don Q, Son of Zorro*. It was named by the *New York Times* as one of the ten best films of the year. The finale showed a bit of technical split-screen wizardry, as both father and son fought side-by-side to the delight of fans. The film returned more than $1.6 million in profit for Fairbanks. *Don Q* also secured Fairbanks's claim to the swashbuckling throne. Other matinee idols tried to get in on the dual-identity masked hero game; Rudolph Valentino, for example, starred in *The Eagle* that same year. While women flocked to see Valentino in a black mask, Zorro was who kids wanted to be. "It is guaranteed to drive little boys into frenzies of stunts," wrote one reviewer of *Don Q*, "until they break an arm or a new fad comes along." A young Marion Morrison, the future John Wayne, almost did just that after watching *Don Q*. "I ruined a beautiful grape arbor," Wayne later confessed, recounting his youthful jump out a second-story window while swinging on a vine.[17]

The frenzied Zorro worship of kids aside, Fairbanks's swashbuckling days were numbered. He made no other Zorro movies after *Don Q*. And McCulley didn't write another Zorro novel until 1931—*Zorro Rides Again*. Imitators began in earnest, pilfering story elements, using dual identities, masking alternate heroes for different films. In 1927, Paramount Pictures released the first Zorro satire, the film *Señorita*, starring the actress Bebe Daniels. "Not Douglas Fairbanks in another *Mark of Zorro*," reads one caption of a photo of Daniels dressed in drag for the film. "Pause and hesitate before you write 'fan' letters to this handsome lad. It is none other than Bebe Daniels in *Señorita*."[18]

In the movie, Daniels (Francesca Hernandez) travels to her ancestral home in Argentina, where her grandfather is under the (obviously mistaken) assumption that he had had a grandson instead of a granddaughter. To oblige grandpa's prejudices against women, Francesca dresses in a faux Zorro costume, replete with head scarf and a fake mustachio, all in order to make grandpa happy, but also to calm a violent feud between her family and a rival clan, the Oliveroses. In the process, she falls in love with the favorite son of the Oliveros family and comic high jinks ensue.

One reviewer noted:

> *Señorita* is a lusty burlesque of the Fairbanks school of acrobatic bravado. More specifically, it pretends to broad satire of Doug's *Don Q, Son of Zorro*. You'd hardly recognize your usual décolleté Bebe as, blade in hand, she holds a staircase against a horde of snarling Oliveros, or as she swings menacingly across a room on a tapestry to land smilingly on a table to confront her bewildered enemies."[19]

Señorita was the first in a long line of satires, farces, and spoofs of the Zorro character. Bebe Daniels's cross-dressing role only hinted at the wide spectrum of sexualities inherent in the fop-hero alter ego of the masked avenger.[20]

By 1929, McCulley and Fairbanks were both suing Warner Bros. for plagiarism in the studio's talkie film version of the Broadway musical *The Desert Song*. The movie has a masked character, the Red Shadow, whose alter ego is the son of a French governor of Morocco. As the Red Shadow, Pierre assists the maltreated Riffs, an Arab rebel group, in getting justice from the corrupt colonial government. The film's plot is an awful lot like *The Mark of Zorro*, set not in California but in Northern Africa. And the characters sang, to the sonorously deprived delight of many audiences. The suit was eventually settled out of court.[21]

Yet it wasn't the imitators or the satire that killed Fairbanks's shtick—sound movies did. *The Jazz Singer* (1927) heralded the twilight of silent films and the new world of synchronized sound on film. With sound films, both Fairbanks and Pickford faded as the most famous Hollywood couple. The two made a movie together, *The Taming of the Shrew* (1929), in full sound. It flopped at the box office.

Pickford fared better than Fairbanks in talkies. She won an Oscar in 1929 for her film *Coquette*. In the case of Fairbanks, his high-pitched voice didn't strike viewers as a match to his heroic silent persona. And the pair's marriage fell to pieces, as well. Both strayed from the relationship with other partners. The couple divorced in 1936 after being estranged for a few years. Although both remarried, the zenith of their fame had passed.

Fairbanks sold the Zorro rights to Darryl Zanuck for a reported $50,000, an unheard-of sum for movie rights at the time.[22] The first king of Hollywood died in 1939, at the age of fifty-six. Years later, Douglas Fairbanks Jr. remembered his stepmother Mary Pickford telling him of Doug Sr.'s decline in the marriage, as well as in the movies. "She told me she woke up one morning at Pickfair, looked out the window, and saw Pete"—that was the name Doug Jr. used for his father—"sitting on the diving board by the pool. And he was sobbing. He realized he'd lost it all."[23]

After Fairbanks, Zorro lived on, of course, but in a different form. And that's why I'd come to the Margaret Herrick Library at the Fairbanks Center. Zorro was partially unmoored from the character's Fairbanksian beginnings. He was a free agent, so to speak; free, or mostly so (McCulley still got his share), but available to provide fodder for the 1930s and '40s era of Zorro remakes, serial B films, and, notably, the character's transition from a swashbuckling hero to a western icon.

All that to say, it's the story of how Zorro became the Lone Ranger.

14 | THE LONE RANGER: OR, HOW ZORRO GETS WHITEWASHED

THE LONE RANGER, as a fictional icon in the American imagination, possesses a pedigree about as good as Zorro. Western master writer Zane Grey authored the first of many novels featuring the Lone *Star* Ranger in 1915.[1] Grey's character, and the novel, wasn't the "Hi-Yo Silver, Awa-a-ay!" Lone Ranger we've come to know, but that first novel did center on a western cowboy who has to work outside the law to bring justice to a local community. In the second half of Grey's novel, the hero, Buck Duane, joins the Texas Rangers in order to secure the governor's pardon for some of Duane's former peccadillos, namely killing in self-defense.

Grey dedicated his novel to a real-life Texas Ranger named John Hughes. Hughes would later claim, with some plausibility, that he was the inspiration for the Lone Ranger because of his association with Zane Grey's first novel.[2] In one sense, then, the Lone Ranger's pedigree extends back further than Zorro, encompassing Grey's character but also a whole host of frontier writing all the way back to James Fenimore Cooper.

The Lone Ranger *we* know—with a horse named Silver, a sidekick named Tonto, and his trademark silver bullets—is part of the long tradition of the western genre. "The masked rider of the plains," notes one authority, "was the culmination of nearly a century of frontier fiction."[3] The Lone Ranger has a debt to earlier frontier figures, such as Cooper's Leatherstocking and Owen Wister's *The Virginian* (1902). One could also cite O. Henry's "The Caballero's

Way" (1907), which inaugurated the Cisco Kid cycles of novels and films. And the Lone Ranger also owes something to early cinematic cowboys like Tom Mix, who starred in many silent-era and early sound films, and who defined the filmic western with clear tropes: white-hatted good guys, stunts, and even a loyal, trusty steed—in Mix's case, his horse was called Tony. Four films with the Lone Star Ranger appeared between 1919 and 1942. Mix starred in the 1923 version of the film.

But the Lone Star Ranger wasn't *the* Lone Ranger. And so, while it's true that the Lone Ranger and the Lone Star Ranger shared many characteristics—including three of four words in the character's title—and while it's true that the Lone Ranger clearly was part of a long tradition of frontier fiction and cowboy films, the Lone Ranger was also influenced by Zorro. Simply put, Zorro, too, appeared at the Lone Ranger's birth in radio in 1933 and at the character's cinematic debut in 1938. Zorro gave the Lone Ranger his mask and his mystery.

But there was an irony at work. Once created, the Lone Ranger, in some sort of pop culture feedback loop, would help shape Zorro's western image thereafter.

Enter one George W. Trendle, Detroit-area lawyer and entertainment promoter extraordinaire. Trendle managed a chain of movie theaters for Adolph Zukor's Paramount Pictures. He once entertained Mary Pickford when "America's Sweetheart" breezed through town on a speaking tour.[4]

Trendle was a balding, bespectacled moneyman with less artistic talent than a nose for what would sell. While still managing his theaters, he moved into radio in 1929. It was on his new station, Detroit's WXYZ, that the Lone Ranger made his debut for the first time. The masked rider appeared out of necessity and financial pressure. Trendle and his business partners had begun their broadcasting endeavor as an affiliate of CBS.[5] It gave their station exposure to a broader listening audience, yet it limited Trendle's revenue due to airtime being taken up by the network. He took a risk and decided to go independent.

The move meant Trendle needed a hit, something that would draw advertising dollars to the new show. The program forming in his mind was a western, a genre that had always played well at the theaters he managed. "We never did bad business with a good western," Trendle told business associate Howard Pierce in late 1932. "In fact, we did good business with bad westerns."[6] Trendle had some vague ideas in mind. He called a meeting of his program managers and producers to discuss options, to hammer out something more concrete. Something western, but what?

Westerns had potential to make money. The merchandising opportunities were there—hats, holsters, toy guns, boots. You could emblazon your character's name on merch. And westerns were popular—most radio stations had their own versions of frontier cowboy adventures. Westerns appealed to kids, especially as they often expressed some golden virtue of their honest, faithful, self-sacrificing heroes.

At the meeting, the head of the artistic department, James Jewell, played a clip of his own *Curley Edwards* show, which followed the semi-adventures of an "honest cowpoke." Trendle wasn't impressed. What he had in mind, he told his producers and managers, was something "like Douglas Fairbanks in *The Mark of Zorro*."[7] The station manager, Harold True, had already mentioned "some sort of modern Robin Hood" in an earlier meeting with Trendle.[8] It was very much like Trendle to take his employees' ideas, tweak them just so, and then pass them off as his own stroke of brilliance.

However the idea originally formed in his mind, Trendle imagined a western show with a Zorro-like hero. Trendle liked the mystery and aura of romance associated with Zorro. Spitballing ideas, Trendle told his station managers and producers "he had especially liked the masked avenger, Zorro, as played in the silents by the great actor and athlete, Douglas Fairbanks Sr."[9] He liked Tom Mix too—the stunts and trick riding done by the actor. Trendle remembered Mix had been in a mask in one movie, *The Great K & A Train Robbery*. A masked rider Trendle liked, but he needed a better name and more compelling story than *Curley Edwards*.

"A name something like . . . The 'Lone Star Ranger,'" James Jewell suggested, perhaps wanting to remain relevant in the discussion after his *Curley Edwards* idea had just been shot to pieces, and in cold blood.[10]

Harold True, station manager, seconded the suggestion, but added: "Zane Grey owns that one—wrote a book of that title. They made a movie, too." True paused a moment, thinking. "Maybe shorter," he said, "more to the point. Maybe 'The Lone Ranger.'"[11]

As with most of these sorts of origin stories, where creative people are depicted struggling to come up with what we the audience know is that famous character, title, song, catchphrase, etc., and they are almost there but not quite, and then they finally stumble on the right combination that will change everything, it's really not clear whether it actually happened that way—somehow so dramatic and definitive all at once, as if everyone immediately grasped the greatness of the moment. Memory has a bad habit of always telling the story from the knowledge of the present. At any rate, Trendle liked it enough that he told James Jewell: "Okay, Jim, get me up some scripts on this 'Lone Ranger.'"[12]

And that's exactly what Jim Jewell did, except that he contracted out for the scripts. Pulp writer and radio scripter Fran Striker, then living in Buffalo, had already been writing shows for Detroit's WXYZ. One program was called *Manhunters*, a western anthology series. There was even one episode that starred a mysterious masked hero who had to operate in secret; he apparently wore a mask on the *bottom* half of his face. At that point, in late 1932, Trendle and Striker hadn't yet met. Both would be credited as the main creators of the Lone Ranger—the Ranger's biggest promoter and the guy who wrote the scripts, and later pulp stories.

But Jim Jewell also deserves credit. He was the main go-between connecting Trendle and Striker. Striker was a prolific writer—pumping out five thousand, even ten thousand words a day. He had no problem writing, adapting, and generally crafting his stories to meet the needs of his clients. But if Trendle proposed the idea of a masked rider à la Zorro, and Striker formed those ideas into stories (adding ideas of his own, in the process), Jewell was the project manager who honed those ideas and those scripts into the actual show that was heard on the radio.

Not long after the spitball idea meeting where Trendle, Jewell, and True came up with the name the Lone Ranger, Jewell wrote Striker:

> Will you write up three or four wild west "thrillers" using as the central figure the Lone-Ranger including all the hookum of the masked rider, rustlers, killer Pete, heroine on train tracks, fight on top of box cars, Indian bad-mud [*sic*], two gun bank robbers, etc. I have an idea that this type of thing might command a large audience among the fourteen or fifteen year old kids and if they are successful, we might

alternate them with the *Manhunter* series, (which, no doubt, will be a relief to you).[13]

Jewell asked for the scripts as soon as possible. Striker, busily writing other stuff, reworked a few stories he'd already created for a different series called *Covered Wagon Days*, which he hadn't yet been able to sell. Such was the process by which the Lone Ranger was given life.

Striker's first scripts for the Lone Ranger weren't exactly what Jewell had in mind. The main character was a happy-go-lucky swashbuckler type. The allusion to Fairbanks was there, but the Ranger wasn't mysterious enough for Jewell and Trendle. Jewell wrote up the interludes and picked the iconic music—the *William Tell* overture and *Les préludes*. But Jewell wasn't satisfied with Striker's treatment. He wrote Striker on January 21, 1933, with notes. "Regarding the character of the Ranger," he suggested, "I feel that we can make more of him if we keep him more as a mystery man inclosing [*sic*] his identity only to the audience and never to the characters in the story—*a la* 'Mark of Zorro.'" Jewell mentioned that the Lone Ranger would be publicized as a "Tom Mix type—always doing good, never doing wrong." The Ranger was never to kill anyone, Jewell stressed to Striker, so that it would remain a children's show. And Jewell added, "Continue to use the silver bullet and silver horseshoe gag—it's good."[14]

The ever-amenable Striker obliged. But the process of producing the Ranger went back and forth between Jewell and Striker. Striker's original idea for the Ranger's closing words, for instance, were, well, close but not quite on the mark. "Come on, Silver!" one draft stated. "That's the boy! Hi-yi-ha-ha-ha-ha-ha! Now cut loose, and away!"[15] In retrospect, James Jewell's decision to shorten it to just "Hi-yo, Silver, Awa-a-ay!" was a good one. The Lone Ranger's creation, in other words, was a process. Yet, by early February 1933, the Lone Ranger was formed enough to ride into living rooms throughout the Detroit area.

But even *lone* rangers don't have to be all alone. It was clear to Jewell and Striker that they needed a sidekick, someone to whom the Ranger could confide, as well as an audience proxy with whom the Ranger could share his internal monologue. Tonto was born to fulfill both needs. An origin story developed in which six Texas Rangers, led by Captain Daniel Reid, are ambushed by a gang of outlaws and only one survives, albeit just barely. Daniel Reid's younger brother is dragged to a hidden cave to convalesce by an Indian who takes pity on him. When the younger Reid—his first name isn't given—gains consciousness, he sees a tall man standing over him.

"Me . . . Tonto," the Indian says in broken English.

"What of the other Rangers?" asks Reid. "They were all my friends. One was my brother."

"Other Texas Rangers all dead," says Tonto. "You only Ranger left. You lone Ranger now."[16]

The details for Tonto, which is a Spanish word that means "silly" or "stupid," were worked out between Jewell and Striker. "It might be a good idea, also," wrote Jewell in February 1933, "to have an Indian half-breed who always stands ready at his command to help him make his changes. . . . It adds a lot of romance and mystery to the character of the Lone Ranger."[17]

If Zorro became the Lone Ranger, then Zorro's trusty Indian manservant, Bernardo, became Tonto. However, while Bernardo was mute, Tonto, at least, could speak—albeit in halting pidgin English. On the other hand, Tonto's term of endearment for the Ranger, Kemosabe, has a less clear meaning. One linguist identified it as a derivation of the Potawatomi word "gimoozaabi," which was traditionally translated as "trusty scout" or "faithful friend" on *The Lone Ranger* TV series. I have always been partial, however, to Gary Larson's definition, given in a *Far Side* cartoon. The Lone Ranger, long in retirement, finally finds out that all along, Kemosabe meant the rear end of a horse. Though perhaps a man of few words, Tonto could say so much with so little.

———————

At the Fairbanks Center, I'd been able to piece together this story—how Zorro influenced the creation of the Lone Ranger. But there was more. As I'd come to discover, the similarities between the masked riders only grew over time. The merging of the two characters was the product, in particular, of Republic Pictures' treatment of both Zorro and the Lone Ranger in the film serials of the late 1930s and '40s.

Republic was a second-tier studio that specialized in low-budget serials and B westerns. Formed in 1935 from the merger of five small Poverty Row studios, Republic made up for in quantity what it lacked it quality. The studio occupied the old Mack Sennett lot in the San Fernando Valley, where the Keystone Kops once did their antics. For almost twenty years, Republic grew to encompass some seventy acres with twenty-four soundstages. There were scores of offices and technical buildings—a legion of office girls pedaled bicycles around the lot carrying messages, musical scores, scripts, and interoffice memos from one building and department to another. Large call boards indicated what films were shooting on a particular day and where. A host of contract actors played similar characters from picture to picture—some always cast as heavies, some cast as heroes, some with numerous bit parts with the hopes of moving up to lead heavy or, even, to stardom. Four, five, sometimes six writers worked up scripts, often dividing the different "chapters" of the serials, shown weekly with features, newsreels, and shorts, between themselves. Second and third units might shoot stunts, while actors filmed parts of multiple scenes in each location used in the serial. Republic was excellent at economizing all aspects of the filmmaking process.

The studio made sixty-six film serials between 1935 and 1954. Most were shot in twenty to forty days. Each had twelve to fifteen chapters of fifteen minutes each. Stock footage was used extensively, especially in serials released in the 1950s. Each chapter usually ended on a cliff-hanger with the hero in peril; the next episode would begin with the hero somehow effortlessly resolving the problem, all with an easy roll, jump, or other some such deus ex machina—in the nick of time.[18]

Although most of Republic's versions of Zorro were serials, the studio's first attempt was actually a feature film, called *The Bold Caballero* (1936), starring Robert Livingston. It was the first sound film, and the first film in color, to feature Zorro. But because Darryl Zanuck at 20th Century-Fox owned the rights to remake *The Mark of Zorro*, Republic was forced to change its working title from "The Mask of Zorro" to *The Bold Caballero*. A few plot changes also became necessary, so as not to completely plagiarize the original story. Reviewers noted it was entertaining but that Livingston didn't hold a candle to Fairbanks in the portrayal of Zorro.[19] Notwithstanding, Livingston got another shot to play Zorro. In 1936 he played a thinly veiled Zorro-like character called "the Eagle" in the Republic serial *The Vigilantes Are Coming*.

Zorro's trajectory toward the western genre began in earnest as the next two Republic Zorro serials bookended two of Republic's Lone Ranger serials. *Zorro Rides Again* was released in late 1937, *The Lone Ranger* in 1938, *The Lone Ranger Rides Again* in February 1939, and *Zorro's Fighting Legion* in December

1939. All four scripts were worked up by an overlapping set of Republic contract writers. All four films were shot by the prolific William Witney–John English directorial team. Witney was a doughy faced twenty-two-year-old in 1937—one publicity photo shows him smoking a pipe and sporting a sweater vest stretched over a not-insubstantial paunch.[20] Despite his youth, Witney and English are credited as some of the first directors to create tightly choreographed action scenes and stunts for their movies.

With writing and directing done by the same group of creatives at Republic, it's little wonder that all four films revolve around one basic plot. A masked rider, whether Zorro or the Lone Ranger, has to heroically defend a local community or business enterprise against the forces of greed. In the offing, the masked rider's service at the local level is deemed a patriotic service to the nation as a whole.

None other than Abraham Lincoln makes an appearance in *The Lone Ranger* (1938). Lincoln worries that Texas has fallen to lawlessness after the conclusion of the Civil War. He therefore sends a commissioner to investigate. Meanwhile, the Lone Ranger has already formed a legion to fight an imposter tax collector who is bleeding the region dry of the local citizens' honest gains.

Likewise, in *Zorro's Fighting Legion*, made a year later, a famous president again makes a cameo appearance. This time, however, it's Mexico's President Benito Juárez, who entrusts the protection of the fictitious San Mendolito gold mines to none other than Zorro himself. "I cannot tell you how much this gold means to us," Juárez tells Don Diego, whose secret identity is a commonplace to the Mexican president. "The very existence of the Republic of Mexico depends on the establishment of our foreign credit for the purchase of arms and supplies. . . . Your legion has no legal standing. If you run into trouble with the San Mendolito authorities, there is nothing I can do to help." Duly noted, Don Diego laughs, as he sniffs a scented hanky.

All four films, but especially *The Lone Ranger* and *Zorro's Fighting Legion*, operate in what we might call today a precursor to the multiverse of many comic book superheroes and superhero films. Benito Juárez didn't become president of Mexico until 1858, but the film is set in 1824, just after Mexican independence from Spain. Abraham Lincoln, likewise, looks particularly healthy in *The Lone Ranger*, considering that his assassination took place just five days after the surrender of General Lee at Appomattox Court House, which officially ended the Civil War.

To the modern viewer, though familiar with the comic book world-building trope of alternate timelines taking place on different earths, Republic's use of historical anachronism is intriguing. Republic serials influenced comic book creators. The writers and artists who developed Batman and Superman, almost all avid watchers of the Republic serials, would shortly begin to work on their own superhero multiverses in a few short years.[21] At any rate, Republic Pictures was famous for melding the Old West with modern automobiles and sky scrapers. The Zorro and Lone Ranger serials were no exception.

In the Republic serials, Zorro and the Lone Ranger became interchangeable characters. Only *Zorro's Fighting Legion* follows Don Diego Vega, the original Zorro, in his mission to help save Mexico's foreign creditworthiness. In the serials, he was just as likely to be an Anglo-American descendant, a great-grandson, or some other ambiguous familial offspring of the original Zorro. In *Zorro Rides Again*, he is James Vega, great-grandson of the masked rider who has to protect the construction of the fictional California-Yucatan Railroad. We encounter Zorro set not in the Old California of the 1820s but in contemporary Los Angeles of the 1930s. James Vega (John Carroll), is a suit-and-tie-wearing man of business. Vega returns to Mexico, not as himself, at least not at first, but as a Zorro reborn. Zorro wears a full-faced mask and has twin six-shooters and a bullwhip—he's Zorro, but he looks like a cowboy in fancy get-up. Zorro has lost his sword and replaced it with two guns strung on each hip.

All is not as it seems, of course. For behind the local villain, El Lobo, is the true criminal mastermind, J. A. Marsden (Noah Beery Sr.), banker and financier, who pulls the strings from his high-rise office in Los Angeles. He remains in contact with El Lobo, a.k.a. Brad Dace, via wireless radio. Beery played none other than Sergeant Pedro Gonzalez in Fairbanks's *The Mark of Zorro*. The actor talks in the Republic Pictures film, usually quite slowly, punctuated with a few exasperated exclamations over radio waves: "Zorro, Zorro, Zorro! . . . What do we do with Zorro!" The chapter play introduces both the modern western and the gangster genres into the Zorro story. One glimpses the American disaffection with shadowy robber barons who built their kingdoms of money and power under the guise of business and finance, and who became targets of American anger in many films during the Great Depression.

Zorro Rides Again somehow mixes cowboys with the energy and feel of the not-yet-created superhero genre. It blends the singing cowboy with an early urban dynamic-duo vibe. In other words, the serial is a bit of a mess. It exists in the Old West as well as in contemporary urban Los Angeles. But that's not surprising. For instance, the Lone Ranger and Tonto replicated into the Green Hornet and Kato in the 1930s.

Green Hornet's backstory casts Britt Reid, a modern-day version of the Lone Ranger, as a descendant of the original Ranger. Under Trendle and Striker, who created both the Lone Ranger and the Green Hornet for the radio, the masked rider could operate in both settings—in the West and in the city—both fighting corruption and greed, but in different contexts. So, in *Zorro Rides Again*, James Vega sings the rousing theme song of the film to Joyce in one scene (like the best of the signing cowboys), while in others Zorro hops around the rooftops of skyscrapers like the not-yet-created Batman. There are plenty of shoot-outs, horse chases, hold-ups, snipers with rifles on clapboard awnings—in short, lots of the basics of the western genre. And yet—this was 1937, before Superman and Batman hit the nascent comics pages—Zorro ventures into the city where white-collar crime boss Marsden has his lair. Zorro dresses in his cowboy costume, while he leaps across buildings—he even uses his trusty whip as a sort of protean Batrope when a cliff-hanging fall is averted by a quick-acting throw-and-coil that arrests his descent to the urban street, preventing a Zorro *splat*.

Zorro Rides Again is a lot like the Lone Ranger. The serial is also a lot like the Green Hornet. It's also a lot like Batman, especially as James Vega has to do quite a lot of detective work with his sidekick, Renaldo (Duncan Renaldo), aided by his black-and-white pinto horse called El Rey. The chapter play is the first appearance of a nearly self-aware horse, who always comes when whistled for—like some remote-controlled Batmobile device—and who, perhaps not so much like the Batmobile, has a vengeful streak, as El Rey kills not one but two villains in the film, one of whom was the chief henchman himself, El Lobo. It's as if Zorro was in some sort of strange evolutionary moment in Republic's *Zorro Rides Again*. He's an ungainly, somewhat gruesome hybrid character, who, in the film, looks like his Lone Ranger western descendent, as well as like the masked vigilante superheroes who were born in the gritty cities of late-1930s America.

The Lone Ranger, however, would be the evolutionary descendant most immediately recognizable in the subsequent Zorro serials of the 1940s. *Zorro's Black*

Whip (1944) stars Linda Stirling as the masked hero who has to take up where her slain brother left off after his murder at the hands of a group of villains trying to impede the statehood of Idaho.

It was the second time a female protagonist had essayed the role of a Zorro-like character (Bebe Daniels, in 1927's *Señorita*, being the first). George J. Lewis, a Republic contract actor, and the male lead in *Zorro's Black Whip*, remembered that because of World War II there was a shortage of suitable leading men to play in Republic's serials. Linda Stirling, a former showgirl and model and fresh off her first starring role in the serial *The Tiger Woman* (1944), was cast in the role of the Black Whip.[22]

Zorro, in fact, is never mentioned in the film, except for in the title. Republic's contracted attorney, Fulton J. Brylawski, cleared the title for release as simply *The Black Whip*, but after negotiations with McCulley, it was decided a "Zorro" enhancement of the title would be feasible and could provide an additional draw at the box office. "Let me point out," McCulley wrote, "that credit must be given on screen in the usual manner with the words 'based on the character created by Johnston McCulley' or words of the same import. This was neglected on a Zorro serial made by you, and I allowed it to pass after consultation with the general manager at that time." *Zorro's Black Whip*, in fact, is the only Republic serial that does carry a credit for McCulley, even though Zorro is nowhere mentioned in the plot.[23]

Indeed, by the 1940s, even producers at Republic Pictures recognized some of their plots were growing a wee bit stale, repeating themselves, whether in serials featuring Zorro or the Lone Ranger. The characters signified the same thing to the studio—a western with a masked rider for hero. One executive producer noted that casting a female lead could spice things up a bit. The studio memo noted:

> This story is essentially the Lone Ranger or Zorro set-up, with a masked girl playing the lead. The basic plot, a masked rider coming to the aid of a community disrupted by war and terrorized by a gang of crooked politicians, has been used a number of times, and this treatment presents no new angles. However, the character of a masked girl lead has never been used in a Republic serial and has definite possibilities.[24]

One possibility was certainly Linda Stirling's sex appeal. Her first role as "Tiger Woman," in the eponymously titled serial, saw her costumed in skimpy animal skins. (They are actually cheetah print, as the Republic costume department apparently couldn't come up with a tiger outfit on such short notice.) Stirling's outfit was pretty modest by today's standards—her legs are really the only thing bared—but young boys flocked to the theaters to see her jump, kick, and wrestle with villains. And although it exists mainly on the level of subliminal undercurrent, Stirling, as the masked Black Whip, certainly has a dominatrix quality about her, what with her whipping and hog-tying all those naughty bad boys. And yet, Stirling pulled it off without incurring the wrath of the motion picture censors. She had, as one film historian notes, a "presence, wholesomeness, beauty and versatility" that allowed her to play roles, such as a tiger woman or a black-clad whip vixen, with a surprising amount of aplomb and decency.[25]

Stirling wasn't long for the movies. She did six serials for Republic and some television work in the 1950s. But she left Hollywood eventually, had a family, went back to college, and became an English professor for the rest of her career.[26]

By the late 1940s, then, Zorro's western hero stature was well established. McCulley began writing Zorro stories again. He published fifty-one "yarns," as he liked to call them, for the magazine *West* between 1944 and his death in 1958. While still technically set in Spanish California, many of the stories deal with the issue of Zorro's secret identity. Sergeant Gonzales becomes Sergeant Garcia, and Garcia displays far more skill and cunning than any previous incarnation of the character. Don Diego is always suspected of being Zorro, but somehow he manages to foil the sergeant or one of the string of corrupt commandants who show up in Reina de Los Ángeles. There are more horse chases, more tavern ne'er-do-wells, more shiftless drifters, and more mysterious plots in these stories than in the swashbuckling early days. Zorro even deals with an American in one tale, a character who turns out to be not half bad in the end.[27] Bernardo's role in aiding his master increases in the later Zorro short stories. He's always presented as born "dumb," by which was meant he was born without being able to speak. But Don Diego uses that quality to his advantage, as Bernardo spies for Zorro, as well as often becomes a decoy black-clad rider to aid Zorro's swift escapes in the opposite direction. As Guy

Williams, star of Disney's Zorro television series in the 1950s always put it, Zorro was essentially "a *south*-western."[28]

Republic Pictures did two more Zorro serials in the late 1940s—*Son of Zorro* (1947) and *Ghost of Zorro* (1949).[29] The so-called son of Zorro is actually a vaguely defined distant relative of the original Zorro, named Jeff Stewart. On returning to his hometown after fighting in the Civil War, Stewart decides to don the mask of his ancestor to fight corruption. It's a lot like the plot of Republic's first Lone Ranger serial in 1938.

But the last serial, *Ghost of Zorro*, provides perhaps the best example of Zorro's merger with the Lone Ranger. *Ghost* stars an up-and-coming actor named Clayton Moore as the male lead. Moore is Ken Mason, an engineer tasked with bringing telegraph lines to Arizona. The villain, George Crane (Eugene Roth), doesn't want this because, of course, the telegraph will bring with it the forces of law and order to the region, which would put a damper on his dastardly plans to rule the area as his private fiefdom. In one scene, Mason finds the long-vacant secret cave of his ancestor, Zorro. The descendant of Zorro's sidekick is also there with Mason, a Native American man called Moccasin, played by none other than George J. Lewis.

"Your grandfather, Don Diego, wore this to become known and feared among bandits as Zorro," Moccasin tells Mason in the opening chapter.

"And your grandfather helped him," Mason replies. "Was he who saddled Firebrand in this cave each time it was necessary for Zorro to ride."

"In that stall stands another Firebrand." Moccasin points to the stabled horse. "Ready for you."

"I'll ride as my grandfather rode," Mason oaths resolutely. "I'll become the living ghost of Zorro and drive these renegades from the land. We'll work together, Moccasin, just as our grandfathers did."

Moccasin smiles approvingly at this.

"Wait here until Zorro needs you," Mason adds.

"*Buena suerte, amigo.*" Moccasin pats the newly minted Zorro on the arm, perhaps not having entirely understood that Mason just told him to wait in the Zorro cave for an undetermined length of time. "Good luck," Moccasin adds, in case Mason, and the audience, can't understand what "*Buena suerte*" means.

The "living ghost of Zorro" was just a somewhat Latin-inflected version of the Lone Ranger. The mask worn by both mystery men was the same in the Republic serials—a larger than normal domino-style face covering with a black mesh material that draped over the lower part of the face. (It's likely Republic's low budgets helped influence that feature of interchangeability.)

Clayton Moore's role in *Ghost of Zorro* caught the attention of George Trendle, cocreator of the Lone Ranger and the guy who envisioned his masked rider as a Zorro-like character. Trendle was then busily trying to move the Lone Ranger radio series into television.[30] Clayton Moore, star of *Ghost of Zorro*, became the most iconic actor to play the Lone Ranger on TV, from 1949 to 1957. The series became the highest-rated program on the fledgling ABC television lineup, its first hit, and the series went out of production the same year Disney began airing, also on ABC, the first Zorro TV series.

The whitewashing of Zorro happened in a couple of ways. First, the Lone Ranger drew inspiration from Zorro—the idea of the masked rider, Zorro's mysterious identity, even the Native sidekick. But the Lone Ranger did away with any of Zorro's potential ethnic Mexican, or even Spanish, heritage. The Lone Ranger was a *Texas* Ranger, and unambiguously Anglo.

Second, the whitewashing of Zorro further developed as the Lone Ranger's story world fed back into the Republic Pictures' Zorro plots. The original Zorro was a vaguely defined antecedent to the new Zorros of the Republic serials, portrayed as an Anglo hero, without any noticeable ties to a Latinx past, outside the surprising appearance of Zorro's name and signature costume. Only *Zorro Rides Again*, the earliest serial, follows a character named James *Vega*—in other words, a character who still has some tie to Mexico, or a link to anything particularly Mexican, in his modern American identity.

The whitewashing of Zorro is a vision of ethnic forgetting. Ties to the past, to the country of origin, are lost. Assimilation has won. The past molders away like some old black costume and mask in a secret cave. It gets worn as a plot trope, no longer signifying anything other than itself. With Murrieta, the dual identity—the dangerous and recalcitrant Mexican behind the facade of a gringo dandy—operates as a critique of violent, coerced assimilation. That's not the case with Zorro in many of the Republic serials. With Ken Mason, in *Ghost of Zorro*, the mask is simply a useful and convenient plot device designed to provide the hero with an interesting set of weapons and a claim to legitimate violence. The hero is fighting *for* the forces of law and order, which are represented as being on the side of a United States–backed telegraph line.

But whitewashing also worked in another way. At this point in Zorro's history, there had been no Latinx actors who played the role of Zorro. Yet, scratching the surface, there were Mexican American actors who played supporting roles in the Zorro films.

Consider George J. Lewis, a longtime character actor, often cast as the heavy, sometimes as the Indian sidekick, and only rarely as the hero.[31] Lewis was actually born in 1904 in Guadalajara, Mexico. His mother was Mexican and his father was an Anglo-American. He lived in Mexico until the violence of the revolution there caused his family to relocate—to Illinois, briefly to Brazil, then to Wisconsin, and finally to Los Angeles. After graduating high school, Lewis learned to act in several West Coast theatrical stock companies. He made the leap to silent films in the early 1920s. Under contract to Universal, he played the role of the all-American athlete in more than a dozen film shorts. When sound film came, his all-American status evaporated. Universal felt he had a slight accent, which meant he could no longer play the roles he had in the silent era.

Throughout the 1930s, Lewis appeared in several Mexican movies and as a supporting cast member in Hollywood B films. For a time, studios produced Spanish-language versions of English-language Hollywood pictures. They were often shot at the same time, using the same sets, and often shared some of the same cast. Lewis appeared in several of these Spanish-language Hollywood films, directed at the emerging Latin American market. But as dubbing technology improved, Hollywood stopped producing concurrent Spanish-language versions. Lewis was once again looking for his next break.[32]

At Republic Pictures, George Lewis found a niche. He lost any trace of a Spanish accent. He played a Nazi in 1942's *Spy Smasher*. He starred with Linda Stirling in *The Tiger Woman*, cast as the main villain. Then, in 1944, Lewis had his first rendezvous with Zorro, or better said, with the Black Whip. He played Vic Gordon, a government agent sent to aid Idaho's bid for statehood. He discovers Barbara Meredith's (Linda Stirling) secret identity and decides to help her. In the process, the two fall in love. But Lewis actually wears the mask and outfit of the Black Whip at one point, in order to lead suspicion away from Stirling's character. (Somehow none of the villains are astute enough to discover that the black-masked individual they've been "wrastlin'" is actually a woman—it's just another odd facet of the Republic multiverse.) And so, George J. Lewis, in the role of Vic Gordon, who briefly dons the costume of the Black Whip, was the first Latinx actor in an English-language film to portray Zorro—or, at least, the Zorro-like Black Whip. A few years later, Lewis again appeared in a Zorro serial, this time as the unfortunately named sidekick Moccasin, in *Ghost of Zorro*. To round out Lewis's Zorro ubiquity, we find him as Don Alejandro, Zorro / Don Diego's father, in Disney's television series.

The career of George J. Lewis—always in supporting roles in Zorro films and television, and only accidentally as a Zorro-like character—pretty much sums up the dominant hue of whitewash applied to the original masked avenger. Zorro, despite Latinx origins, was a character developed for a US entertainment audience. The ethnic aspects of Zorro provided a bit of exotic allure to the character, a dash of mystery, perhaps—that's all. The story was never meant to do anything but confirm the ideal of Anglo-American heroism, innocence, and resilience. The Lone Ranger was Zorro, but a fully assimilated Zorro, without the potentially dangerous issues raised by ethnic American identities, however veiled or vague those Spanish or Mexican portrayals might be in Zorro films and television. Zorro's black hat and black horse became the Lone Ranger's white hat and white horse. The Lone Ranger, in short, didn't want to confuse audiences—behind the mask was a white hero.

15 | FOX DOES THE FOX

Research Log #5
Beverly Hills, California
6:02 PM

AS I DESCENDED the Kirk Douglas Grand Staircase and passed by the unpupiled white marble bust of Douglas Fairbanks at the Academy archives, I thought about Zorro's journey from swashbuckling hero to western icon. Part of that story is about changing tastes in US popular entertainment—the era of westerns was emerging and would only increase in power and ubiquity during the 1950s with the domination of television. Zorro still was a swashbuckler, and would be revived as such, but Zorro also kept up with the demand for western heroes. Zorro began to multiply—the swashbuckler, the western icon, and, soon enough, his superhero descendants.

And yet, part of the story of Zorro's evolution was about the kind of legend Americans wanted to hear. Heroes who operated in a gilded bygone era confirmed the story many US audiences wanted to believe about their past—that they were part of a nation of do-gooders, that justice was on their side, and that, sometimes, heroes had to work outside the law in order to uphold truth, justice, and, even, the American way. The "bad guys" in these stories were just "bad apples," aberrations, the unfortunate one-off. The "bad guys" were very rarely the institutions of American democracy. The system wasn't the problem, in other words; individual bad men were the problem.

"A few unscrupulous Americans had not hesitated to enrich themselves at the expense of the Californianos," reads an opening title sequence to 1937's *The Californian*, a film distributed by 20th Century-Fox. The movie stars Ricardo Cortez as a Zorro-like character. But don't get excited—Ricardo Cortez was actually the stage name for Jacob Krantz, a Jewish American actor typecast to play "Latin lover" roles because of his dark eyes and complexion.

There are many examples of this kind of film in the late 1930s to the 1950s—movies that set out to tell the story of Zorro, or Zorro-like masked avengers, even films about Murrieta himself, but all of them take out the annoying fact that the masked vigilante avenger emerged out of racial violence, particularly created out of US policy and institutional racism. It wasn't just bad apples that spoiled the bunch—the rot went deeper than that.

MGM's *Robin Hood of El Dorado* (1936) is a good example. Warner Baxter, who played the Cisco Kid in previous films, was cast as Joaquín Murrieta in the picture. The title comes from Walter Noble Burns's 1932 novel of the same name.[1] At the Fairbanks Center, I found hundreds of pages of production files on *Robin Hood of El Dorado*. There were alternate titles suggested, such as "I Am Joaquín" and simply "Joaquín Murrieta." There were multiple scripts, comparisons between the screenplay and the different versions of the Murrieta legend as told by the *Police Gazette* in 1859, as well as Burns's novel. There were historical synopses done by MGM researchers, even a bibliography of books on Murrieta that could be checked out at the Los Angeles County Public Library.[2]

Hollywood, in this period, was growing sensitive to Latinx themes, knowing they had an audience in Latin America for their films. It's as if MGM really wanted to get the story right. And, in my view, Baxter plays a pretty good Murrieta, despite being an Anglo-American actor playing a Mexican part. He is sufficiently made into a victim of forces beyond his control: his whipping at the hands of Americano bad men, the lynching of his brother, the rape and murder of his wife—all become eminently understandable causes for the revenge he takes on scurrilous gringos who did the crimes. The film sympathizes with his plight. MGM made the movie into a tragedy more than anything else. (An early script had the famous "I am Joaquín" tavern scene all set to go, but in the final edit it was cut.)[3]

But despite all the research, the quest for authenticity, and Baxter's nuanced portrayal of the bad-good man, the film undercuts its indictment of California history and the Mexican-American War by its opening title sequence. "Part of the spoils of war—lately ceded to the United States by its Mother country—Mexico—the uneasy stepchild in a new family." Clunky sentence structure aside, the sentiment justifies many of the wrongs done in the film as the inevitable consequence of the "spoils of war" or, even more oddly, as the reasonable abuse heaped upon a stepchild in a blended family. But no fairy godmother gets Cinderella out of her predicament in this story.

Murrieta's revenge on those who murdered his brother and wife is defensible enough within the framework of the film—but Murrieta's ultimate sin, according to the movie, is that he didn't stop at revenge on the individuals responsible. In one scene, the notable Californio dons are all assembled and debate about what course to take in the face of the American annexation of California. One demands that the only way to deal with aggression is to fight. Another Californio caballero responds to the call to fight with wide-eyed horror. The music swells behind him and the camera begins to zoom into a close-up while he begins his speech. "Please, please, my friends," he appeals to reason, "let us use wisdom, instead of words. A dignified appeal instead of useless force. We cannot fight the United States"—the patriotic-themed music is really going now—"We would be but a handful against a powerful nation. Our destiny lies in the hands of the new government. We must be patient and pray fervently that, in the end, justice will prevail. If we foolishly take up arms against the Americanos, they will look on us as outlaws, no better than Murrieta, who has done so much to hurt our cause." Murrieta, in contrast, creates an army of aggrieved Mexican Americans who visit their fury on the system itself—that's the unforgiveable trespass in the movie for which there can be little forgiveness.

Hence, the finale: Murrieta's one-time Anglo-American friend, Bill Warren (Bruce Cabot), a man who continues to understand Murrieta's proper anger throughout the film, finally turns against Murrieta because of a personal tragedy inflicted by the bandit. Murrieta's one-time friend, therefore, leads the posse that puts an end to the Mexican outlaw. Bill Warren is a character who acts as an audience proxy. We, the audience, are supposed to be on board with Murrieta until the bandit's activities result in the death of the bride-to-be of Bill Warren's younger brother. An innocent white woman has died because of Murrieta. Bill Warren, and the audience, turn against him and his cause.

In other words, Cinderella might understandably kill her stepmother and stepsisters, but taking the fight to the magic kingdom itself, where other stepchildren are most likely being abused as well, is simply too far. Individuals were the problem, according to *Robin Hood of El Dorado*, not the system itself. Murrieta merely didn't wait long enough for American justice to establish itself in California. "I am cold—it's growing dark," the Murrieta character says as he lays dying on the grave of his beloved Rosita "Put your arms around me."

One reviewer scoffed at the film after seeing it at New York's Capitol Theatre. "It is a grim story that the Capitol's picture tells," he wrote, "for all its window-dressing of gay fiestas and romantic interludes. Warner Baxter plays the title role—although Murrieta was far from being a Robin Hood—with such sincerity that we cannot help regretting Metro's decision to lighten the tragic quality of its theme by inserting sequences not appropriate to light-hearted operetta." The reviewer was uneasy with Murrieta as an antihero, but even more galling to him was what he saw as Hollywood's pandering to Latin American audiences in portraying Murrieta with any sympathy at all. He chalked this up to the superior quality of American free speech:

> Perhaps the most satisfying part of the picture is the realization we bring from it that America, for all its charged suppression of free speech, is dispassionate enough to accept even so camouflaged a reflection on its morals as this. In a sense it is ironic, too, that Hollywood, unable to make films of "It Can't Happen Here," "Paths of Glory," or "Forty Days of Musa Dagh" through fear of treading on foreign sensibilities, is not restrained at all when it comes to pointing an accusing finger at certain unpalatable phases of our national history. It would seem that the only toes we safely may tread upon are our own.[4]

The film only mildly criticizes American policy in California, and instead it indicts "bad apples" primarily, including Murrieta himself, for the violence. But even at that, the reviewer saw it as not sufficiently representative of the United States' track record of freedom and justice. The United States, even in its dark-ish hours, the reviewer argued, was still better than other nations.

As I packed my things to leave the Academy archives, I remembered that even while Zorro headed off in the direction of the Lone Ranger in Republic's serials, Zorro remained an A-list commodity. In 1936, Darryl Zanuck at 20th Century-Fox acquired the film rights from Fairbanks to remake *The Mark of Zorro*. I found a letter McCulley wrote to his literary agent, Mitchell Gertz, in April 1939 that explains how both studios, the A-list Fox and the B-list Republic, had the rights to Zorro:

> Dear Gertz,
> A few facts to clarify the Mark of Zorro thing. . . . About three years ago, I was approached by Republic. They wanted to buy the right to use the character Zorro in a couple of screen plays. At that same time, there was some talk of Fox remaking Zorro. Before answering Republic, I got in touch with Mr. Zanuck by letter, and he referred the matter to Julian Johnson. I suggested that it was the ethical thing for me to let them know and have a chance to stop any other studio making a Zorro yarn by making a deal with me. A letter from Mr. Johnson finally told me they were not interested.[5]

McCulley had assigned the rights to *The Mark of Zorro* (a.k.a. *The Curse of Capistrano*) to Fairbanks. That agreement was updated in 1929 to include talkie rights, although McCulley denied that fact in his 1939 letter. Fairbanks then sold Zanuck his rights on February 18, 1936. When Republic approached McCulley about using Zorro, he told Zanuck about it. But 20th Century-Fox was happy with its option to remake the original. McCulley, therefore, "loaned" the character to Republic for an initial two-year period (1936–38) for $800. The loan was renewed, for another $800, for the period 1938–40; then for $600 during 1940–45; and a final extension, for $500, for 1945–50.[6] Fox owned the rights to *The Mark of Zorro*, but not rights to the character. Republic, in contrast, owned rights to the Zorro character, but not *The Mark of Zorro*. That split, between the original story and the character property, helps further explain how and why Republic Pictures went in the direction it did—Zorro as western—with its five Zorro serials.

But Fox had plans for the Fox that didn't include the Lone Ranger or anything of the sort. Fox had been working on a big-budget remake of *The Mark of Zorro* since the studio acquired the rights in 1936. In development for four years, with the working title of "The Californian," Darryl Zanuck wanted to use his remake of Zorro as a way to edge out his rival studio Warner Bros. Warner had scored a huge success with *The Adventures of Robin Hood* (1938), starring Errol Flynn. The swashbuckler film was back, and Zanuck knew he had the original swashbuckler, Zorro, in his back pocket. He therefore ignored McCulley's letter about Zorro rights, and mostly didn't care that Republic was making B-list serials with the character. Zanuck wanted to remake the original Fairbanks classic, not create a brand-new storyline.

Zanuck played tough with Warner Bros. when he heard that Warner was perhaps planning a similarly themed film. Zanuck wrote Jack Warner in July 1939:

> I read that you were preparing a story on the history of early Los Angeles during the days of Mexican rule. I want to call your attention to the fact that we own the [Johnston McCulley] story and picture *The Mark of Zorro*. We have been working on this story consistently for the past year and it goes into production as a Technicolor feature starring Tyrone Power when he returns from his honeymoon in Europe."

Zanuck was essentially firing a swashbuckling warning shot across Warner Bros.'s bough. Warner would proceed in the direction of Zorro at the studio's own risk. "*The Mark of Zorro*, as you know," Zanuck continued, "recalling the old Fairbanks picture, deals exclusively with incidents in the city of Los Angeles under Mexican rule." Zanuck, like other Americans, was perhaps a little hazy on Zorro's original "under Spanish rule" setting. The distinction, however, was lost on Zanuck, as Zorro's Spanishness was now seen as an extraglossy version of California's Mexican past. At any rate, Zanuck told Warner to keep his hands off the subject. He didn't want the rival studio to "be put to any unnecessary expense" as Fox's picture would come out before Warner's and was, in his words, "apt to take the edge off your proposed production."[7] After he did Zorro, Zanuck believed, no one could come close to the subject. He planned on making his remake a hit, the perfect one-upmanship to Warner's *Robin Hood.*

If, as one historian writes, "the 1940s belonged to Darryl Zanuck," the Zorro remake was Zanuck's entrée to the decade.[8] He had managed to make 20th Century-Fox one of the top three Hollywood studios, along with MGM and Paramount. He'd assembled a host of stars: Betty Grable, Gene Tierney, Carmen Miranda, Henry Fonda, and Don Ameche, as well as the up-and-coming young lead actor, Tyrone Power. Zanuck also had virtuoso directors like Elia Kazan and Joseph L. Mankiewicz.

Zanuck was a Hollywood mogul, a word based on a term used for the Muslim rulers of India in the 1700s, who were reputed to have autocratic powers. It was an apt word to describe studio bosses of the era like Zanuck. He had things his way. Zanuck's office was always painted a particular shade of green—"Zanuck green," as it was known at the time. He had sycophants and cowering employees. He had a bedroom built that adjoined his office suite. The boudoir's stated purpose was so that he could work late, reading and commenting on every A-list script the studio produced. But the unstated purpose, and fuel for rampant Hollywood gossip, was that Zanuck used the plush boudoir for his afternoon liaisons with beautiful actresses under contract to him. The rumor was denied assiduously by Zanuck's children in later years, who claimed they themselves had often been in the famous bedroom at prime-time assignation hours, but is often asserted by the studio mogul's biographers. As one authority notes, "Having a bedroom for casual sex at the office is certainly mogul-like."[9] Zanuck was a hands-on administrator at Fox, and, it would seem, many of his female stars suffered as a result.

In terms of creative control, Zanuck wanted the ultimate say—in almost everything from initial film treatment to script, casting, and final edit. Zanuck said at the time "he was not the type of producer who stands on the side-lines and hires people to express their views for him and takes screen credit." He acquired film properties, supervised his directors, oversaw musical scores, and made, or unmade, countless stars in the process. "I expect every picture that I have been associated with to equally represent the views of the writer, the director and myself," he insisted.[10] And if there was a conflict between these views, Zanuck's view usually won.

The problem for the studio mogul was that he wanted a sure-fire hit with the remake of Zorro. But to get a hit, he couldn't just proceed with business as usual. He would, perhaps, have to take a risk. The biggest films of 1939 had been with other studios, a fact galling to Fox's studio boss. It was truly a history-making film year, something recognized even at the time. Columbia produced *Mr. Smith Goes to Washington*; Samuel Goldwyn and United Artists released *Wuthering Heights*; MGM scored with *The Wizard of Oz*, and then, of course, scored again with *Gone with the Wind*, which MGM jointly produced with David O. Selznick's independent company.

The mogul of 20th Century-Fox didn't want his rival studio competitors to unseat him from his comfy green office. A risk, indeed, was necessary. Zanuck needed a director who could handle the Zorro legacy. And not just a competent journeyman director who would pull off a good, though ultimately second-rate treatment of a film, which had, by then, become so associated with the Fairbanks persona that it would inevitably call forth comparisons. He contemplated choosing a director with a clear cinematic vision. Zanuck needed a director who could do Zorro for a new generation.

Fox's mogul had options within the studio for the director's job. But instead he picked Rouben Mamoulian, best known at the time for spearheading the use of moving cameras in his early sound features, as well as being the first director to shoot a movie in three-strip Technicolor, *Becky Sharp* (1935).

Given Zanuck's peculiar sort of megalomania and domineering personality, Mamoulian was far from a safe choice for the canvas chair. The Georgian-born director had been one of the founding members of the Screen Directors Guild (today the Directors Guild of America), established in 1936 to increase director salaries, as well as to promote greater autonomy among filmmakers over their pictures. Mamoulian was the sort of director—headstrong and independent—that Zanuck loathed. Mamoulian was an auteur, an artist, who chafed against Hollywood's assembly line mode of production. He got his start as a stage director on Broadway. When he moved to film, he was hailed by critics for such pictures as *Applause* (1929), *City*

Streets (1931), and, what has become the defining film classic version of the material, *Dr. Jekyll and Mr. Hyde* (1931). Mamoulian had had some practice with Latin-themed films, like 1936's *The Gay Desperado*. He had also done historical costume dramas, like 1937's *High, Wide and Handsome*, about the founding of the first US oil well.

Luckily for Zanuck, Mamoulian was somewhat unhappy with his lot in 1939. He'd traded *Mr. Smith Goes to Washington*, a film he'd been slated to direct, to Frank Capra, who was ready to film *Golden Boy* (1939), which Mamoulian ended up doing instead. He regretted the switch, given Capra's huge success with *Mr. Smith* and his own relatively insignificant outing with *Golden Boy*.[11] It was at that moment that Zanuck offered Mamoulian the chance to direct *Zorro*. He jumped at the opportunity.

For Mamoulian, it was an occasion to showcase California's beauty, as well as a way to explore themes he particularly liked. "I had fallen in love with California as a boy," Mamoulian later said, "through the stories of Brett Harte [on the gold rush days], and *The Mark of Zorro* was set there, at a time when it was Spanish, when it had a great picturesque quality and languor, and wonderful haciendas and oak-trees and manor-houses."[12] To Mamoulian, the Spanish fantasy he'd imbibed as a youth was the vision he set about to create for *Zorro*'s remake. He also wanted to do it because of *Zorro*'s theme of fighting oppression. In many of the establishing scenes, for instance, Mamoulian used close-ups of the frightened peons facing their corrupt leaders. He wanted "to show it the way these villains look to the poor peons," he said. "So I showed a large close-up of a peon trembling and then cut to a large close-up of the monsters. After a few of these, I went to long shots."[13]

Zanuck chose a director with cinematic vision, but also one, at least in his view, who could be a real pain in the ass. In one early meeting, Zanuck absolutely refused to grant Mamoulian final say over the last cut of the movie. Mamoulian called the bluff and began to walk out of the office. Zanuck relented—at least a little. When it came time for final edits, he simply left the studio entirely, so that no one could accuse him of giving Mamoulian undue autonomy on the picture. He didn't want to set a precedent, after all. If he had to give a little, risk a little, to produce the box office hit he wanted, Zanuck didn't want his compromises to undercut his future control in relations with other directors.[14]

Meanwhile, Zanuck worked and reworked the script. He wasn't much of a writer, but he had a keen eye when it came to editing. He hated the early versions written by William A. Drake and Dorothy Hechtlinger. At one point, Mamoulian also voiced his disgust with the current state of the screenplay and demanded more latitude with it during filming. Two new writers were brought in—Garrett Fort (known for his *Frankenstein* adaptation) and Bess Meredyth (who had worked on *Charlie Chan at the Opera*). John Taintor Foote wrote the final screenplay, with heavy influence from Zanuck himself.

All the writers had initial difficulty in adapting McCulley's original novel. Fairbanks, stunts aside, had done a fairly one-to-one film version of the story. Zanuck and Mamoulian didn't like it. They had no desire to do a Fairbanks copy, nor did they want to fail in making a valiant new swashbuckling adventure, which held out the promise of out-swishing and out-swashing Errol Flynn's *Adventures of Robin Hood.*

Zanuck met with his scriptwriters on June 20, 1939, shortly before shooting on the film began, in an effort to discuss how to make their Zorro pop. Zanuck cited Fox's recent release *Jesse James* (1939) as a model for their Zorro picture. "*Jesse James* is an example of a story where there was an impending suspense underlying the whole thing," Zanuck pointed out, "a man riding to his eventual doom—a situation which gave us a definite emotional feeling about the story." Zanuck admitted that Zorro was a different story than their western bandit film, a sentiment not shared by, for instance, Republic Pictures. Fox's studio boss wanted "an emotional undercurrent which will take the story out of the standard track." The conventional story in *The Curse of Capistrano* was that Zorro's father, as well as his love interest, Lolita Pulido, are both persecuted by corrupt Spanish authorities. That was too boring for Zanuck. In the meeting, *The Prisoner of Zenda* (1937) was mentioned as an example of how a "hokey story was saved by a superb treatment." They needed a new angle. There had to be "a personal element," according to Zanuck, "that gave the story the added element that helped make it a success."[15]

Ideas about what this "personal element" might be seemed to flummox Zanuck and his writers. The solution finally settled on was adding an additional female protagonist to tempt Don Diego away from his Zorro mission. Zanuck wrote in a memo after the meeting:

Here is the drastic revision I suggest, which will supply the personal emotional element which we now lack. Instead of there being just one girl, Lolita [contract player Linda Darnell], there will be two girls. The older girl (I'll call her Juanita) [freelance player Gale Sondergaard] will be the Governor's daughter [subsequently changed to wife] and Lolita, the niece or ward. . . . She [Juanita] wants to go back to Spain with its glamor, its court life. . . . When Diego [Tyrone Power] comes into it, she will fall for him and consequently be less anxious to get out of there.[16]

That change, rearranging the family relations, adding multiple love interests, and, in the final script, adding another villain, affected the basic Zorro narrative. Ever after, the 1940 script treatment became the foundational Zorro story. The McCulley and Fairbanks versions were basically wiped away. Under Zanuck's script, and Mamoulian's direction, Lolita Pulido became Lolita Quintero, the niece of the corrupt *alcalde* (mayor), Luis Quintero, who has recently unseated Don Diego's father in the position. Luis is married to the flirtatious Inez Quintero, who aches to go back to Spain until Don Diego arrives and catches her eye as a potential new boy toy. Part of the emotional undercurrent of the new treatment, then, is that Don Diego / Zorro falls in love with the niece of his enemy. It creates a tension whereby Don Diego has to decide—only briefly, as it turns out—between duty to his family and loyalty to his heart. Moreover, the Zanuck/Mamoulian version adds a new villain, the army comandante Esteban Pasquale, who was Captain Ramón in the McCulley/Fairbanks original. The reconfigured story created a whole new dynamic of love interests for Diego/Zorro to choose between, and also multiple villains for him to contend with. It doubled down on the romance and the action, in other words. And it would be to this basic plot, not McCulley's novel, that subsequent writers would turn in creating their own new Zorro tales. The traces of Murrieta, or a Latinx imprint, became increasingly remote with each reinvention.

When the story came together, the cast soon fell into place. Zanuck first chose Richard Greene to play the lead. (Greene would come to fame later for his portrayal of Robin Hood on British TV in the 1950s.) But the role of Diego/Zorro eventually went to the young heartthrob, and vaguely "Latin" looking, Tyrone Power. Power had never swashbuckled in a film before, despite his stardom in such 20th Century-Fox films as *Lloyds of London* (1936), *In Old Chicago* (1938), *Suez* (1938), and the film Zanuck mentioned to his scripters, *Jesse James* (1939). Power, however, had done some costume dramas and westerns, which spoke well of his Zorro potential. And Power sort of looked like a more compact version of Errol Flynn, especially after growing his mustachio for the role. Power also cast a dashing silhouette in the skin-tight pants he had to wear as Don Diego, giving Flynn a run for his money in the midcentury Best Man's Bottom category.

For the female lead, Linda Darnell—not yet eighteen—was cast as Lolita Quintero. Her performance sits comfortably in the dainty ingénue mode rather than the fiery I'll-kill-myself-rather-than-marry-you Lolita Pulido vein. *The Mark of Zorro* was Power and Darnell's third feature together, and the pair would go on to star in one more film opposite each other, Mamoulian's *Blood and Sand* (1941), a remake of the Rudolph Valentino picture.[17]

With the leads set, Zanuck had no qualms about investing *The Mark of Zorro* with some of Errol Flynn's *Robin Hood* supporting cast strength. For the role of Fray Felipe, the kindly yet irascible Franciscan monk, Zanuck picked the gravel-voiced and rotund Eugene Pallette, who had played Friar Tuck in Flynn's *Robin Hood*. Pallette basically did the same part in *Zorro* that he'd done in that film—he's big, boisterous, and a bit of glutton, yet with a heart of gold. He's always asking for God's merciful forgiveness after just having clunked a villain on the head or after having, once again, called down damnation on the politically corrupt. In one scene, as Fray Felipe, Pallette absolutely eviscerates an apple—chomping loudly in bite after bite—as a sort of alternative channel to release his rage against Alcalde Quintero. "May God forgive me," he intones before laying into the fruit with abandon. Pallette's endearing Friar Tuck persona worked once again in *Zorro*.

For the role of the villain comandante of Reina de Los Ángeles, Esteban Pasquale, Zanuck also purloined a *Robin Hood* cast member—British actor Basil Rathbone, who played the scheming Sir Guy of Gisbourne in that film. Rathbone had fallen into a series of archvillain roles, but he had also played the master detective Sherlock Holmes. He had ten years of fencing experience, and it was put to good use in *The Mark of Zorro*. Master fencer Fred Cavens, who had worked with Fairbanks on *The Black Pirate*, was brought in to train Tyrone Power, who had never before so much as picked up a sword, let alone learned the art of strip fencing. Cavens also coached Rathbone and

Pallette. "Eugene Pallette," one magazine reported, "who tips the scales at 250, lost 18 of those pounds during three weeks of fencing with Basil Rathbone."[18] With filming taking place during a heat wave, Power drank quarts of milk to maintain weight, but still dropped pounds because of the training. When Rathbone, the one experienced fencer among them, a man who had crossed swords with Errol Flynn, was asked about Power's abilities with a blade, he was unequivocal. "Power was the most agile man with a sword I've ever faced before a camera," said the British actor. "Tyrone could have fenced Errol Flynn into a cocked hat."[19]

Mamoulian hoped all that fencing training would pay off. He scratched his head, perhaps not a few times also wiping his rounded spectacles with a handkerchief, all while in pensive anticipation of just how he could top both the Fairbanksian Zorro and the superior swash-swish of Flynn's *Robin Hood*. "Those Errol Flynn films had duels through castles," Mamoulian later remembered, "up and down stairways. Where do you go from that?"[20] The solution, Mamoulian realized, was to stage the final duel between Don Diego and Esteban Pasquale in the confined space of the alcalde's office. Mamoulian was often a less-is-more sort of director. If he couldn't top Fairbanks's stunts and couldn't outmatch the sprawling duels in *Robin Hood*, he would distill the swordplay in *Zorro*, making it more potent in its brief but pungent form.

The constricted field of action heightens the scene's dramatic power. Notably, Power is not dressed as Zorro in the finale. He begins the duel in his popinjay persona. But when the swordplay heats up, so, too, does Don Diego. After a scratch from Pasquale's sword, he fully comes to life with all of Zorro's energy. "I needed that scratch to awaken me," Diego says while pushing Pasquale away. The scene is fast paced but deliberate—it looks and feels like a real fencing match. Each clang of the sword reverberates as most of the finale happens with no background score. It's virtually silent, except for the sword whips, the clatters, the smash of breaking glass at a missed thrust, and the grunt of Diego's near tragic trip over a misplaced pillow on the floor—all punctuated with occasional taunting dialogue from our two duelists.

"That's a good effort, my capitán," Diego says as their swords lock blades, giving both a moment's rest.

"The next will be better, my fencing clown!" Pasquale retorts, releasing their grappled swords and beginning a counterattack.

Mamoulian manages, in the finale, to unmask Zorro through the sword fight without the aid of the Zorro costume. As the duel progresses, Diego's inner Zorro manifests in his skilled swordplay and bravado. Any of the fop left in his Diego mask is torn away through combat. The alcalde, Luis Quintero (J. Edward Bromberg), cowers in the corner, periodically asking if Diego has grown tired. By the end, Diego, energized as Zorro and exasperated by Quintero's needling, quips that the alcalde will be next.

"Ah," Diego chuckles, "the capitán's blade is not so firm." Somehow the double entendre escaped the meddling film censors.

"Still firm enough to run you through," Pasquale replies, clearly having lost his composure.

Backed against a wall and fighting like mad, Pasquale swishes his sword back and forth, flailing to find Diego's blade, which is clearly too quick and skilled for the comandante. With a final lunge, Diego runs his sword straight through Pasquale's heart. A pool of blood appears on the comandante's white satin shirt. His eyes go wide. He slumps to the floor, dead. But his slide to death reveals something else besides Diego's superior skill: Pasquale's fall to the floor knocks loose a wall covering, behind which a large *Z* had been carved by Zorro previously in the film. Quintero looks at the defeated Pasquale—looks at the wall where the carved *Z* is revealed—then looks back at Diego. Diego is unmasked as Zorro in a truly novel manner. Mamoulian didn't even need a black costume to do it.

The film, then, has a proper climax, with the final duel, and an extended denouement, when Diego is still faced with the task of taking control of Los Angeles. He rouses the peasants and caballeros to his side and forces Luis Quintero—always truly a weak-kneed bully who hid behind Pasquale's now vanquished sword—to abdicate and return to Spain. The sniveling Quintero leaves in short order, as Inez Quintero skulks off in tow. With a clever nod to the Fairbanks version, Diego looks at his sword and tosses it upward; it sticks firmly in the ceiling. The line from the Fairbanks original, *Till I need you again*, is implied but not said. Diego embraces Lolita, and the peasants rejoice as Don Alejandro, the benevolent aristocrat, has now replaced Luis Quintero, the corrupt aristocrat. Zorro's brand of revolution was always pretty conservative as revolutions go. This is no social uprising or race war—it's the return of the king, a reversion to order.

There was nothing particularly radical in Mamoulian's film. According to one *New York Times* reviewer,

> Director Rouben Mamoulian has kept the picture in the spirit of romantic make believe, with a lot of elegant trifling, some highly fantastic fights and flights, and one jim-dandy duel between Mr. Power and the villainous Basil Rathbone, which ends about as juicily as any one could wish. Once or twice, it is true, there creeps in a note of seriousness, as though Mr. Mamoulian or some one were sincerely concerned about poor oppressed peons. But mostly it bounds along at a lively, exciting clip, the way all extravagant fictions should.[21]

The extravagant fiction of the film was by design, as was the desire on Zanuck's part not to offend Mexican and Latin American film audiences with his treatment of Zorro. And it wasn't just Zanuck. All Hollywood top-tier studios had become more sensitive to Latinx portrayals in their films. Censorship in Hollywood had been formalized in 1922, with the establishment of the Motion Picture Producers and Distributors of America (MPPDA). William Hays, the former postmaster general in President Warren Harding's administration, was selected to run the new organization, which became known as the Hays Office.[22]

But it wasn't until the 1930s that censorship added more bite to its bark. Part of the MPPDA's mandate was to unify and establish morality guidelines that would be applied to movies *before* their release. The familiar G, PG, PG-13 ratings, and so on, wouldn't be established until the 1970s. In the 1930s, then, if a film didn't pass muster it wouldn't receive approval for audience viewing. The Production Code Administration (PCA), created by the MPPDA and run by individuals such as Joseph Breen, read scripts and offered potential edits so that the movie could receive the code's seal of approval. Without that seal, a film would be practically barred from a wide release, as all MPPDA members agreed not to produce or distribute such a movie. Sex, violence, anti-Americanism, and religious irreverence all came under the PCA's editorial purview.

But a new development materialized in the late 1930s. As the threat of war increased in Europe, studio moguls like Zanuck realized a new war could hurt box office returns. Approximately 35 percent of the movie industry's gross revenues came from foreign markets—and 60 percent of that was made in Europe. The film market south of the border seemed entirely promising, especially as the Mexican film industry had increased its vigor. Mexico churned out numerous homegrown productions and had built its own star system, creating, in the process, what is today known as the Golden Age of Mexican cinema. Making sure Hollywood films like Zorro didn't offend Mexican moviegoers, or generally put off film audiences throughout Latin America, just made good dollars and cents.[23]

The threads of censorship—the one moral, the other nationalistic—woven together with a pragmatic market approach, came together by 1939. President Franklin Roosevelt wished to win the hearts and minds of Latin Americans and so, too, did the movie studios. Roosevelt created the Office of the Coordinator of Inter-American Affairs with the intent to "harmonize all official relations with Latin America in order to shore up economic ties and thwart Nazi influence" in the region. The Inter-American Affairs Office created a Motion Pictures Division, which endeavored to promote films that won those hearts and minds, but also hoped to convince US citizens of the "benefits of Pan-Americanism." The result was essentially an added layer of censorship at the PCA. New films had not only to be free of rampant sex, violence, and other forms of so-called "deviance" but also to be read for particularly unhelpful stereotypes of Latinx characters. A specialist on Latin America, Addison Durland, fluent in both Spanish and Portuguese, was hired to fill this role at the PCA.[24]

Under Durland's editorial eye, all hints of derogatory portrayals of Mexican characters—poor, uneducated, uncivilized, etc.—in Hollywood scripts were flagged as needing revision or removal. In one unproduced script, a proposed remake of Don Q, Son of Zorro, which never made it to the silver screen, Durland noted:

> Page 1, Scene 1: "a few peons sleep along the wall under serape and sombrero . . ." We earnestly recommend the elimination of these

characterizations, since they would prove offensive to Mexicans. The same applies in Scene 3 of the same page, as to the "two tequila-soaked musicians, sweepings of a taproom."[25]

Ironically, the push to minimize negative stereotyping of Mexicans in films resulted in movie portrayals that erased Mexican-ness entirely. "We also wish to recommend," Durland noted, "in order to avoid any other possibility of offending Mexican audiences, that all characters in this story be clearly presented as *Spaniards* and in no way identifiable with *Mexicans*."[26] The strategy to avoid stereotyping Mexicans, in other words, was to erase all Mexican identity entirely and present the characters as Spanish. And that's exactly what happened in the 1940 remake of *The Mark of Zorro*.

Zanuck hired Ernesto Romero, a cultural attaché to the Mexican Consulate in Los Angeles, to act as a technical advisor on the new Zorro film. As an employee of the Mexican government, Romero had been working as a stereotype watchdog on Hollywood films since the late 1920s. The new mandate from the PCA only increased demand for his services. He advised producers and directors of films with Mexican themes and worked with the studios to eliminate, or minimize, gross characterization of Mexico and its people. Lupita Tovar, a famous Mexican actress who worked for a time in Hollywood, described Romero as "a very nice man, very polite—and very short." (Tovar, it seems, was a particular fancy of Romero's, which sentiment was not reciprocated by the actress.)[27]

For *The Mark of Zorro*, Romero was daily on set. He made sure, for instance, that the cast correctly pronounced the twenty-five words in Spanish used in the film. "South Americans are sensitive about mispronunciations," wrote one film magazine, "and a wrong-placed accent may cost the studio the market for which it hungers!" Set designers and costumers, seconded by Zanuck, assisted by Romero, and incentivized by the lure of Latin American revenues, made sure *The Mark of Zorro* erased any hint of Mexican California from the film. "Set in Spanish-ruled Los Angeles of 1820," reported *Modern Screen* magazine, "the picture is admittedly a celluloid lure for South American shekels."[28]

Tyrone Power's wardrobe cost $15,000, all in silks, brocades, satin shirts, and tight velvet trousers. For his look as Don Diego, hairdressers primped his curly locks, taking advice from Romero, who said that aristocratic Spaniards of the day wore their hair that way. "Come hell or high water," Power stated on set, "I'll be damned if I'll permit Alice Faye's personal hairdresser to fingerwave *my* hair every morning and sit me under a dryer, loaded with hairpins! Who do they think I am?" Despite protest, Power did just that—his hair bobs and waggles with aristocratic flamboyance in the film.

"Hollywood's European markets have bitten the dust," stated *Modern Screen*, "and the studio's frank winks at the dollars below the Rio Grande are prompting it to behave like a lovesick boy before the lady of his heart." Zanuck mandated that the film be made "as flattering as possible to Spanish eyes and ears and that authenticity is to prevail only whenever it is pleasant."[29] A fully and completely Spanish Zorro—one more Spanish than Spain—was much easier for the film to pull off than a Mexican Zorro.

In keeping with the Spanish fantasy heritage of Los Angeles, *Modern Screen* magazine had no ability to conceive of an authentic, and inoffensive, Mexican heritage for the region. According to *Modern Screen*, it was a "hot, dry, dusty town, inhabited mostly by Indians and half-breeds whose health required a street brawl before and after each meal. When Fox introduces Los Angeles, however, it will be a replica, not of the original, but some modern-day architect's dream. It will be shinning, white and beautiful and boast a select population of dashing caballeros and flirtatious señoritas."[30] The only way to avoid offense, in other words, was to create an extravagant fiction—California's past was a Spanish fantasy, with a gallant, handsome Spanish Zorro.

And it worked. As the film exhaled the romance and adventure of exotic Spain, reviewers and audiences inhaled deeply. One reviewer wrote, "Director Rouben Mamoulian has captured all the danger, beauty, romance and thrills of Old California's most exciting days in 'The Mark of Zorro.'"[31] Another enthused: "It's all very thrilling, really!—and amusing!"[32] It was escapist fun, "nothing in it to strain a brain," noted another critic.[33] "Well, it just doesn't seem possible," remembered one reporter, "20 years have passed since every kid in our neighborhood had a lath sword and a stick horse and played Zorro from dawn to dusk."[34]

For the older generation, the film breathed nostalgia; for the younger, it presented a new heartthrob. "Tyrone Power now steps into the boots, tight pants and bolero of Don Diego Vega," wrote the *New York Daily News*, "and, while he might be a bit of a disappointment to oldsters who remember the elder Fairbanks's Zorro as something out of another world, Tyrone is a devastating and heroic figure to the youngsters of today." "Squeals of delight," were heard from young girls and boys, according to the *Daily News*.[35] Zorro traditionalists, like Bosley Crowther at the *New York Times*, moaned that "a Zorro without at least one leap from a balcony to the back of a running horse, is gravely suspected by us."[36]

But moviegoers were not, in the main, like Bosley Crowther. Many were more like the reviewer for the *Hollywood Reporter*, who noted she had not seen the Fairbanks original, but said it didn't really matter, since Power looked particularly dashing in his tight pants.[37] The famous pants, in fact, were mentioned time and again. "Bits about it," the reviewer from the Nebraska *State Journal* wrote. "Tyrone Power is proof that a skinny man in 1850 wasn't as lucky about hiding his physical deficiencies as now. Those skin-tight pants were revealing."[38]

On balance, reviews recognized that Power was no Fairbanks, but that Power played the role with more romance than did Fairbanks. Moreover, "In contrast to so much of Hollywood's recent war-inspired product," wrote a reviewer from Ogden, Utah, "it doesn't stress deep social and economic problems."[39] Zanuck and Mamoulian pulled off the Zorro remake. But, to do it, they turned up the volume on romance, they made Power's pants skin-tight, and they didn't "strain a brain" in entertaining their audiences. In short, it was a hit.

Mexican audiences loved it as well. Presenting Zorro as thoroughly "Spanish" connected with Mexican moviegoers who were fresh off a twenty-year high of nationalistic fervor. The Mexican Revolution included a period of violent civil wars (1910–1917), and then two decades of cultural reconstruction (1920–1940). Art and artists played a large role in that reconstruction. Figures like Diego Rivera, David Alfaro Siqueiros, and José Clemente Orozco made their brand of public art in an effort to symbolize the indigenous, authentic roots of Mexico. These so-called muralists visualized Mexico's past in vivid tableaus that adorned public buildings, schools, and museums. Artist Frida Kahlo, married to Rivera, wore traditional Mexican clothing styles, fought for self-expression, and painted deeply personal self-portraits. She rejected labels; for instance, when French surrealists tried to claim her as their own, Kahlo refused to accept the description. She was doing Mexican art, *her* art, not aping European styles.

The Mexican film industry, likewise, produced nationalistic movies that idolized local community life, such as *Allá en el Rancho Grande* (*Out on the Big Ranch*, 1936). The Spanish past, in other words, represented Mexico's journey from oppression to freedom and self-definition. That *The Mark of Zorro* depicted the "bad guys" as the corrupt Spanish government of Old California was no stretch of the imagination for many Mexican audiences. Zorro, for many Mexicans, could therefore symbolize the seeds of revolt and resistance that finally flowered into independence from Spain in 1821, an event that took place just a few years after the setting of *The Mark of Zorro*. "Zorro," wrote one reviewer in *Siglo de Torreón*, "avenged the mistreatment inflicted on the miserable by the powerful. . . . He was loved by the humble and by Lolita" but "hated in equal measure by traitors and the powerful."[40] Zorro was readily assimilated into a language of Mexican nationalism.

Zorro's entrance to the Mexican world of pop culture took place after the 1940 film. Reviewers remembered Douglas Fairbanks's portrayal, but in 1920 film was far less ubiquitous as it was in 1940. There were only some five hundred movie theaters in Mexico in 1938. Approximately 76 percent of movies shown in Mexico had been made in Hollywood.[41] But Mexico's industry was strengthening. It went from producing 5 movies in 1930 to 125 in 1950. Among the early type of film that Mexican audiences loved were ranch comedies, *comedia ranchera*, which focused on the return of urban migrants back to their local roots—female purity was preserved and there was a happy ending. And there was always plenty of song and dance. (*Allá en el Rancho Grande* helped set the pattern for this type of film.)[42] Zorro easily integrated into the ranch comedy genre.

Directors José Benavides and Raúl Martínez Solares followed on the success of *The Mark of Zorro* and produced their own Mexican version, *El Zorro de Jalisco* (*The Zorro of Jalisco*, 1941). Pedro Armendáriz was cast as the lead, Leonardo, a big-city lawyer who returns to his small town in Jalisco after the death of his father. He finds his childhood home overtaken by unscrupulous bandits, led by Ernesto (Emilio "el Indio" Fernández). The plot mimics the basic Zorro story. In this instance, the ineffectual lawyer demands that everything be done according to the law, but he is eventually revealed as Jalisco's own Zorro. The masked avenger becomes a Mexican version of the hero—his defense is of a local community, fighting to restore local order, which has been devastated after several decades of social ferment. Armendáriz, the first Mexican actor to wear the mask, would, by the end of the 1940s, make his debut in Hollywood in several John Ford films, such as *The Fugitive* (1947).[43]

By 1950, Zorro became the object of parody in Mexico. Germán Valdés, better known as the Mexican comedian Tin-Tan, starred in *La marca del zorrillo* (*The Mark of the Skunk*). Hugely popular, it ran in Mexico City movie theaters for several weeks more than a majority of Mexican-made films released at the same time. Tin-Tan's brand of humor fit within the *carpa* style, a Mexican genre of comedy that reveled in vaudeville-esque patter, slapstick, and double entendre. It lampooned the overwrought period costume drama aesthetic. Tin-Tan, like his more internationally well-known Mexican comedian colleague Cantinflas, voiced the sardonic wit of the common man, often hapless but no less capable of survival in the ludicrous situations in which he found himself.

La marca del zorrillo was Zorro's entrance into the realm of irony, where what was said conflicted with what was shown. One beautiful court lady is presented as "the Countess of Tijuana," for instance, a town not known for its aristocratic origins. The joke in the film is the ostentatiousness of the high class. Tin-Tan puts on the dress of the rich, the powerful, and the nobility in order to critique it. Many of these sorts of parodies of Western classics, including famous works by Dante, Shakespeare, and Dumas, appeared in Mexico at the time. Lampooning Zorro was a way to work out what it meant to be Mexican in an era when cosmopolitan culture came in movies exported from Hollywood.[44]

But that was basically it for Zorro from 1940 to '50 in Mexico. Only two Mexican films were made—one, a more serious Mexican version of the story; the other, a parody of the whole idea of aristocratic pretention in the Zorro tale. More Zorro films appeared in the 1950s to the '70s, but these were often Zorro knockoffs or riffs on the masked avenger characters then popular in Europe. Zorro was never really a pop culture icon in Mexico.

More important, in terms of Mexican pop culture, were the masked characters of *lucha libre*—free wrestling—which took hold of the Mexican cultural imagination in the 1940s. Starting as a live sport, and continuing as such today, lucha libre also became a genre of film beginning in the 1950s. *Luchadores* fit into two main categories—*técnicos* are the good guys, who always follow the rules, while *rudos* are the bad guys, who don't. Only by selectively breaking the rules are the técnicos able to overcome the tactics of rudos, who flaunt their roguish behavior. The most famous of these luchadores was El Santo (Rodolfo Guzmán Huerta), who starred in fifty-two films from 1958 to 1982. The films often pit a masked El Santo against various "threats" to the nation, such as monsters, mad scientists, and the like.[45]

The Latinx origins of Zorro weren't born in Mexico City—they were born in the borderlands of California in the gold rush. That was a long way off from Mexico City's film culture—a long way also from the concerns of Mexican nationalism after the revolution of the early twentieth century. The Mexican legend on which Zorro was based was formed in the troubled history of California colonization, annexation, and racial violence. That region—California—was cut off from the dominant story of Mexican history when the borderlands territory became a US state. Zorro's ghost haunts the American past, but not really the Mexican past.

In the 1940s, the only pop culture figure to use a Zorro-like character to critique California's history of American annexation was not Mexican—he was Spanish. Spanish author José Mallorquí Figuerola created the hero El Coyote in a series of novels (eventually a series of films from the 1950s to the 1990s) that present the hero as a Californio who takes up mask and costume in order to avenge wrongs done by the Americans in California. It is, perhaps, a just irony. Both Mexicans and Americans had so long pointed the finger at Spanish corruption in California. But it was ultimately a Spanish author who sought to correct the record.[46]

And yet, the mainstream of US pop culture paid no attention to what was happening with Zorro in Mexico or in Spain. In 1950, Hollywood films continued to focus on the "bad apple" version of California history. One of the last films I researched at the Fairbanks Center was a 1950 film called *Bandit Queen*, starring Barbara Britton. Britton plays Lola Montalvo, the daughter of a Californio landed family. The film, surprisingly, mentions the Foreign

Miners' Tax, which accounted for a lot of the racial violence in the period. The Montalvos are killed by the county sheriff in cahoots with a land baron who wants to steal gold-rich lands from the "Spanish" population after US annexation of California. Lola swears revenge, takes the sobriquet of Zara (her mother's name), learns to use the bullwhip, and dons a black charro costume and black mask. By day, she assumes the alias of Lola Belmont, and convinces the town she is merely a respectable young woman. She gets revenge on those who killed her family while leading a band of other aggrieved Mexican Americans. She leaves her calling card—ZARA—written on her victims. And guess who her love interest is? Joaquín Murrieta! The film basically mixes the Joaquín legend with Zorro, but with a female lead. The narrative descendant (Zorro) teams up with the narrative parent (Joaquín)—or, in this case, the narrative affinities are powerless to remain apart, drawn together by bonds of mutual amour.

The funny thing is that reviewers at the time didn't comment on it in the press. Advertising, of course, focused on the sex appeal of Britton with a bullwhip—"She sought revenge with a whip . . . a gun . . . a kiss!" reads one lobby card from the era. Another newspaper announcement pictures Britton with whip in hand while a ripped bodice exposes more of her body than is actually shown in the film. Britton herself made sure to mention (probably for copyright reasons, as Lippert Pictures, which produced the film, didn't own the rights to Zorro), "I play the part of Zara. Any resemblance to Zorro [is] purely coincidental [and I] wear a caballero's costume and mask and have to manifest all the characteristics of strong leadership. But that is only one phase, because at times in the picture I appear as a very genteel lady of early California."[47] Both characters, Zara and Joaquín, introduce themselves to one another using alter egos—Lola Belmont in Zara's case, and Carlos del Rio in Murrieta's. When they finally reveal their true identities in each other's arms, they decide to leave their lives of banditry and revenge behind.

For all the film's romance and adventure, it shows that when Zorro, or a character like Zorro, is placed within the context of racial violence and Anglo-American settler colonialism, Zorro becomes a story, like that of Murrieta, that critiques the US policies of westward expansion. And the inverse is also true—when Zorro appears outside of that context, the character is often a justification for American annexation. Zorro, in that formulation, represents a kind of precursor American sensibility—an avenger fighting the corrupt Spanish authority, which found its culmination in US rule over California. *Bandit Queen*, then, suggests that the era of the gold rush was a sticky time for American storytelling, as once US annexation took place, justice did not come to all of the new state's citizens.

As I left the Fairbanks Center, I headed toward Hollywood Boulevard. There were a few stars on the Walk of Fame I needed to visit—Bob Kane's, cocreator of Batman, for one. But there was also Walt Disney's. He created the most enduring Zorro through Disney's 1950s TV show. The Spanish fantasy Zorro, I knew. The Zorro masquerading as the Lone Ranger, I'd also come to know. The swashbuckling Zorro, thanks to Fairbanks and Power, was there too. But Disney made Zorro into a commodity.

16 | DISNEYLANDIA

ON THE EVENING OF SEPTEMBER 11, 1957, Walt Disney revealed his Zorro—Disney's Zorro—to a TV audience for the first time. As cameras rolled, a dozen or so mouse-eared, bright-eyed, and manifoldly white child stars of *The Mickey Mouse Club* clamored for space around Walt Disney while he sat cross-legged and bemused in a canvas director's chair. These eager Mouseketeers cajoled, nigh demanded, some tidbit, some crumb, some skosh of news about which programs would appear on the new season of Walt's own *Disneyland* television show, then in its fourth season, and that very episode being "The Fourth Anniversary Show." Walt Disney gave a simple shrug and decided, in what was clearly rehearsed nonchalance for the cameras, to appease his disciples.[1] *Was it not to them, these faithful Mouseketeers*—along with the thirty-five million viewers, we should add—*that Walt Disney had his good pleasure in revealing the secrets of the Magical Kingdom?*[2] It most certainly was.

Before speaking, as Disney shifted in his chair, he glanced around at his assembled Mouseketeers—the faces of American enchantment personified. There on Disney's left hand, the youngest of the bunch and not even a Mouseketeer per se, who preceded Madonna and Prince by being best known to history by a single personal noun, was Moochie.[3] He, like the others, quietly waited for Walt Disney to speak, as cameras rolled.

This excerpt from "The Fourth Anniversary Show" is included as a DVD extra on one of the discs containing the first season of the *Zorro* TV series.[4] The excerpt, at only 3 minutes and 15 seconds long, shows the first time Walt unveiled *Zorro* to his TV audience. The excerpt was aired just a few weeks before Zorro premiered.

Zorro would become an immediate hit on ABC for Walt Disney. Part of that instant success started with his eager Mouseketeers, who outlined to the kids at home the kind of delight they could, and should, have when the show finally came on the air. And, of course, there was Moochie.

In the segment, Disney proceeds to tell the Mouseketeers about *The Saga of Andy Burnett*, the story of Johnny Appleseed, and others. "Then," Disney goes on, "you'll meet some interesting cartoon characters . . . uh . . . Little Toot and Susie the Little Blue Coupe."

The kids laugh at that. All, that is, except Moochie.

"What about Zorro?" Moochie demands in a tone that hits somewhere between aw-shucks and heel-dug-in petulance.

Disney ignores the interruption, continues, "And you're going on a very unusual sea voyage called 'The Wake of the Cucuy.'"

"*Gee!*" one Mouseketeer cries in rapture.

"What. About. ZORRO!" Moochie says again, with extra petulance.

"Zorro?" Walt Disney questions, sounding like some distracted father who finally realizes his smallest child has been jumping and bobbing at his feet for some time now. "As a matter a fact . . . uh . . . I don't think I should talk about him. You see, confidentially, Zorro won't be on the *Disneyland* show."

"Ohhhh . . ." Sounds of pain come from Moochie, crestfallen.

"Well, Zorro's on an entirely separate series"—Walt tries to win his smallest disciple back to his devotion—"on the air at a different time."

Walt Disney takes that as his cue to leave, but all the Mouseketeers shout the Messiah of the Magical Kingdom down: "WAIT . . . tell us about ZORRO!"

"OK, hold it, just a moment." Walt sits back in his canvas director's chair. "A little about Zorro and you've got to let me get back to my own show."

"It's a deal!" says Moochie.

The camera starts a slow zoom on Disney. He's the storyteller now.

"Well," he begins, "a long time ago there was a masked rider who rode the countryside. This was in Old Spanish California, back in the time of high adventure and low Spanish guitars."

The camera cuts to the opening song and title sequence for the *Zorro* show. The Chordettes, a musical group famous for their hit song about Davy Crockett, sing a Latin-inflected ballad.

> *Out of the night when the full moon is bright*
> *Comes a horseman known as Zorro . . .*

We see a masked Zorro fencing, riding his horse, doing . . . what Zorro does. The sequence ends with Zorro backlit on horseback, Tornado rearing up on two legs—a lightning bolt splits the sky.

The camera cuts back to Walt, looking pretty satisfied.

"And that's the little bit I promised you about Zorro," says Disney.

"Boy oh boy," Moochie enthuses. "Was Zorro a real person?"

"I'm afraid not, Moochie. You see, Zorro's a mythical character . . . he's something of our imagination."

Suddenly, Guy Williams, the actor who would become the most famous Zorro ever in the history of Zorros, comes out on the soundstage, but in an area of the soundstage set to look like Old California.

"What's that?" Walt says.

"That's your imagination," Moochie drolls.

A dashing and mysterious Zorro addresses Walt Disney's disbelief in his existence. "As you say," Guy Williams begins, with only the slightest hint of an affected Spanish lilt, "perhaps I am only a part of the imagination. I remember that's what they said about me in California. Some would smile and say: Zorro—*poof*—he's a ghost, a dream, a myth, a something of the imagination."

Zorro shadow fences with a dastardly villain who sneaks up from behind. He quickly dispatches the opponent and returns to the camera.

"So, you see, my friends," continues Zorro, "it is entirely a matter of opinion. This is a personal thing between you and me. Whether I am real or not is for you to decide. Each of you in your own mind and heart. Meantime, till we meet again!"

Zorro swirls his cape and laughs heartily: *ha-ha-ha-ha-ha*. He takes his sword and cuts a *Z* in the air.

And then a magical thing happens. Moochie, with outstretched arm and a slightly crooked, though extended index finger, becomes what is, to my calculation, the first recorded kid giving an air *Z*—*zft zft zft*. All the Mouseketeers follow and the excerpt ends.

What Moochie didn't know, along with the millions of other kids watching on their televisions, was that Walt Disney had wanted to make a Zorro television show for the better part of the last decade. He just hadn't been able to do it. Until now.

Zorro, under Walt Disney's purview, would ride through the nostalgic aching of lost childhoods and become a nigh on totemic embodiment of everything that appears for an instant but gets lost forever, receding out of reach—like Zorro, rearing his black stallion, Tornado, up on hind legs, a wave from the masked rider, for a moment backlit in moonlight, and he's gone.

In other words, Zorro was huge. He was back again in a major way. But not any Zorro. Disney's Zorro. Walt Disney did for Zorro what Hershey did for chocolate, what Kleenex did for facial tissue, what Coca-Cola did for sugar water. Disney made Zorro a recognizable brand. Disney made Zorro a household name. Disney made Zorro consumable in that singularly twentieth-century American way: Zorro became purchasable. You could now buy Zorro, thanks to Disney.[5] It was the Spanish fantasy heritage on sale in so many board games, socks, wallets, lunch boxes, and thermoses—but also toy swords, whips, hats, capes, and of course, masks. The domino mask had a boon never before seen in its varied and rather long history.[6]

But, for all that significance, from the perspective of hindsight, Zorro wasn't the goal for Walt Disney. Zorro was simply what happened on Walt's journey toward a far loftier dream. Zorro, actually, was what happened on Walt's way toward Disneyland. Or, better said, basically Walt Disney dreamed of making Disneyland, and—like the Matterhorn and the Lilly Belle Train, like the replica Swiss village of Zermatt, and like, of course, those nausea-inducing spinning tea cups—Zorro was just one of the attractions.

Disneyland was the true distillation of Walt's particular form of American magic. For Walt, like the tikis of exotic Adventureland, like the castle of Fantasyland, like the Jules Verne–inflected futurist visions of Tomorrowland, and like Davy Crockett of Frontierland, Zorro was a citizen of a larger universe.[7] Zorro was just a part of Walt Disney's world-building. And once he had Disneyland and Zorro became part of it, Walt moved on from Zorro in order to build other corners of that universe.

What Moochie and millions of other little moppets across the country didn't know was that Zorro would be gone in just two television seasons (1957 to 1959)—sixty-eight half-hour shows, four one-hour specials, and a theatrical release of edited material from the first thirteen episodes.

It was gone too quickly for many of America's Moochies. But the cultural idea of Zorro was set. Like the dogged way the Batusi clung to Batman, so, too, Disney's television series stuck to Zorro. Although Zorro as a character continued to evolve, and devolve, over the next five decades, Disney's Zorro became the true essence of Zorro-ness. All other Zorros beware.

———————

By 1950, Walt Disney had built an empire on cartoons. Born in Chicago in 1901 but raised in Missouri, Walter Elias Disney loved to draw. He took art classes and got a job as a commercial illustrator. He moved to California in the early 1920s.[8]

It seems likely that Walt was first introduced to Zorro through Douglas Fairbanks's leaps, jumps, and skylarks. With his business-savvy brother, Roy, he created Disney Brothers Cartoon Studio in 1923. Then: the Mouse. With a talented artist, cartoon-animator Ub Iwerks, Walt created Mickey Mouse in 1928.

Always a visual innovator, Disney wanted color and sound to accompany his moving cartoons. Full-color three-strip Technicolor, with feature-length animations, followed. There was *Snow White and the Seven Dwarfs* (1937); *Pinocchio* and *Fantasia* (both 1940); *Dumbo* (1941)—and then the classic kill-the-mother-in-the-first-five-minutes *Bambi* (1942). All these features developed new techniques for animated films, including special camera work, new processes for transferring illustrated concepts into moving images, and basically creating a narrative formula for heroic journeys had by simple characters, often animals, with whom kids could identify.[9]

In the 1940s the US government turned to Walt and his studios for propaganda, much as the government looked to Hollywood for public relations assistance in Latin America. And who better to sell war bonds in a time of global conflagration than Donald Duck? As President Roosevelt rolled out his policy of the friendly relations with Latin America for fear of Japanese and

Nazi influence south of the border, Disney assisted the effort through cartoons amenable to hemispheric solidarity.

One historian writes: "No sooner had the United States military seized the Southwest from [Mexican] inhabitants in the mid-nineteenth century than our popular culture added insult to injury by transferring Latinos in general, Mexicans in particular, into a brutal, mindless people."[10] About six Latinx types developed: the bandit, the harlot, the male buffoon, the female clown, the Latin lover, and dark lady. Female characters had passionate natures—they were fiery sexpots, often with loose morals. Male Latinos, in contrast, were violent, ill-tempered fools. One early silent film, *Broncho Billy and the Greaser* (1914), is but one example. The Anglo character, the hero, slaps down the "swarthy" Mexican villain.

Walt Disney's approach was always a bit different. The second cartoon Mickey Mouse appeared in, for instance, *The Gallopin' Gaucho* (1928), cast Mickey as a Latin American who has to save Minnie Mouse from Pegleg Pete. It's here that we can also see the influence of Douglas Fairbanks. The film star had just released *The Gaucho* in 1927, and Disney's version with Mickey was a cartoon parody. By the 1940s, then, Nelson Rockefeller at the Office of Inter-American Affairs thought Disney's lighter touch with Latinx characters would be helpful to the overall American policy of good neighborliness.[11]

Disney's Latin American cartoons of the 1940s were all, well, caricatured depictions of Latin American people. In hindsight, that seems problematic. Yet, as in *The Three Caballeros* (1944), Latin America is treated with respect, albeit also with a fair dose of exoticism. It was the first feature-length film to combine live-action actors with animation—for instance, singer and actress Aurora Miranda appears. (Aurora was one of Carmen Miranda's younger sisters). The film plots a swath through Latin America from the very south, to Uruguay, to Brazil, and finally to Mexico. Donald Duck plays an ugly American tourist, while more sympathetic cartoons take on the role of guide through their countries. It gave a US audience, at the very least, a sense of geography as the viewer follows the journey up Latin America by returning to an illustrated map of the region. As a shout-out to hemispheric brotherliness, it does the trick. It ends with fireworks and THE END written in Spanish, Portuguese, and English. At the time, it was considered a paean to multiculturalism.

By 1950, then, Walt Disney had built an empire of cartoons, he had some credibility in dealing sympathetically with Latinx themes, and he solidified his genius that year with the popular film *Cinderella*. Walt had classic fairytales down cold. He'd reached an audience beyond US borders, and his idea of creating characters with non-American identities had now been done.

The time for Zorro had arrived—but first, Disneyland.

A cartoon empire was expensive and time-consuming, as Walt and brother Roy had discovered. Live-action features were attractive to make content faster, and at a reduced price. Disney experimented with live-action in the late 1940s, kicking off the series *True-Life Adventures* (1948–1960), which followed the doings of real animals. In terms of feature films, *Treasure Island* (1950) and *The Story of Robin Hood and His Merrie Men* (1952) were the first to appear. Critical acclaim followed. *Variety* called *Treasure Island* "sumptuous," and the *New Yorker* called it "absolutely first-class."[12] Disney's adaptation of the Robert Louis Stevenson classic became the sixth-highest grossing film in the UK box office in 1950.

All of that—the cartoon stories, the fairytales, the adventure classics in live action—were amounting to something in the mind of Walt Disney. Always a tinkerer, a guy who made little miniature models of potbellied stoves painted in red, gold, and green, a guy who built a miniature steam engine train in his backyard in the Holmby Hills of Los Angeles, Walt Disney imagined a place where people could come to experience his brand of magic in person. The idea came first as a kind of carnival train, which would take the magic to San Francisco, then to the Midwest, and on to the rest of the country. But that was really expensive, as it turned out, and Roy Disney hated the idea.[13] Walt persisted.

The original Imagineer did research. One Disney associate remembered a visit he had with Walt to Coney Island.

> He rang me up one day and said, "Come to Coney Island with me." I could feel my face falling. It wasn't my ideal place, but, anyhow, I said, "Yes, yes, thank you!" We had a hell of a good day, actually. That was the beginning of Disneyland. He was going to see what things were that people liked doing. We did everything—the switchbacks [roller coasters], the horse, everything. We ate the fluffy stuff [cotton candy]. We had a lovely day, thoroughly enjoyed ourselves.[14]

Walt had a knack for figuring out what was fun about an experience, and then replicating that experience, but branding it with the Disney stamp.

As the idea of what a Disney-specific theme park might look like percolated in his mind, Walt worked on how to finance it: television. "He would use television," writes one Disney biographer, "as a lever to bring his park into existence, by making a network's investment in it a condition of his providing a program. Then he would use his TV show to promote the park itself."[15] Walt would allow a TV network the opportunity to show Disney content. In exchange, he'd charge the network through the nose for it. The profits would build Disney his theme park.

Before approaching a network, he had to secure the rights to a story worthy of the Disney name. A story of adventure, a story that people knew but that hadn't yet had the Disney magic applied to it. It had to be something that tapped into history, even the history of California itself, where Disney envisioned founding his Magic Kingdom. Walt chose to pursue the rights to Zorro.

It was perfect timing for Johnston McCulley. His contract with Republic Pictures expired in 1950. He'd been writing his short stories in *West* magazine, but Zorro had more or less returned to a print medium. Mitchell Gertz, McCulley's literary manager, made the deal with Disney. *The Mark of Zorro* remake rights still belonged to 20th Century-Fox. But the new short stories by McCulley, as well as rights to the Zorro character, were obtained by Disney through his own WED Enterprises and later transferred to the Walt Disney Company. McCulley wrote of his delight with the arrangement.

> My deal with the Disney Studios is complete in every detail, and I am thoroughly satisfied with the deal. Re: Zorro, they have all the rights in and to the character with the exception of publication rights. In the case of new ZORRO stories, the television rights would go to them after publication, automatically; and all other rights such as merchandising, etc., are handled by DISNEY STUDIOS. . . . It is not in my category to meddle with any of the merchandising. . . . Don't worry about my take; I'll get a percentage down the line.[16]

McCulley continued to write Zorro stories for *West*. He churned out other tales for the pulps. The deal with Disney allowed him greater financial security to some extent. His wife, Louris Munsey, died in 1956. He was also in increasingly fragile health, and died in 1958.

After McCulley's death, his stepdaughter, Beatrix Maurine McCulley, sued both Disney and McCulley's agent, Mitchell Gertz, claiming they had cheated the writer out of royalties.[17] The case was settled between the parties and all rights went to Disney Studios. Later, after Walt's death in 1966, the rights reverted to the heirs of Mitchell Gertz, as Gertz also had passed away. But all that lay in the future. For the time being, Walt Disney had access to make his Zorro television series.

Zorro was now not only in Walt's imagination but also in his back pocket. Walt housed both the Zorro and the Disneyland projects in the same building on the studio lot in Burbank. Richard Irvine, Bill Martin, and Marvin Davis worked on Disneyland. Bill Cottrell, Walt's brother-in-law and a longtime Disney employee, took charge of Zorro preproduction.

The Zorro Building, as it was called—the office built to house the Disneyland team and the Zorro writers—was, according to one employee, made of just "ramshackle walls and thin, very temporary, hot in the summer and cold in the winter." Walt bought period furniture, "heavy dark wood furniture," that he pictured as being part of the Zorro set. Bill Cottrell, the Zorro producer, worked up fourteen initial scripts, hired writers, and thought about casting.

Walt visited often. "He would drop into my office every day and see what I was doing," said Bill Martin.[18] Zorro, according to Martin, was important to Walt. One member of Disney's staff remembered Walt walking around the office challenging employees to a duel with a yardstick—swishing the make-believe sword around, making air Zs as he walked the halls. By 1953, Walt Disney needed TV—specifically Zorro, he thought—to make Disneyland a reality.

The Zorro rights had been obtained. The Zorro Building, with writers and producers working on development, had been constructed. Walt had one last obstacle to contend with: his brother Roy. Walt had just renegotiated his contract with Walt Disney Productions and he held the rights to Zorro personally. He therefore had to pitch Zorro to Roy and the board, along with his bigger plan for Disneyland. "You back my leisure park," Walt described his strategy in approaching the TV networks, "and I'll give you a TV series you can announce as a 'Walt Disney Presents,' with all the prestige and public interest that name will stimulate for you."[19] Roy and the board agreed, although Walt suspected his brother simply wanted a new source of cash for the studio.

Walt made sure his brother, who would be the guy actually approaching the networks, would not forget Disneyland in the deal.

The National Broadcasting Company, which had the largest number of TV affiliates, turned down the Disney offer. The Columbia Broadcasting System, in contrast, replied with a qualified "maybe." One of their sponsors, Johnson & Johnson, wanted to see what they'd be getting for their investment—they wanted to see a pilot for the *Zorro* TV series. "Walt doesn't do pilots," Roy said. "Never has. Says he never will. You know our track record. You'll have to judge us on that and the draft scripts."[20] Johnson & Johnson washed its hands and Roy Disney had to come home with no deal.

The third-place American Broadcasting Company, however, was desperate enough to bite. According to Walt, ABC was the "Little Orphan Annie of the TV airwaves," but ABC was willing to give Disney funding for what he most wanted—Disneyland. But there was a catch: ABC didn't want to risk doing the *Zorro* series—a television show about Old Spanish California was viewed by many as a surefire way to failure. They wanted an anthology show, one where Walt's personality would be on display. "Give us Mickey Mouse, Walt," said one ABC executive, "plus the Disney name, and I guarantee that within two years we'll be one of the big three."[21]

ABC offered $500,000 up front with a guarantee of $4.5 million. Walt agreed. Zorro was shelved for the time being. He planned to do the show once the anthology show, called *Disneyland*, was a proven success. *The Mickey Mouse Club* also went into production. The Disneyland park opened on July 17, 1955, when fifteen thousand people stood in a mile-long line to get in.[22] There was more waiting to get onto the rides, many of which didn't work. Hungry patrons were left without food options after a dishwasher broke. There was a gas leak. In short, Disneyland on opening day was much as we've come to know it at present. But Walt got his theme park. Zorro had to wait for a belated entrance.

17 | GUY WILLIAMS BECOMES ZORRO

THE MAN WHO WOULD BECOME ZORRO in the Disney TV megahit was born Armand Catalano in the Bronx, New York, in 1924. A first-generation Italian American, Catalano's parents were both from Sicily. With hazel eyes, a six-foot-three athletic frame, and a smile that turned heads, by the age of twenty he began to model for print advertisements.

It was Catalano's agent, Pat Allen, who suggested a name change. Allen spent call after call pushing her client Armand Catalano. The feedback for Allen was often *Call me back when you have some all-American types to send over.* One time, Allen decided to try something different.

"I have an 'All-American' type for you," Allen told the talent scout, all while looking at Catalano, who was in the office at the time. "Yeah, his name is Guy Williams."[1]

"Guy Williams" got the job that Armand Catalano couldn't. For those in Hollywood who could pass as white—for many Jews, some Latinxs, Poles, Italians, and a host of others—taking a stage name was part of the deal. If an actor could look like a Williams or a Smith or a Johnson, then an actor took that name. And if an actor or actress couldn't quite look Smith-like, well, at least a French-sounding name could suffice. Americans loved French surnames: Bardot, Gabin, Lefebvre, Aubert—these were acceptable foreign surnames; they added an appropriate exotic flair, but within the boundaries of whiteness. Armand Catalano became Guy Williams, and Guy Williams started to get jobs.

In the 1940s, in an era before the rise of television, modeling often meant doing print advertisements. Photos would be taken of the model or models for the given ad, and the prints were then turned into life-like paintings before being published in magazines. In that mode, Guy Williams appeared in *Look*, *Mademoiselle*, the *Saturday Evening Post*, *Collier's*, and *Life*. On one shoot, for Mum Deodorant, Guy met his future wife, Janice Cooper, then a swimsuit and print-ad model. "Sweaters a problem?" queries the ad. "Not for me"—the painting-from-photo has Guy helping Janice take off her ski jacket, while Janice looks confident that no unsightly pit stains will tarnish her cold-weather attire because of her wise choice in Mum Deodorant.[2] Such were the details of Guy Williams's meet-cute with his future wife.

———————

By the time Guy Williams, along with a hundred other ambitious, hungry actors, got the casting call for Disney's *Zorro* in early 1957, he'd been in a series of "eminently forgettable" roles. Those were his words, and he always used them to refer to his life before *Zorro*.[3]

He had a point. Williams had a bit part in an Arabian adventure film starring Rock Hudson and Piper Laurie, *The Golden Blade* (1953), which cast and crew affectionately called a "tits and sand" flick, owing to the endless imported sand that filled the soundstage and the legion of what one observer described as "beautiful harem girls running around the set in see-through costumes."[4] And then there was his almost breakout performance in *Bonzo Goes to College* (1952), a film whose star—"Bonzo"—was a performing chimpanzee. But topping all of these "eminently forgettable" roles was probably *I Was a Teenage Werewolf* (1957), starring a young Michael Landon. Williams was cast as the lawman who shoots down the ill-fated werewolf in the last scene of the movie.

But, for the history of Zorro, there was one role that mattered: Guy Williams had a guest part on *The Lone Ranger* television series starring Clayton Moore. Moore, who had played Zorro in the 1949 Republic serial *Ghost of Zorro*, became the first TV version of the Lone Ranger. In the episode, "Six-Gun Artist" (June 30, 1955), Williams plays Sheriff Will Harrison. He falls in love with a beautiful artist named Julia Gregory (Elaine Riley). Unknown to Sheriff Harrison, but of course discovered by the Ranger, Julia Gregory is secretly a six-shootin' outlaw, which, while providing the main plot twist, makes Gregory a uniquely unsuitable match for the law-abiding sheriff. The Ranger and Tonto (Jay Silverheels) intervene.

"Woman with pretty face and evil heart always make trouble," Tonto tells Sheriff Harrison.

The masked man and Tonto leave the sheriff's office.

"A masked man, workin' on the side of the law! I still don't get it," says Harrison's deputy.

"I didn't get it either, till the Indian told me," replies the sheriff. "We've been face-to-face with a legend. He's the Lone Ranger."

It was but another instance of the Zorro–Lone Ranger interchangeability. Clayton Moore started as Zorro only to be best known as the Ranger; Guy Williams started out in *The Lone Ranger* and became famous for *Zorro*.

In the middle of Guy Williams's climb through "eminently forgettable" roles, a tragedy almost disqualified him from his Zorro destiny. At least, it seemed like a tragedy at the time. Williams, like many actors in the era of rawhide westerns, needed to know how to ride a horse. The Bronx-born Williams had learned to ride on his first stint in Hollywood in the late 1940s.

In addition to the practicality of keeping up his chops, Guy discovered he actually liked riding. It was a time when the backlots of many Hollywood studios simply blended into the desert scrub chaparral of the Los Angeles hills. Open spaces were just a minute's ride away. One day, Williams took a horse out to practice bareback riding. The horse, slick with sweat, lost its rider and Guy hit the ground hard. He snapped his humerus bone, and it took him a year to recover. He lost his Universal-International contract. It was a low point in his then-brief career. A friend of his, Dennis Weaver, got cast in the *Gunsmoke* TV show during the time when Williams was still recovering. Guy and his wife, Janice, later referred to that era as their "rice days," because rice was cheap, they were poor, and they had to eat.[5]

Tragedy has a way of becoming something else when you're Guy Williams and Zorro's ghost seems to be haunting you. Williams took up swimming, hit the speed bag at the gym, and became an avid walker. He trained, in other words. If the requisite training montage with music had been invented in the mid-1950s, this would've been the time to cue it up in the life of Guy Williams. He wasn't going to let the injury lead to failure in show business.

By chance, Williams noticed a fencing studio near his home—the Aldo Nadi Fencing Academy, led by Aldo and his brother Nedo. Guy enrolled and soon learned to feint, parry, riposte, and coupé with the foil, the épée, and the saber. Guy got in shape while learning the basics of strip fencing, which refers to the fencing floor, fourteen meters long by seven meters wide.

Among those he met at the studio was a young, blond-haired actor and stuntman named Glasé, who went by the stage name of Britt Lomond. Lomond learned fencing while attending New York University and had even been trained by one of the US Olympic fencing coaches. Lomond came to Hollywood in the early 1940s and first got work doing movie stunts. He doubled for Mel Ferrer in the swashbuckling classic *Scaramouche* (1952). *Scaramouche* was known for containing a ten-minute-long swordfight that was, at the time, the longest in swashbuckling history. Britt Lomond did most of that swordfight, and he was proud of the accomplishment.

Guy Williams and Britt Lomond fenced one another in the Aldo Nadi studio without knowing that one would later become Zorro and the other, Capitán Monastario, Zorro's enemy and rival in the Disney series. Lomond helped Williams learn camera fencing, which was different than the fencing done for competition.

"Hold the weapon as delicately as you would hold a small bird," Guy and Britt repeated the mantra of the maestro, "gently enough that you do not crush it, yet strong enough that it cannot fly away."[6]

When the casting call came from Walt Disney Productions in early 1957, Guy Williams was ready. "Once in a while in Hollywood," Williams said in a 1983 interview, "there was a role in town that everybody was talking about. And *this* was one of them. The fact that *Walt Disney*—that's a big start right there—was going to make *Zorro*, everybody immediately thought of Douglas Fairbanks, the original film; the Tyrone Power one, which really made a big splash—so, when you coupled the name Disney and Zorro, it was a *wanted job!*" "Careersville" is how Guy Williams referred to it.[7]

Walt Disney hadn't forgotten *Zorro*. When ABC turned down the original idea in 1953, Walt put it on the back burner, but he didn't forget. The Zorro Building continued to house the *Zorro* staff even after Disneyland became a reality. "Damnit, I love it here," Walt told one of his collaborators at the Zorro

Building. One Disney biographer writes that Walt called it his "sandbox"—a place where he could imagine, work on the small scale, and didn't have any departments to deal with.[8] *Zorro* was birthed out of the same atmosphere of creativity that brought Disneyland to life. When the chance came, especially after a renewed deal with ABC, Walt knew what series he wanted to bring to life: *Zorro*. Disney just needed the right actor to be able to pull it off.

Richard "Dick" Simmons had been Walt's first choice for the part of Zorro. Simmons played a Zorro-like knockoff character in Republic's recent serial *Man with the Steel Whip* (1954). But the Simmons casting fell through. At that point, Walt's chosen director for *Zorro*, Norman Foster, along with producer Bill Anderson, made a general casting call. At least a hundred actors showed up. It quickly narrowed to four front-runners for the two leads—Zorro / Don Diego and Captain Enrique Sanchez Monastario, the villain in the first thirteen episodes. Screen tests were done with the four candidates, including acting as well as fencing. Britt Lomond made the list, as did Mexican American actor Armando Silvestre and Italian Americans Tony Russel (born Antonio Russo) and Guy Williams. To hide his blond hair and "china blue eyes," Lomond used temporary black hair dye and wore dark contact lenses. "Britt! This is a *Spaniard*, you know?" one casting director told Lomond.[9] Lomond's dye and contacts were his attempt at looking the part.

A curated ethnicity is what Disney and his producers wanted for their television show. The production team wanted a vague "Spanish-ness"—which, in itself, was something that freaked Walt out during preproduction, whether audiences would be turned off by a "Spanish" show. In keeping with the still-dominant Spanish fantasy heritage, now sprinkled with Walt's magic, a depiction of Mexican California was not what the *Zorro* producers wanted—at least, not in the main leads.[10]

In Hollywood, at the time, the darkest-looking white actors often played the Mexican roles. Walt Disney's television production *The Nine Lives of Elfego Baca* (1958), for instance, cast Robert Loggia, an Italian American actor, in the role of the Mexican American lawman from New Mexico. Armando Silvestre, a front-runner for the *Zorro* show, had been born in San Diego, California, but as a Mexican American whose first language was Spanish, he had a bit of an accent when he spoke English. As it turned out, Disney and his team envisioned Don Diego in their show affecting a Spanish accent. So, certainly, Silvestre's accent was a selling point, right?

Not so. Walt Disney and his director, Norman Foster, wanted to control the accent.[11] Silvestre had played in the film version of Johnston McCulley's 1939 novel *Don Renegade*, called *The Mark of the Renegade* (1951). It was basically a Zorro plot without the mask. Silvestre had also been in the Mexican film *La sombra vengadora* (*The Avenging Shadow*, 1956), in which he plays a lucha libre–style masked hero. Silvestre was handsome and had all the assets one would want in a Zorro, including a more-than-fit physique—Silvestre barechested it in *La sombra vengadora*. For all that—his acting chops, his experience playing Zorro-like characters, his svelte torso, even—Silvestre's accent was too ethnic for the Disney producers; it was too, well, Mexican.

"The director wanted to be able to control the accent," Britt Lomond later remembered. "'R's got trilled and 'i's were pronounced as 'e's, but otherwise the accent was light."[12] After landing the role of Zorro, Guy Williams recalled, "Nobody told me what kind of accent they wanted. So when I did the test I was all over the place with a Spanish accent—heavy, heavy accent—because no one would say which way they wanted to go. They knew they could always drop it if it was heavy. But, if I were to go too light, that would be worse."

Guy Williams walked around the set for the first several weeks, and he'd get a tap on the shoulder. It would be Walt Disney. "Can you bring it down a little, Guy," Walt would say. At one point, Walt thought Guy should go by his actual last name, Catalano, because it sounded Spanish. Guy ended up keeping Williams but backed off the accent. On the set, Walt kept tapping Guy on the shoulder, sometimes motioning him to bring up the accent, sometimes down. "One day," Williams later remembered, "I had finished a show and he didn't tap me on the shoulder. And that's the one I kept."[13]

Many Latinx actors did get cast in Disney's *Zorro*, just not in leading roles. A good majority of those opportunities came through Norman Foster, the show's first director. Although he wanted the accents to be "just so," Foster championed the careers of several future Latinx stars. Foster was irascible and often clashed with Walt. Disney fired Foster on more than one occasion only to hire him back the next day.

Foster wasn't a Hollywood guy. He'd started as an actor, but liked directing better. He spent quite a bit of time traveling, and lived off and on in Mexico. There, he met Mexican film stars, such as Dolores del Río, whom he directed in *Journey into Fear* (1943), and Ricardo Montalban, best known later as the mysterious Mr. Roarke in *Fantasy Island* (1977–1984) and as Captain Kirk's nemesis in the classic *Star Trek II: The Wrath of Khan* (1982). Foster directed Montalban in *Santa* (1943) and *Sombrero* (1953), and when *Zorro* came up he recommended Montalban for a guest-starring villain in the one-hour special "Auld Acquaintance." By all accounts, Foster loved Mexico and wanted to give Mexican actors a chance in Hollywood.

A number of other actors also guest-starred or had supporting roles in several episodes—Cesar Romero, Perry Lopez, Rita Moreno (from Puerto Rico), and BarBara Luna. The part of Don Diego's father, Don Alejandro, went to George J. Lewis, the Mexican American actor who had been in all those Republic serials, and who had even dressed as the Black Whip. With Lewis, the oddest irony developed, which no one seemed to recognize at the time: a Mexican-American actor who spoke English perfectly with no accent, but who played his role in *Zorro* with an affected Spanish lilt. Latinx actors were all over the Disney *Zorro* series—just not in its main starring roles.

Zorro was Spanish, as conventional wisdom had it, and the Walt Disney series wanted to keep him that way. Guy Williams, a first-generation Italian American, who could pass for the most all-American guy—literally—got the role of Zorro.[14] Britt Lomond, who continued to dye his blond hair black, but lost the contacts because of an awful eye infection, got the role of Captain Monastario.

The character of Zorro masked a lot of things in its history—racial violence, settler colonialism, the context of California's traumatic annexation, even the sexual violence of Johnston McCulley, but it also masked the contribution of a host of Latinx actors, who either channeled their ethnicity into an acceptable "Spanish-ness" or had to play up the Latinx stereotypes familiar in Hollywood—the fiery female sexpot or the enraged macho *bandido* or the fat, lazy, but kindly Mexican peasant.

And yet, it's not as though the writers didn't try. They were writing a western set in the era of Spanish colonialism—a "*south*-western," Guy Williams liked to call it. Within that western genre, where the cowboys were heroes and the Indians were threatening menaces, the writers attempted nuance.

One writer, Bob Wehling, who wrote some 40 percent of the Disney *Zorro* scripts, studied California history. Wehling was born in 1919, the same year *The Curse of Capistrano* was first published. Wehling served in World War II, saw intense action, and then decided upon his return to the United States to try his hand in Hollywood. *I've faced death in the European Theater; what's the worst that could happen in Los Angeles?* seems to have been his thought process. Wehling, without a job or many prospects, had to sleep in a Los Angeles park, making sure to keep his shoes safe so no one would take them in the dead of night. But things improved. He got a break writing for Disney.[15] Wehling and Norman Foster wrote the first script for the show, "Presenting Señor Zorro," which aired October 10, 1957.

The series opening establishes the basic formula originally employed by McCulley, with Fairbanks's changes. Don Diego de la Vega returns from Spain to find his father in trouble. The authorities are the villains. He must act, but how? The direct approach, Diego considers, will endanger his father. It's at that point that he decides, while still on the boat, to take on a bookish dual identity—not so much fey, or foppish, but slightly jovial. Williams thought the audience would soon tire of a pronounced effete or foppish Don Diego over the course of the series. The first draft of the script is set in "1820," with "1830" written in pencil; "1830," however, would've put the setting firmly in the Mexican period, as Mexico had already gained its independence from Spain by that date. Ultimately, "1820" was the date selected.[16] As Diego and his manservant, Bernardo (Gene Sheldon), talk on the ship before disembarking, they work out their plans.

"Yes, Cal-ee-fornia is beautiful," says Diego with only a hint of accent. "Many times I have dreamed of this homecoming, but I'm afraid things have changed since I left. We are in for trouble, Bernardo."

In pencil, a script change included Diego burning his father's letters, so as not to incriminate him should Diego be caught or his things searched. Meanwhile, Bernardo looks questioningly at Diego. Bernardo is mute in Disney's *Zorro*, but he can hear, which is put to good use for Zorro's plans. Bernardo wonders what the trouble might be. Bernardo, according to the script, "pantomimes feathers, war-whoop, and bow and arrows."

Diego laughs. "No, not Indians," he says, "politics. A few corrupt officials using their authority for personal gain. Conditions must be very bad for my father to summon me home."[17]

In an era when "war-whooping" Indians were a mainstay of westerns, Bob Wehling's focus on corrupt politics is interesting. From the start, the corrupt enemy is an extension of a greedy, power-hungry government and its military apparatus. "Presenting Señor Zorro" sets the stage for a western hero firmly in the tradition of vigilante justice so common in US history and memory. But

Disney's *Zorro* is always having to fight both the corrupt government officials as well as the supposedly misguided vigilantes who take the law into their own hands—some of whom look a lot like Joaquín Murrieta.

The first season presents two main story arcs. The first follows the conventional Zorro-battles-corrupt-comandante tale. For many fans, the "First Thirteen," as they're sometimes known by die-hard *Zorro* aficionados, are the best. These episodes pit Diego/Zorro against Captain Monastario and contain some of the best swordplay. In a supporting role is Sergeant Demetrio Lopez García (Henry Calvin), the fat but lovable and well-meaning oaf who is Zorro's enemy but Diego's friend. And, over time, Sergeant García becomes obviously sympathetic to Zorro's fight. Even in the first script, one writer or editor notes in pencil: "Sgt. García sympathetic?"[18]

Although Britt Lomond's run as Monastario was hugely popular, his eventual downfall left a void that got filled by other villains—an anthology of them. For the second story arc of the first season, the writers drew on both Zorro's history in the serials, as well as the superhero genre—and California history. The writers created a supervillain with his own masked identity—the Eagle—who enlists scores of agents throughout California, known to each other only through the presentation of an eagle feather. The Eagle turns out to be a crooked landowner with designs to dominate California. But it's in that second story arc—with the Eagle and his rogue's gallery—that we get a glimpse of Joaquín Murrieta. Or, actually, we should say "Murrietta," spelled with two t's.

A pair of desperados, Carlos and Pedro Murrietta (Kent Taylor and Paul Picerni), ride into Los Angeles.[19] The Murrietta brothers have pillaged the churches of South America and stolen a Catholic relic known as the Cross of the Andes. The story hinges on the Murrietta brothers' scheme to sell the cross and other relics to fund the Eagle's growing criminal empire. Zorro, of course, defeats them both—one dies in the process, although not at Zorro's hands, and the other is placed in jail. Murrieta-the-bandit, with a cutthroat reputation, is the "Joaquín" used for these episodes. But it wasn't the only story that included a Joaquín-like character, revealing that the Murrieta legend continued to influence Zorro.

Season 2 of the Disney TV series moved Diego de la Vega out of Los Angeles for the first several episodes. The move to Monterrey was Walt Disney's doing. He felt a change of scenery would be good for the series. It was the same set, but just a new matte painting for the establishing shots and a new plaza, with vendor stalls erected to make it look different from the original set. Moving Don Diego to Monterrey allowed Diego to have a romantic storyline, as he meets—and has to save—the father of Anna Maria Verdugo (Jolene Brand). The move to Monterrey also allowed for new villains. With Monastario and the Eagle defeated in season 1, the change of locale enabled a repeat of the defeat-corrupt-comandante story. With the governor out of town, the assistant governor takes over and begins to rule with an iron fist, felt most painfully by the peons, played by Mexican American actors.

The show titled "The New Order" begins a four-episode arc.[20] The scene opens on the Monterrey plaza. Theresa (BarBara Luna), "a fiery young woman," according to the script, "is hawking the sale of tamales by singing to customers who pass." "A little refrain reminiscent of 'Pickle in the Middle' as applied to tamales," is what the script directions call for.[21] "Pickle in the Middle" refers to the Artie "Mr. Kitzel" Auerbach and Milton De Lugg tune, which started as a hot dog vendor sketch on *The Jack Benny Show*. The song comes out in the Zorro series as more rhumba than big band.

"Tam-a-les," Theresa sings, "Hot-Hot-Hot-Hot," as she moves her shoulders in time with each "Hot." As she sings, she bats her eyelashes, she mentions that "your tongue will burn," and that the tamales are "sooo del-eee-cious." "For the hottest tamale in Monterrey," she sings, "come to Theresa, the folks all say." One doesn't have to be too astute to realize the various meanings put to the phrase "hot tamale." But at the end of the little song, Sergeant García appears to harmonize with Theresa—blissful peace reigns in the plaza of Monterrey. Until, that is, García tells Theresa of the new orders from the lieutenant governor. All the vendor stands will be torn down. Theresa goes from sweet to extraspicy at this point. She jumps on García, scratching, kicking, and screaming. Don Diego intervenes, with Bernardo in tow, and calms the situation. Theresa shows her gratitude to Don Diego by stealing a kiss. Embarrassed, Diego looks sheepishly at Bernardo, who gives him a concerned look.

Enter Joaquín Castenada (Perry Lopez), the Murrieta stand-in for the episodes. He's Theresa's vaquero boyfriend. When he finds out that the vendor stalls are being torn down, he's ready for a fight. And this sets the dramatic tension over the remainder of the story arc. Diego/Zorro must continually stay Joaquín's impetuousness as Joaquín seeks tit for tat to meet the violence of the government with his own vigilante justice.

"I'm getting a little tired of this," Diego tells Joaquín as Joaquín pulls out a knife. "Put that away," Diego chides.

"Stand aside," Joaquín demands.

"Do you have to be hit on the head again?" Diego says, exasperated, referring to the fact that Bernardo knocked Joaquín unconscious in order to keep Joaquín from acting violently toward the soldiers. Here we have in miniature the basics of the vigilante's dilemma: Zorro has to intervene, both to bring down the lieutenant governor and to keep Joaquín from starting a war. And Joaquín intends on doing just that—he takes to the hills and enlists outlaws to assist him.

Soon, a bounty for Joaquín's capture is levied that rival's Zorro's own price. Joaquín Castenada in the series of episodes becomes a kind of foil for Zorro. All of the original Murrieta's grievances are adjudicated within the Walt Disney TV show. What the show recommends is not resistance but consensus—reasonable men talking it out. Diego and Bernardo try to reason with Joaquín in his hilltop hideout. Joaquín, angry, puts the pair in chains.

"Pay no attention to him," Theresa says to the manacled Don Diego. "When he is angry, he is stupid. And all of the time, lately, he is angry."

"She's right, Joaquín," Don Diego says. "You've let your anger blind you. Why, even your friends, you treat as enemies."

"I will decide who my friends are," Joaquín shoots back.

"Joaquín," Diego continues, "you could be a man of reason. And so could the governor. If only the two of you would get together, talk as reasonable men. There would be no more trouble."

Theresa tries to intervene. Her speech to Don Diego is an acknowledgement of just grievances against Mexican Americans. "You do not understand, Don Diego," she says. "I know you are our friend. But until you have had to live like this, until you have been pursued like an animal, you do not really know."

And, it's true. She's got a point. Don Diego in the Disney television show is played as a wealthy Spaniard. All traces of Joaquín Murrieta DNA in Zorro are gone; Joaquín Murrieta has simply been made into a separate character entirely—namely, Joaquín Castenada, hot-headed Mexican vaquero who can't cool down long enough to talk like a reasonable man. It's as if the writers meant to render a verdict on a whole period of history via Zorro's intervention.

In the end, after four episodes, Zorro manages to capture both Joaquín and the governor. He chains them together, giving each the other's key that will free them. Zorro makes the two talk, to build enough trust, in order to give one another the other's key. The governor realizes he's been lied to by his lieutenant governor—the "bad apple" in this scenario. Joaquín, in contrast, learns of the governor's good intentions. On their return to Monterrey—together—they face the various "bad apples" that are to blame, and peace returns again to the town. Theresa once again sings about her hot tamales with the same rhumba-inflected "Pickle-in-the-Middle" number that started the four-episode story arc.

If only two reasonable men could talk, perhaps the racial and ethnic violence could've been averted in Old California. *Isn't it pretty to think so?* The cynical rhetorical is as true for California's history as it is for a novel's tragic lovers. The only way to keep up the fantasy is to avoid the truth. In Disney's reworking of the Murrieta legend, Zorro provides a buffer between truth and fiction. Zorro, a character birthed out of the Murrieta story, now stands between the outlaw and his fate. Yet, for Zorro to do so, he has to uphold the status quo as just. The problem, according to Zorro, and according to the popular myth about California's history, was that just a few "bad apples" were to blame. Simply remove the rotten fruit, in other words, and all would be well. This was Disney, after all. One could hardly expect America's magic maker to do anything less than uphold popular myth.

"This was in Old Spanish California," Disney told the Mouseketeers on "The Fourth Anniversary Show," "back in the time of high adventure and low Spanish guitars."

It was Walt Disney who killed the *Zorro* television series. Legal disputes between Walt and ABC, which aired the show on Thursday nights, centered on ABC's sponsors. Walt wanted to do color television. NBC now wanted Walt, and NBC had color television capabilities. But ABC wouldn't release Walt from the seven-year contract that had bankrolled the Disneyland park.

"Walt was very upset with ABC," remembered Bill Anderson, a Disney producer. "[*Zorro*] was doing well. 7-UP, one of the sponsors, told Walt and ABC they were looking for a show with a broader audience."[22] Yet, *Zorro* had increased its Share of Audience from 32 percent in the 1957 season to 38.9 percent in the second. Especially popular were the so-called Annette episodes.

For her sixteenth birthday present, Walt arranged for Annette Funicello to guest-star in a number of *Zorro* episodes.[23]

The real issue, besides the desires of the sponsors, was Walt's desire to do something new. He told one associate at the time that he'd felt put in a "straight jacket," as networks demanded westerns and more westerns.[24] Walt Disney had moved on.

To be fair, Walt wanted to bring *Zorro* back in color on NBC, but ABC said absolutely not. Disney claimed he owned the sets, the actors, and the scripts for *Zorro*. How could ABC make *Zorro* without Disney? A final price of $49,500 per episode for a *Zorro* third season was proposed to ABC.[25] The network said it was too high; the audience potential, mainly young children, didn't warrant that high of price tag, came ABC's reply. Walt sued ABC to get out of the contract on July 2, 1959—the same day as the last *Zorro* show aired.

While production of *Zorro* and *The Mickey Mouse Club* halted, Walt's own anthology show continued. His contract with ABC didn't extend to *Walt Disney Presents*, and so several one-hour specials of *Zorro* were shown. An edited version of the first thirteen episodes was theatrically released as *The Sign of Zorro*. *Zorro, the Avenger*, another edited version of Disney episodes, was sent to the foreign markets—Japan, Holland, Denmark, France, Italy, Finland, Brazil, Portugal, and the United Kingdom.

Walt bet that ABC would back down. The bet failed. ABC was even then, secretly, working with Warner Bros. on new shows. When the 1960 season began, ABC unveiled its new programs and *Zorro* was dead.

Guy Williams, with a tinge of bitterness, told one interviewer in 1983, "Well, Walt got into a little fracas with the network and, well, that's the way Walt did things—he pulled the show off the air."[26]

Guy Williams, however, still had four years left on his contract with Disney. He did numerous public appearances. A YouTube video shows one of the first public appearances the cast from *Zorro* did at Disneyland. The fox finally made an entrance at the park. Thousands in masks, kids as well as well-adjusted adults, squint into the sun as Guy Williams fences with Britt Lomond on a Disneyland replica set.

As the litigation with ABC continued, Guy appeared at a horse show in Cincinnati. He visited Fort Smith, Arkansas; the Calgary Stamped; Madison Square Garden. There were rodeos and parades galore. He signed autographs, sometimes in oddly suggestive places for adult women who showed up at his public appearances.[27] Guy Williams feared that if he broke the Disney contract, no other studios would give him a chance. He wanted to do films, but by and large, *Zorro* would haunt his career. He played Professor John Robinson in *Lost in Space* (1965–1968), the science fiction reimagining of the Swiss Family Robinson classic. But *Zorro* was the height of his success.

"[Walt] took it away from the network," Guy later said of the *Zorro* television series. "He took it away from himself, and certainly took it away from me!"[28] In one guest appearance on the gameshow *Password* in 1967, Guy told the host that he'd played a "Super-Spaniard" in his role as Zorro. He laughs, but he also looks like he's cringing.

Eventually, Williams embraced his Zorro role. He moved to Argentina in the 1970s because of the immense popularity of the masked avenger in that country. He toured in a circus for several years, giving fencing demonstrations while dressed as Zorro. There were plans to do a Zorro feature film, with Williams as an aging Zorro bequeathing his mask to a new generation. That plot would have to wait another couple of decades to make it on-screen. But it wouldn't be Guy Williams who would play the role. Williams died in Argentina in 1989 of a brain aneurysm. It was several days before his body was discovered, alone, in his Buenos Aires apartment.

———————

At the height of Zorro-mania, the show got canceled. One *Life* magazine multipage spread from the era shows just how deep *Zorro* had reached into the psyche of American children.[29] Kids in random towns throughout America, in Hingham, Massachusetts, for example, were depicted running around neighborhoods in their Zorro merch provided by the Walt Disney Company. Johnston McCulley, just a few months before his death, was pictured teaching young moppets how to scratch a proper Z on the wall of a building. *Life* showed two kids from Denver, Colorado, fighting a duel perched atop wooden horses on a merry-go-round.

As far and as fast as Zorro could seemingly travel, in reality the character was forever going in circles, ending up where he started. Perhaps a new generation of riders hopped on as one generation hopped off, but Zorro was, for the average American kid, just an entertaining fiction. "As you say," Guy

Williams dressed as Zorro told the Mouseketeers on "The Fourth Anniversary Show," "perhaps I am only a part of the imagination. I remember that's what they said about me in California. Some would smile and say: Zorro—*poof*—he's a ghost, a dream, a myth, a something of the imagination."

And, yet, Zorro rode on. There was an arc to Zorro's evolution. Representations of the character became whiter over time, more distinctly Anglo-American. He upheld consensus over conflict. He defended the established order. The recalcitrance and rebelliousness of the bandit Murrieta was gone. Zorro the idea remained, even while the cultural commodity was an ever-changing quantity. Zorro, too, was always good at hiding in plain sight, shape-shifting to keep up with the times. There were new fads on the horizon, and new icons to influence . . . like Batman.

18 | ZORRO, ALIAS BATMAN

Research Log #6
Hollywood Boulevard
7:15 PM

ALL ROADS LEAD TO THE HOLLYWOOD WALK OF FAME—well, all Zorro roads, that is. There are tons of stars on Hollywood Boulevard dedicated to celebrities whose careers, at some point, became associated with Zorro. Basil Rathbone, villain of the 1940 remake of *The Mark of Zorro*, was one of the first to catch my eye. His star is right outside the TCL Chinese Theatre, the rebranded name for Sid Grauman's Chinese Theatre, established in 1927. Ricardo Montalban has a star—so, of course, does Walt Disney. Guy Williams only got added posthumously. But his is not in the forecourt of honor, separate from the Star Walk, where the biggest stars are immortalized—the hands and footprints of almost one hundred years of Hollywood's most holy celebrities are here, preserved in cement blocks.

The first thing that struck me about the Chinese Theatre, and its cement memorials, was how very much like Rome it all felt, despite the fact that the architecture is more art deco than classical. Tourists, like some sort of modern-day pilgrims, seem to be searching for meaning among the ruins. One can see tourists combing over the names of the cement impressions. And then—*Oh, my! Here are the hands of Tom Cruise!* Or—*Come, look, dear! There are the lovely impressions left by Marilyn Monroe and Jane Russell.* ("Gentlemen Prefer Blondes," the pair wrote on their shared cement slab.) In Hollywood, tourists genuflect and kneel with all the ardor of the most pious pilgrims seeking the relics of the saints. It's some sort of connection to greatness. The slanted roof, the stone pagodas, the enclosed space of the Chinese Theatre and forecourt—all of it adds an aura of secular entertainment sacredness.

And so, here, quite near the theater's entrance, I stood next to Tyrone Power's handprints and footprints: "To Sid," Power wrote in the cement, "Following in my father's Footprints." And then even closer to the theater's ornate door, I found the handprints and footprints of Douglas Fairbanks and Mary Pickford. Fairbanks and Pickford are equidistant from the entrance, but also separated from each other by the central walkway.

The earliest prints all give messages to Sid Grauman, the Chinese Theatre's first owner. Before the footprints were an "honor," or were anything near a marker of Hollywood saint status, they were, well, just fun footprints marked in wet cement to celebrate their friend's new swanky theater. All kinds of saints began that way. Just regular people with above average abilities to look good, whether in the paintings of saintly icons or on the silver screen. What matters is the stories we tell, whether of saints or stars.

I was reminded of a line from Mel Brooks's 1974 spoof of the western genre, *Blazing Saddles*.[1] It's a movie as smart as it is hilarious. The villain, Hedley Lamarr (Harvey Korman), gets shot (in the crotch!) at the end of the film while he stands in the Chinese Theatre's cement forecourt of honor. Before he dies, he falls on the footprints of none other than Douglas Fairbanks. "How did he do such fantastic stunts," Lamarr says nearly on his last breath, "with such little feet?"

Yes, indeed, I thought. *They do seem slightly smaller than one would think, for all the skylarking he could do.* Fairbanks, in many ways, had an outsized influence on Zorro—he set the standard for the earliest swashbuckling image of the masked avenger in black. But Fairbanks, too, had an outsized influence not only on the film version of Zorro but also on the creation of Superman and Batman.

———————————

I thought about those two earliest comic book superheroes as I began walking down Hollywood Boulevard. So much ink has been spilled about the origins of the American superhero, and especially about Superman and Batman. What's missing is an account of Zorro's influence.

Superman made his appearance in June 1938 in *Action Comics* #1. Writer Jerry Siegel and artist Joe Shuster had been working on their character for quite a few years before their bodysuited hero hit the comics pages. But among the many influences the pair pointed to, they often mentioned Douglas Fairbanks. Siegel, in particular, was an insatiable consumer of Fairbanks movies.[2] He told interviewers later that Fairbanks's *Mark of Zorro* and Rudolph Valentino's *The Eagle* were both influences on Superman.[3] Yet, even here, Valentino's film was itself a riff off the masked, dual-identity success of Fairbanks's own *Don Q, Son of Zorro.*

Zorro keeps popping up when Superman is mentioned. For instance, film producer Alexander Salkind remembered that it was Zorro who influenced him and his father, Ilya Salkind, to do a feature film (*Superman*, 1978, with Christopher Reeve). "I was walking down a street in Paris in 1974," Alexander Salkind told an interviewer, "and I saw a poster advertising Zorro. . . . The next day out of the blue I said to my father, 'Let's do Superman.'"[4]

Zorro's always in the mix when superheroes are talked about. Comics nerds and comics historians—not necessarily a mutually exclusive bunch—usually gloss over Zorro's importance. For instance, when the dual-identity aspect of Zorro is pointed out, a nerd might say: *What about the Scarlet Pimpernel? He was obviously created before Zorro, wasn't he?* And it's true. But Zorro didn't just get his dual identity shtick from the Pimpernel. It's deeper than that. It's part of American history. He got it, too, from Joaquín Murrieta, a character steeped in the history of *America*, not in the history of aristocrats from Europe. The dual identity is an inheritance of American diversity, glimpsed in a character like Zorro, and then changed and rearranged for use by comic book superheroes.

I arrived at my destination: 6764 Hollywood Boulevard, the address of the Guinness Book of World Records store. Outside, on the sidewalk, is Bob Kane's star. He was honored posthumously and placed outside the Guinness World Records store because he holds the record for the most film and television adaptations of his most famous creation—the Batman. Kane's best articulation of Zorro's influence on him came in an interview he did with John Tibbetts, one of Douglas Fairbanks's biographers:

At the movies I saw *The Mark of Zorro* with Douglas Fairbanks, Sr. who was my idol as a child, a kid growing up in New York, in the Bronx actually. Zorro was the most swashbuckling daredevil I've ever seen in my life. He out-acrobated Batman a thousand times, but he gave me the idea of the dual identity. During the day he posed as a foppish bored Don Diego Vega, the son of one of the wealthiest families in Mexico around 1820. But they were under the domination of the Conquistador government at that time, and they robbed the poor and levied the high taxes and really caused all sorts of terrible injustices against the poor people. So at night he donned this mask, kind of a handkerchief mask with slits in the eyes; and he'd attach a trusty sword to his side and he'd exit from a cave on a black horse. I think the black horse's name was Tornado. And actually, there you can see the reference where many years later to the idea of a bat cave and the bat mobile, instead of the horse. That had a profound influence on me, on the dual identity. There are other dual identities, like the Scarlet Pimpernel, but I got mine mainly from Zorro.[5]

According to Bob Kane, it's a pretty open-and-shut case: Zorro was there at the beginning.

"But," as one sage comics historian notes, "Bob Kane said a lot of things."[6] And he did say a lot of things. Many of them, however, weren't exactly true. Bob Kane, for instance, wasn't the sole creator of Batman, even though that's exactly what he told his editors at National (later DC Comics), and what he told just about anyone who would listen to him in later years. In fact, Bob Kane had help creating Batman. Kane's longtime collaborator, Milton "Bill" Finger, was equally as important as Kane in coming up with Batman. But also, others: Sheldon Moldoff, Jerry Robinson, and Gardner Fox. Yet Finger had an especially pronounced role in bringing the caped crusader into existence. When Kane brought Finger his first idea sketch for "the Bird-Man" (which later historians have uncovered as a tracing Kane made of a Flash Gordon comic), Finger helped his buddy out. The red underwear and weirdly uncool stiff bat wings had to go, Finger told him. Also, the name. "The Bat-Man" was better. Finger continued with changes, in color and style, which moved the idea closer to the recognizable character we've come to know—the cowl, a gray-black color scheme, and a scalloped, flowing cape.[7]

It wasn't as though Bill Finger was above appropriating work from others for his own purposes. He was just better at it than Bob Kane. Like all young aspiring artists and writers at the time, they lifted bits and pieces from the pulps and comic strips that they loved, and used those as inspiration for their creations. Finger drew liberally from a host of pulp characters and radio dramas; the Shadow, for example, but also the Phantom. The pulp character Doc Savage had a utility belt that was eventually bequeathed to Batman. The 1930 film *The Bat Whispers*, which follows a crazed, masked guy in a bat mask as he kills his victims one by one, also was an influence. Kane and Finger even used a 1938 children's book called *Gang Busters in Action* to help fill in their first Batman issue, "The Case of the Chemical Syndicate."[8]

Despite the diffuse array of sources for Batman, Fairbanks and Zorro keep showing up in the masked crusader's origins. Finger told comics historian Jim Steranko that "Batman was a combination of Douglas Fairbanks and Sherlock Holmes"—the swashbuckler and the master detective.[9] One editor of the iconic fanzine *Alter Ego* wrote: "Bill maintained (well into the 1960s) a file of Douglas Fairbanks, Sr. photo stills. He showed me the file and said that he would attach selected photos to finished scripts for Bob and his assistants to use as models. The stills I saw (and had never seen before that date) were the familiar swinging poses that characterized the Acro-Batman that was popular in my youth."[10]

If Finger loved Fairbanks, he also loved McCulley's pulp fiction—and not just the Zorro yarns. Finger, for instance, lifted part of Batman's backstory directly from one of McCulley's stories. In 1934 and '35, McCulley penned a series of short fiction for *Popular Detective*, published by Street & Smith. Those stories centered on a crime fighter with the dual identity of . . . the Bat. When Batman appeared in May 1939 in *Detective Comics* #27, he was already "the Bat-Man," already in action busting heads and killing goons. (Batman lost his hyphen by the third issue, but he continued being a gun-toting badass for a bit longer.) It wasn't until *Detective Comics* #33 (November 1939) that he finally got a backstory. McCulley's Bat stories are prominent in that backstory.

Young Bruce Wayne and his parents, so issue #33 tells us, are just out from the movies when a mugger shoots and kills Bruce's parents, setting the now mentally rattled youngster on the road to becoming Batman. But note: in the earliest tellings of the backstory, *The Mark of Zorro* was not the movie the Waynes had just seen. The movie, in fact, was never named until Frank Miller rebooted Bruce Wayne's origins in *The Dark Knight Returns* (1986).

Miller's retroactive continuity—with *The Mark of Zorro* being the movie—has since been made a more-or-less canon feature of Batman's origins. So great was Miller's influence on the character's development—he basically resuscitated Batman—that Miller's Zorro references in *The Dark Knight Returns* are viewed as having always been part of the story, even though it was Miller who articulated them. One example: in *The Dark Knight Returns*, a mostly dark and angry Batman rides down the streets of Gotham on a black horse that looks nothing if not like Tornado!

But all that would come later. When Finger wrote the original backstory for Batman, McCulley's influence was on display. The backstory ends, after the scene of the double murder of the Waynes, with a now-grown Bruce sitting in his study, contemplating his decision to become a crime fighter. A bat flies in the window, and he chooses that symbol as alter ego. "A bat! That's it! It's an omen! . . . I shall become a bat!" In McCulley's short story "The Bat Strikes!" (November 1934), written before Finger wrote the Batman backstory, the protagonist, private eye Dawson Clade, has the same experience when a bat enters his room. "That's it!" Clade exclaims aloud. "I'll call myself the Bat."[11]

McCulley, for all his personal loathsomeness, had a large role in the burgeoning superhero genre. McCulley, writes one pulp historian, "is the spiritual father of all 1930s avengers who administered bushwhack justice from the night and strewed the scene of their exploits with scarlet spiders and paste-on bat decals."[12] Fairbanks and McCulley were there at the birth of the superheroes.

But what about Murrieta? Murrieta is harder to see than those other two influences on Zorro. As I stood atop Bob Kane's star, I could almost hear nerd critics saying, *No one even knows about Murrieta. How can he be an influence on Batman?* Just like in Zorro, Murrieta's mark on Batman is covered up by so many other stories. But when you strip Zorro's and Batman's stories down to their most basic, something of Murrieta's dual identity, his search for justice, his uncomfortable relationship to his heritage and his present, becomes apparent. Consider one such basic synopsis written by a comics commentator.

> You may never have read that story, but you know the main character. He's a fop who luxuriates in wealth and irresponsibility by day, but by night dons a black mask and strikes terror into the hearts of those who prey upon the less fortunate. His symbol is known throughout the land. He struggles with the duality of his existence. He's forced to

endure disdain and disappointment from his loved ones because their safety demands that he hides his true self from them. In carrying out justice from the shadows, he shames the hapless and corrupt people who purport to maintain order by the light of day. They call him by the name of a beast because his capabilities seem beyond human.[13]

The synopsis works equally well for Batman, for Zorro, and even for Murrieta.

Murrieta's legend is, of course, a myth. But it represents the history and experience of Latinx people and also many other minorities who have lived a hyphenated existence. The superhero story allows for those dual identities—the difference between what one seems to be and what one really is—to be noble, heroic, and used for the greater good. There's power in the hyphenated existence of American diversity. Legends are deep wells. We return to them in order to draw up fresh stories to quench our thirst for meaning in the present. But to draw out freshness from the well, sometimes you have to dump out the old stale water first. The old stories have to be put to rest before new ones can live.

It was only then, after my (somewhat) long journey to understanding the Zorro legend and its meaning, that I realized the old Zorro story had grown pretty stale. As I stood on Bob Kane's star, with tourists begrudging my immobility in the middle of Hollywood Boulevard's busiest sidewalk, I came to a realization: to live on, Zorro had to die.

19 | ZORRO REBORN

ZORRO TURNED ONE HUNDRED YEARS OLD IN 2019.[1] The masked man in black is older than Wonder Woman (a spry seventy-eight years old in 2019), older than Batman (he was eighty), older than Superman (eighty-one), and even older than the Shadow (eighty-nine). Zorro had been fighting corrupt governors and politicians in Old Alta California for a century. Zorro the swashbuckler, Zorro the western hero, and Zorro the superhero were the three most recognizable trajectories of the character. But his death was heralded, perhaps, with the sheer ubiquity of his likeness.

Disney's *Zorro* placed him on every kind of kids' swag imaginable. From the 1950s to the '70s Zorro began to go global to a larger degree. Part of this was due to Disney leasing rights to foreign film productions. Almost thirty films were produced in Italy, France, and Spain. Peplum films, often known as "sword-and-sandal" flicks, featured Zorro alongside any number of strongmen—Hercules, Samson, Goliath, and the Italian classic hulk Maciste. Zorro could appear with the Three Musketeers or at the Court of Spain, but also in Bollywood (*Zorro*, 1975).

Zorro died from sheer exhaustion. He was just played out.

It's at that point, when a genre or icon becomes so common that it loses its power to move audiences in the traditional way, that it dies. Parody and satire are usually not far behind. In 1981 actor/producer/comedian George Hamilton swept in to mock Zorro's ailing health as a pop culture has-been. Hamilton was fresh off the success of his first film satire, *Love at First Bite* (1979), which spoofed the vampire film.[2] Looking for a new vehicle, he settled on Zorro. Melvin Simon Productions financed the film, and scriptwriter Hal Dresner was hired to pen the screenplay. Dresner was best known for his erotic fiction. He put those chops to good use in the new film, which came to be called *Zorro: The Gay Blade.*

The title was a riff off the enormity of "Gay Caballero" titles from the mid-twentieth century. There were tons of "Gay Desperados," "Gay Cavaliers," and "Gay Bandits" featured in classic films. By the early 1980s, *gay* had come to mean something else. That was the central double entendre of the film, and Dresner peppered his script with plenty of others. The plot hinges on the twin sons of Zorro—Diego and Ramón. Diego is the stereotypical Latin macho, whom we first discover in bed with a married woman back in Spain. Called to California by his dying father, Diego discovers the costume of Zorro and starts gallivanting as the masked hero. Soon, Diego's twin brother returns, after a twenty-year hiatus in England. Dresner describes his entrance in the script:

> His voice—how to put this—has a certain arch gentility about it. No—a hint of sibilance. No—a fey, ironic quality. Of course, coupled with a British accent, it was perfectly acceptable then. But now we'd have pegged the guy as obviously gay.[3]

And stereotypically gay he was in the film. George Hamilton plays a dual role in the film, both as the macho, not-so-smart super-Latin-lover brother Diego, as well as the returning Ramón, who, we learn, now goes by the name Bunny Wigglesworth.

The film is a play on the 1940 version of Zorro. Thus, there are two female leads. The first is the wife of the corrupt alcalde, played by Brenda Vaccaro. Her nattering performance is often the one cited by people who remember it. The other lead is Lauren Hutton, who plays the protofeminist suffragette Charlotte Taylor Wilson.

For all the film's fun and one-liner humor—"It's no shame to be poor," Bunny says while dressed as a plum-colored Zorro, "just poorly dressed!"— the movie aims at a deeper critique of Zorro's ambivalent sexuality. For instance, Dresner's script imagined Bunny Wigglesworth as the film's hero—a gay hero. Dresner's description of the final scene for Bunny, where he rides off after saving his brother, paints Ramón/Bunny in such terms:

106. Ext. Grassy Hillock—Day

It overlooks the verdant valley and also the cemetery. Charlotte Taylor Wilson and Diego are there on horseback. (On separate horsebacks, actually.) And down in the valley below, we see the figure of Ramón, alone still but looking quite valiant. In the fig. now is the plaque of his father, horse rearing, lance high and now Ramón duplicates that pose, and waves. Diego and Charlotte Taylor Wilson wave back and, supported by the most heroic music since 'The William Tell Overture,' the screen's first homosexual hero rides off into the sunset.[4]

Dresner and Hamilton truly tried to bring off a satire of Zorro that would both ennoble the gay hero, as well as poke fun at that same gay hero, throughout the entire movie. That's a tall order. For satire to work there has to be a clear understanding on the part of the audience on the purpose of the satire. Otherwise, the audience can simply mistake satire for meanness, parody of stereotypes for the stereotypes themselves.

The ennobling qualities of the gay hero, despite Dresner's attempt in the script to highlight them, go largely unnoticed in the actual film. And they went unnoticed by many reviewers too. One commentator, who identified himself as gay, wrote for the *Village Voice*:

> What was the point of the title—and that fruity [movie poster] of Hamilton? To scare away the straights and get the gays? But in 1981 gays are hardly likely to support a movie about a mere fop who never actually makes sexual (or even romantic) contact with another man. They may, in fact, be insulted. As an expert on the question, I am here to tell you that *Zorro the Gay Blade* evoked no interest whatsoever on Christopher Street."[5]

Zorro seemed to be so culturally dead that even the parodies of the character failed to hit the mark.

But still, even stronger than parody is nostalgia. Vague and often convoluted memories of Zorro filtered into pop culture. In the 1980s, movies were full of nostalgic references to classic swashbuckling films that nodded to Fairbanks or to Zorro or to both. *The Goonies* (1985) portrays a misfit bunch of outsider kids who find a lost treasure map in their Astoria, Oregon, attic. They follow it to find the pirate horde of the infamous One-Eyed Willie, even while being pursued by the murderous, and dysfunctional, Fratelli family. Part bildungsroman, part ensemble comedy, part wistful wink to childhood dreams of adventure, the story was written by Steven Spielberg, and his production company, Amblin Entertainment, financed it. Richard Donner, director of *Superman* (1978), also directed *Goonies*. It's no wonder, then, that in Spielberg and Donner's hands, all sorts of classic film tropes show up in the movie. And there's a direct link, once again, between Fairbanks and Superman. The misshapen Quasimodo younger Fratelli brother, named Sloth, turns out to have a heart of gold (and a soft spot for Baby Ruth candy bars, as well as for Chunk, one of the Goonies' gang). In the climactic battle between the kids and the Fratellis on-board the hidden pirate ship, Sloth rips his button-down open to reveal a Superman T-shirt underneath. He then proceeds to knife-slide his way down the main sail on the ship in a direct nod to Fairbanks's own stunt in *The Black Pirate* (1926). The film score in *The Goonies* is the same one used by Hamilton in *Zorro: The Gay Blade*.

Wherever classic film nostalgia appeared in the 1980s, Zorro seemed not far behind. Nostalgia also hovers over 1987's *The Princess Bride*, based on William Golding's eponymous novel (1973). A clear Fairbanks/Zorro character is found in the Man in Black (Cary Elwes), who is also known in the film as the Dread Pirate Roberts, Westley, and the Farm Boy. Another character, Inigo Montoya (Mandy Patinkin), resembles D'Artagnan from *The Three Musketeers* but also Zorro as well, since he is a Spanish master fencer. The film mixes and shakes together genres from classic cinema—the fairytale with the swashbuckler with the love story.[6]

By the time Spielberg rebooted Peter Pan in 1991's *Hook*, starring Dustin Hoffman and Robin Williams, the time had come for Zorro's seeming resurrection on screen. While shooting *Hook* for TriStar Pictures, Spielberg got his inspiration for a new Zorro film. Between takes directing Robin Williams's swordplay, he had an assistant begin to inquire about getting the rights to the Zorro character.[7]

It would take seven years, three directors, and three teams of writers to make what would become *The Mask of Zorro* (1998). At one point, Spielberg faced dire warnings from the studio about the prospects for the film.

After receiving another unsatisfactory script, Spielberg himself faxed pages of notes to the writing team and studio producers over how to fix it. Zorro was a character Spielberg loved as a kid. He just couldn't figure out how to bring him back to life.[8]

———————

As the new Zorro major motion picture project languished in development, Zorro had something of a rebirth in comics. Zorro in comics was sporadic until the 1990s. A few Zorro comics appeared in the early 1950s and early 1960s. They mostly rehashed McCulley's stories or repeated Disney's episodes. Everett Raymond Kinstler's art stood out—so, too, did the work of the great Alex Toth.[9]

Then Don McGregor, with heartfelt nostalgia, brought Zorro back from oblivion in the 1990s. Frank Miller, who brought Batman back to his man-in-the shadows, badass roots, drew the cover art for *Zorro* #1 (November 1993). Sex and violence and a darker Zorro emerged. Zorro became a true comic book hero: he fought not just the third-rate corrupt henchmen of Spanish California but also the original nighttime skulker himself—*Drah-cu-lah*—in a two-part series wherein Zorro just can't understand why the Count has so much game with Zorro's lady! Luckily, for Zorro, a bit of the real Crown of Thorns is at hand for a makeshift weapon against the bloodsucker par excellence.[10] He faced Buck Wylde, a crazy, bloodthirsty trapper; he fought Moonstalker, an aggrieved Native American who had no desire to be saved by Zorro. In short, if Zorro was to become a comic book superhero, he had to fight supervillains.

And not all of the villains were men. Zorro fought, in '90s comics fashion, Lady Rawhide, a scarlet-haired femme fatale, dressed in a barely there red-and-white tie-up corset—*because you gotta maintain period dress, right?* Lady Rawhide was drawn with thigh-high laced leather boots and elbow-length leather sleeves and rodeo gloves. Her cleavage spills out from what might be described as a pair of whip-thin boob suspenders. It was as if Annie Oakley shopped at Frederick's of Hollywood.[11] No joke.

The '90s were a boon for overly sexualized comic book bodies—male and female, but especially female. Sex and violence. Out-of-proportion breasts and behinds, and men with dozens of rows of abs. The juiced body was in during the '90s. *Baywatch*, with hard bodies and oiled skin, was in. And comic book artists, who'd been traditionally underpaid and with little artistic license, now were the main show. They drew their bodies big, beautiful, and buxom as if drawing in a fit of freedom after years of repression.[12] And, of course, sex sells. When artist-led Image comics started producing eye-catching sexy comics, the whole industry began to follow suit.[13]

"Men aren't the only ones with dual identities," writes Don McGregor in *Zorro* #3, which introduces Lady Rawhide.

It seems no one could figure out if it was sexual liberation—*women can now fight and punch, do acrobatics, and handle weapons, so they're actually feminists*—or if it was just a newly fetishized female dominatrix sexploitation. Often, it was a little bit of both, depending on author and audience reception. "It's interesting to note here," writes comics historian Trina Robbins, "that throughout the 1990s, 'bad girl' comics—the kind produced for adolescent and teenage boys, and starring hypersexualized women with large breasts and little clothing—are often preceded by the word lady, as in *Lady Death*, *Lady Justice*, and *Lady Rawhide*, while the feminist comics have the world girl in their titles."[14]

Lady Rawhide got her own comics series after the success of the Zorro run. "Hey, want to read a comic that's *not* just for *little boys*?" an alluring Lady Rawhide says on the cover of the first issue. "Don't *peek* inside now!" says a startled Lady Rawhide on the cover of issue #3. She's drawn topless, but facing away from the viewer, apparently changing into her masked avenger costume in a bathroom!

Zorro was back and sexier than ever, albeit with a hefty dose of objectification and misogyny thrown in.

Cartoons and another TV show brought Zorro back to the small screen. A new live-action series launched by the Family Channel ran in the early 1990s. *Zorro: Generation Z* (2006), a cartoon placing Zorro in the future, gave the masked man—now a teenager—a lightsaber and a motorcycle, instead of a Spanish cutlass and a black horse.

But where was Murrieta in all of this? Steven Spielberg and the writers for *The Mask of Zorro* were ready with an answer. Notably, Spielberg's Amblin Entertainment, with TriStar distributing, took a chance on a maverick Latinx director for the new Zorro film—Robert Rodríguez. Rodríguez's *El mariachi* (1992) made a big splash despite the film's tiny budget (under $10,000). It follows a gun-toting musician through a melee of bullets and death. The sequel/remake, *Desperado* (1995), made an even bigger dent in the marketplace, especially as it brought Spanish actor Antonio Banderas to the public's attention.

Rodríguez jumped at the chance to direct the Zorro movie. "This is cool, a Mexican Zorro!" he remembered thinking at the time. Zorro's Mexican identity was already in the working script when Rodríguez came on board. "I wanted to take it even further that way," he later remembered, "and make him a Mexican bandit running around, you know, like Joaquín Murrieta."[15]

Ultimately, Rodríguez quit the project, mainly since the studios involved (Amblin, TriStar, DreamWorks) were already losing money on the film and they didn't want to pay anything more to "fix the script," according to Rodríguez. New Zealand film director Martin Campbell (*GoldenEye*, 1995) eventually got the nod to direct it, as well as the 2005 sequel, *The Legend of Zorro*.

Casting for *The Mask of Zorro* also took time to get right. The story follows an aging Zorro who ends up bequeathing the mask to the next generation. For the original Zorro, Diego de la Vega, Sean Connery was attached to the role for a time.[16] When that fell though, mainly because Mikael Salomon, the first director on the film, backed out, Anthony Hopkins got the part. For the young Zorro, who begins the film as a Mexican bandit, Alejandro Murrieta, the fictitious brother of Joaquín, Antonio Banderas was selected. Newcomer Catherine Zeta-Jones, from Wales, like Hopkins, got the part of Zorro's love interest, Elena Montero.[17]

The film is the clearest cinematic nod to the influence of the Murrieta legend on Zorro. And yet, it reinforces many of the tired stereotypes of California's annexation to the United States as did the mid-twentieth-century films. It opens in 1821, in California on the eve of Mexican independence. The corrupt Spanish governor Don Rafael Montero (Stuart Wilson) and Zorro (Anthony Hopkins) fight in the main plaza for the last time before Mexican troops are about to take over. Zorro is injured in the duel, but escapes to his wife and infant daughter. Montero has suspected Diego de la Vega is actually Zorro for some time, and when he shows up at the de la Vega hacienda, he finds the same wound on Diego's arm that he'd just given to Zorro in the plaza. Zorro is unmasked, and when the two begin to fight, Diego's wife gets in the way and is mistakenly killed. Montero, who has been in love with her these many years, puts Diego in prison and takes Elena, Diego's daughter, back to Spain to raise her as his own.

The film then skips to twenty years later. We see Alejandro Murrieta (Antonio Banderas), his brother Joaquín, and Three-Fingered Jack fleecing Mexican soldiers out of money. A rogue American soldier, Captain Harrison Love (Matt Letscher), kills Joaquín, while Alejandro gets away. Meanwhile, Montero returns to California and comes up with a plan to mine gold from the region and buy California from Santa Anna, Mexico's president. Diego de la Vega escapes from prison and finds a drunk Alejandro Murrieta. Diego decides to train Alejandro into the next Zorro.

The Mask of Zorro, while nodding to the Murrieta legend, loses the main context of the Murrieta story. The racial violence of Americanization and the gold rush are nowhere to be found. The story takes place when California is still under Mexican rule. There's no rationale given for why Joaquín and Alejandro became bandits in the first place. The inclusion of Captain Harrison Love, a clear nod to the California Ranger who actually led the posse to kill Joaquín Murrieta, is an interesting historical detail. And yet, Captain Love in the film is not an active-duty American soldier. He's simply a former army officer hired to provide muscle for Montero, who is seeking to buy California from Mexico.

Once again, the proverbial "bad apples" are the enemies, not the policy of American annexation and Manifest Destiny. One scene even oddly replays the grisly "Head of Murrieta" story. Captain Love has kept Joaquín's head in a jar of alcohol, just as the legend stated in real life. Captain Love confronts Alejandro (Banderas) with the head, because he suspects that although Alejandro is now dressed in fine clothes and is a well-mannered fop, he is actually the brother of the man in his alcohol jar. Alejandro denies this is the case, and in a truly symbolic moment—although super weird—Alejandro actually takes a drink out of the alcohol liquid that is preserving his brother's head. Thus we see Zorro literally consuming the legend of Murrieta.[18] He toasts Captain Love, biding his time; his revenge is taken later, when, as Zorro, Alejandro scratches an *M* for *Murrieta* on Captain Love's cheek.

All that sounds pretty good, right? Finally, a film that acknowledges Zorro's debt to Murrieta, and also, through a bit of symbolism where the new Zorro drinks the ghastly pickled head juice, Murrieta becomes Zorro. But consider the larger context. The film depicts, like so many early Zorro stories, Murrieta's whitewashing. "Zorro was first constructed as Spanish from Mexican narrative and mythic building blocks," writes one critic of the film, "only to be reconfigured and re-imagined in the film as Mexican."[19] But he's transformed in the film as a hero by losing his rebelliousness. He loses his ruggedness. He sheds his last name and background and trades them for the comforts of affluent life. Alejandro Murrieta changes his name to Alejandro de la Vega. He's taken somebody else's last name and heritage. And he makes allegiance to a country that has historically mistreated his people. In *The Legend of Zorro* (2005), Alejandro de la Vega (Banderas) actively fights *with* the Americans for California's annexation into the United States. His enemies, like the villains in the first film, are Europeans with designs on California. The American villain in the film is another "bad apple"—in essence, not representative of the United States. Zorro's struggles in these two films symbolize the American yearning for freedom from European oppression and the wink to the old fiction that true liberty came to California when the region was saved *from* Mexico by union with the United States of America.[20]

That's messed up.

The Mask of Zorro and its sequel in 2005 essentially tried to resurrect a corpse. Despite the references to Murrieta, and the acknowledgement of Murrieta's influence on Zorro, the films rehash the fantasy that Zorro's struggle heralded the eventual annexation of California by a virtuous United States.

The Mask of Zorro and its sequel did, however, provide a positive service to the Zorro legend. The films were significant in that they made Zorro a serious action hero again. Zorro was brought back from mere parody and nostalgia. Although the films attempted to nod to Zorro's Latinx origins by including the Murrieta legacy, the films only managed to reinforce the whitewashing of Murrieta into Zorro.

But all was not lost for Zorro. In 2005, the same year that *The Legend of Zorro* flopped, Chilean novelist Isabel Allende wrote a new origin story for Zorro. The eponymous novel recast Diego de la Vega as a mestizo, the son of a Spanish father and an indigenous mother. Allende's novel became the new Zorro ground zero.

———————

It's in the comics that Zorro has been reborn. Allende's novel provided a new starting point for the character. Zorro, as a masked, dual-identity hero with a mixed heritage soon thrived in the comics. He soon joined forces with other diverse avengers. What happens when you team up an African American avenger with a Latinx vigilante?

Justice, my friends. Or, at least, spaghetti western justice.

In 2015, Dynamite Entertainment published a *Django/Zorro* seven-issue crossover graphic novel. At this writing, it is the first and only official sequel to a Quentin Tarantino film—*Django Unchained* (2012)—and a movie adaptation of the *Django/Zorro* graphic novel is slated for a 2022 release. The art, by Esteve Polls, was magnificent. Iconic. Just putting Zorro and Django side by side looked, well, really cool. The colors, by Brennan Wagner, were mood driven and helped the reader navigate flashbacks and cuts; they conveyed filmic emotions. The story was by Quentin Tarantino and by Zorro-writing veteran Matt Wagner (the *Mage* trilogy, among many others). Wagner wrote the Zorro trilogy published by Dynamite (2008) and based on Allende's 2005 novel, *Zorro*. So *Django/Zorro* was a sequel both to *Django Unchained* and the Zorro storyline by Wagner.

And that teaming showed. Tarantino invited Matt Wagner to his Los Angeles home, and the two spent a few days brainstorming the story. They watched old Zorro movies in Tarantino's home theater. The two became buds. Tarantino especially liked the Republic serial *Zorro's Fighting Legion* and used it as inspiration for the graphic novel.

What readers get with *Django/Zorro* is a tension between competing visions. On the one hand, Django continues as an ex-slave ready and willing to kill anyone who stands in the way of freedom. And, in *Django Unchained*, Django Freeman is the *only* one who is fighting for freedom, it seems. Everyone else is simply subservient or too oppressed or, in the case of Stephen the House Slave (Samuel L. Jackson), too drunk with the power that collaboration has given him.

On the other hand, we meet Don Diego de la Vega, in his hoity-toity carriage, playing the fop. He just so happens to cross paths with Django. (This is an element taken from the *Django Unchained* film, where he crosses paths with Dr. King Schultz, played by Christoph Waltz.) Don Diego is old. It's the late 1850s, and so we catch up with Zorro in the winter of his life. Yet, he's still trying to protect the oppressed. He's traveled to Arizona—where the action begins—to deal with the so-called Archduke Gurko Langdon, who has forged his wife's lineage and propped himself up as ruler in an alternate history of pre-US Arizona.

And here's the tension: Django exists as a one-man riff on a false mythology of American slavery—that, for instance, enslaved people didn't fight back. That the enslaved were all more like Stephen the House Slave than like Django Freeman. Anyone who didn't fight back was ultimately a collaborator in his or her own enslavement. Yet, the reality is that enslaved people did fight back. They ran away. They resisted—some might say Frederick Douglass truly gained his freedom when he hit an overseer who wanted to whip him, not when he later escaped. Slave owners lived in constant fear of uprisings and rebellions. Django might inspire cheers as he kills racists and slave owners. But he wasn't the only one who fought back.

Zorro, in contrast, becomes another mentor for Django. He hires Django, but really intends to enlist him in his cause to bring down the Archduke of Arizona. There is growth for the Django character. He understands that perhaps there are others ready to stand up to injustice, like he is. The tension lies in the ends that both characters seek. Django seems intent on blowing everything to hell, whereas Zorro has a subtler, chess-like approach. He intends to bring down the archduke and help the Indians, but leave the social order as it is.

What is justice? in other words. That's the subtle conflict at the heart of the *Django/Zorro* graphic novel that's never really settled by the end. Sure, the archduke is taken out, but so are others. For instance, Bernardo, Zorro's trusty manservant, is killed in the graphic novel while helping the two avengers, but his death is never really commemorated. He'd served Zorro for decades, and with one shot, he's dead.

Both Django and Zorro are encumbered by a weight of history. The history of slavery. The history of Spanish, Mexican, and American outrages in the West. Perhaps, when viewed within each of their respective stories, justice is done according to each. But, when placed together, one wonders what justice looks like now that Django and Zorro inhabit the same universe. For all the killing and death the two masked avengers unleash, is it justice or simply revenge?

———————

In 2015, Zorro had another first: he finally died. The Dynamite comics crossover *The Lone Ranger: Death of Zorro* actually kills the original Diego de la Vega. It's *Death of Superman* epic in its finality, albeit temporary. Zorro, like Superman, doesn't actually die forever. These characters always come back, because audiences keep going back to the well of those legends to draw up new meaning. In *Death of Zorro*, a legion of masked heroes band together to avenge the death of Zorro. In the process, a new Zorro gets the mask, this time an indigenous young man whom Diego de la Vega had mentored as a surrogate father.

But Zorro's resurrection in the comics was not yet complete. To celebrate the original caped avenger's one hundredth birthday, American Mythology Productions released *Zorro: Swords of Hell*. It's a four-part miniseries that's smartly written and gorgeously drawn and colored. *How do you tell new stories about Zorro, the fox, after one hundred years?* Answer: hordes, like actual hordes, of the undead. Westerns are sort played out these days, according to Mike Wolfer, writer of an upcoming Zorro storyline:

> Zorro was one of the earliest American literary heroes, created during the time when Westerns were enjoying immense popularity, but with each passing decade, we're farther and farther away from the age when Western themes, and the mystique of the "wild west," were still within living memory of many readers.[21]

Many readers, in short, don't get excited about the West anymore. "A century later," says Wolfer, "modern readers are a bit reluctant to embrace western themes, so basically, we're appealing to more modern tastes by skewing our tales toward horror, and the fun aside is that we're introducing the 'Old West,' its settings and themes to readers who have never seen it."[22]

Correction: *herds*, like actual *herds*, of the undead.

The writer of the new series, David Avallone (*Bettie Page, Elvira, Twilight Zone / The Shadow, Doc Savage*), gives us a one-page setup, and then the aforesaid hordes of undead crawl out of the La Brea Tar Pits looking for slaughter, and to slaughter, in particular, Don Diego de la Vega, Zorro's wimpy, primpy alter ego.

But that one-page setup is classic. It's a nod to Zorros of the past, but with a twenty-first-century gender sensibility. We find Don Diego fencing with his fiancée, Lolita. It's a scene evocative of the Banderas/Zeta-Jones duel in the 1998 film *The Mask of Zorro*.

The opening scene in *Zorro: Swords of Hell* has the fire we expect in Zorro stories. It has the sexual tension mixed with challenge. It has the you-can't-bed-me-if-you-can't-beat-me sorta vibe. But, under Avallone's direction—with great framing by Roy Allan Martinez—it's not clear who has bested whom. They emerge together, Diego and Lolita, as two formidable equals who have the steel and mettle to face all human foes.

"Your wish was not so foolish that it could not come true," says Diego to Lolita while they fence. "No man is more like Zorro than I."

"The garb of Zorro," replies Lolita, "well suited the romantic dreams of a girl . . . But this WOMAN happily takes Don Diego de la Vega to be her husband . . . without his mask."

But, of course, human foes are not what they will face.

Man and woman, evenly matched, expect a wedding to shortly take place. It's a recurring theme in Zorro stories. Don Diego is always about to marry his love, but then—enter bad guys who require the wedding to be postponed.

So then, enter bad guys: the undead horde.

Virtuoso swordplay and derring-do just might not be enough this time, we find out. Not when Zorro faces an unknown evil. "I had not known when I started the series that the great South American novelist Isabel Allende wrote a Zorro novel," says writer Avallone. "When I pitched my story, which involves the deposed alcalde, the mayor of Los Angeles who Zorro defeats in the origin story, making a deal with a warlock, or should I say brujo, to make the dead rise out of the La Brea Tar Pits and conquer L.A. for him, I thought, *Well, what's Zorro going to fight that with?* It's not *The Walking Dead*; he's not going to cut all their heads off. You've gotta come up with a challenge that you can't stab your way out of."[23]

And that's the main challenge Zorro faces in *Swords of Hell. How do I fight these creatures, who look eerily reminiscent of sixteenth-century Spanish Conquistadors?* (They are drawn immaculately, these undead conquistadors, by Roy Allan Martinez—*Son of M, Immortal Iron Fist, She-Hulk*. The coloring, by Emmanuel Ordaz Torres, is also spot on, from Lolita's red dress to the shadowy menace of the creatures.)

Zorro: Swords of Hell, comes with three alternate covers, a common practice these days. There's the Demon Cover, by S. L. Gallant; the Nostalgia Cover, by Jon Pinto; and the Toth Ltd. Edition Cover, by none other than the Zorro god himself—Alex Toth. There's even a blank cover edition for the aspiring comic artist out there to add her own take on *Swords of Hell*. You're in for a real treat, in other words.

The reader, at the end of *Zorro: Swords of Hell*, part I, is left without knowing the fate of our heroine, Lolita, or whether Zorro will be able to figure out how to kill these undead enemies.

A horde of the undead is not the only enemy Zorro faces. The myth of forced diversity—it's the other important, and perhaps even more insidious, villain Zorro battles in *Swords of Hell*. It's also an important enemy for the book's writer, David Avallone.

"There is no such thing as forced diversity," Avallone told me in a phone interview. "There's only forced lack of diversity. Any all-white, all-male state has been created artificially by white males."[24]

Forced diversity is the derisive criticism of historical or fictional renderings of the past wherein the writer supposedly "forces diversity" by creating the presence of so-called nonnormative peoples. In other words: gay people, people of color, people of diverse sizes or abilities. All these people weren't really part of the past, so this theory goes, because "that's not how it was *then*." White people, especially white men, were those who held power, those who made history. And if we're saddened and shocked by that, well, that's because that was reality then. We shouldn't, according to critics of diversifying the past, simply create diversity in the past that wasn't there, all because we, in today's world, value diversity.

Take, for instance, criticisms of the hit Broadway musical *Hamilton* or snipes at the film *The Greatest Showman*. Or, perhaps, even the lesbian relationship presented in the Netflix series *Anne with an E*, the reimagining of the classic Anne of Green Gables novels.

Forced diversity! cry those who criticize others for writing such characters into history or art of the past.

They might say the same of *Zorro: Swords of Hell*. (We're still leaving aside the hordes of undead, by the way.) Zorro, as written by David Avallone, is a mestizo. He's a product of mixed origin. His mother was of the Tongva tribe. His grandmother was a *curandera*, or spiritual healer. Avallone began to write Zorro this way before he realized that novelist Isabel Allende had done similarly in her 2005 take on the masked avenger. In the conventional story, started by Johnston McCulley one hundred years ago and picked up in countless iterations and films, Zorro always had a Spanish, or pure, "blue blood," heritage, unsullied by admixture. No Indians or Mexicans in *his* blood.

In Isabel Allende's rendering of the story, said David Avallone in our interview, "Diego is mestizo, making him an appropriate protector of Southern California, you know, by representing all of the people. But also that, canonically, his grandmother was a *curandera*. Better to use grandma than a random witch doctor!"

All that is to say that a Zorro of mixed heritage better represents the reality of the diversity that was actually part of Southern California's history. Also, Avallone uses the Tongva tribe as the indigenous people who inhabited the geography that would become present-day Los Angeles. And it's the Tongva tribe, Avallone told me, who hold the key to Zorro's victory over the undead hordes. "When they said make it supernatural, I was actually relieved," Avallone told me. "That I haven't seen before. That's a fun way to go with Zorro. You have to give Zorro a challenge he can't just swing a blade at. He has to draw on other resources, or ways of approaching the world. I have his grandmother saying, 'You can't just stab it to death.'"[25]

David Avallone has written a story that makes sense. "What would the Tongva have called a witch doctor?" he told me. "So, that's where you get the Jaguar Brujo in the story. And that's where you get the *curandera*." The underworld, he told me, is connected to the La Brea Tar Pits; he recalled reading in Allende's novel a comment made by characters that it was a place of spirits.

Diversity, in other words, is not forced in the new take on Zorro. If you take seriously the social context, the ethnic makeup of Southern California at the time, and the ways in which spiritual worldviews mixed and overlapped, then *Zorro: Swords of Hell* becomes, ironically, a more accurate representation of the time than the strictly white, aristocratic, Spanish fantasy heritage of many traditional renderings of the Zorro story.

"I will say this one thing," Avallone told me in our interview, "which is not an excuse but an explanation, that a lot of sexism and racism in art is a lack of imagination if nothing else. I think if you're a writer sitting at a keyboard and you're writing a scene and the scene calls for a doctor to walk into the room and you're a white middle-aged guy, you go, 'Well, a white middle-aged guy walks into the room.' In the twenty-first century, you have to be really squintin' hard. . . . I mean, I haven't had a white middle-aged doctor in thirty years."

So, the idea of forced diversity is perhaps more fantastical than Zorro fighting the undead, which he does actually do by issue #2. But, he has help. David Avallone was at first reticent to write Bernardo, Zorro's mute manservant, into his new comic series. He always seemed too much like the stereotypical Tonto character from the Lone Ranger. But, here again, Avallone saw Bernardo as an important link to the Tongva tribe and the key to Zorro's salvation.

The incredibly sad part, Avallone told me, is that the Tongva have all but disappeared. There is really no thorough description of their spiritual words. Was the underworld a place of pleasure or of torment? Was the underworld goddess a crone or a beauty? These are issues Avallone tackles in issues #3 and #4. But what is certain is that there is no failure of imagination in Avallone's rendering of Zorro and his worlds.

Zorro is dead—or, at least, Zorro is fighting the undead. And his story has once again become relevant to a society clamoring for authentic representation in the tales we read or watch or listen to.

And there's another reality at play. Latinx comics creators don't necessarily need Zorro to express their identities. Zorro is there as a source of inspiration, but there are many others. I think about an artist and writer like Javier Hernández, creator of the graphic novel *Daze of the Dead* (1998). His character, El Muerto, is the alter ego for Diego de la Muerte, a nod to the influence of Zorro's other self, Diego de la Vega. "Using Zorro as just one focal point," Hernández explained to me in an interview, "I've often told people how amazing it is that during the '50s young white American kids would be sitting in front of their television sets cheering for the swashbuckling

Disney TV hero Don Diego de La Vega. And even earlier than that were the movies and serials from the '20s through the '40s. One can debate the validity of the 'Latinoness' of those portrayals, but American audiences were being exposed to a Latinx character in full superhero attire and adventure."[26] Zorro was the closest thing to an authentic Latinx hero for many twentieth-century kids.

But by the 1970s, there were others—for instance, Marvel's White Tiger, a Puerto Rican martial artist from the Bronx, or El Diablo, created by DC Comics.[27] Hernández writes:

> When I did start toying with the idea of creating my own stories, I instinctively felt, wanted to, create characters that reflected a Mexican background. It was admittedly a response to having not seen many of those type (if any) of characters in the comics and shows I loved as a kid. Not necessarily a defiant "I'll show them!" attitude, but more of a desire to show interesting new things that people were choosing not to tap into, the way they would with, for example, Greek or Norse mythology. I looked at it like, "I'm Mexican, my parents come from Mexico. . . . Why not use this stuff?"[28]

Zorro may have provided early inspiration for Latinx comics creators, but perhaps the largest source of inspiration is simply each creator's own particular experience.

Hernández's work blends Mexican folklore into his story about a regular guy who suddenly receives supernatural powers from a pair of Aztec gods after dying and being brought back to life. He uses his Mexican heritage to add an interesting new twist on the superhero genre. And Hernández is just one of many—just one example—of a multitude of Latinx creators who are simply writing from their own experience of being Mexican and American, Puerto Rican, Dominican, and so forth. As Frederick Luis Aldama, a prominent comics historian, notes: "Latinx authors, artists, and directors are extraordinarily creative and *recreative* in what they do to actively add to and transform mainstream superhero comic book storyworlds."[29] Zorro might just end up refashioned, reshaped, and reborn in new ways—a product of authentic representation, a well to return to in order to draw up fresh new meaning for the present.

As for Zorro himself, at this writing, a major motion picture, tentatively titled Z, is in preproduction (from Sobini Films). Slated to star in the movie are Mexican actor Gael García Bernal and Kiersey Clemons. It's supposed to take place in an apocalyptic future. "The western frontier," reads the current synopsis, "has re-emerged and, as in the past, a hero will answer the people's cry for justice."

Zorro is dead.

Long live Zorro!

EPILOGUE
Zorro in an Alternate Nerdverse

Final Research Log
East Baton Rouge Parish Library
10:46 AM

AT THE MID CITY MICRO-CON, there were no lines. There was no endless queue for some "CON EXCLUSIVE" vintage 1960s Batmobile; no wraparound-twice wait for a celebrity signature; no odd human switchback for limited-edition nerdom paraphernalia. There was no extruded plastic, as far as I could tell. No dealers, no purveyors, no hawkers of generic glossy prints. There were no Agents of Merch, in other words. The Mid City Micro-Con, brought to you by my very own EBR Library at the main Goodwood Branch, in a phrase, didn't suck.

And what was on offer at the Micro-Con was pretty, well, great.

There were friendly librarians who bid you a cordial *Hello, good sir!* from where they sat behind a folding table at the library's entrance. They had everything you needed—schedule, meal tickets, free library swag—all right there for you in a premade plastic tote. There were scores of Micro-Con buttons for the taking, all of which instantly proclaimed the con's mission of intentional inclusion. Each button displayed a diverse superhero—Miles Morales (Spider-Man), Kamala Khan (Ms. Marvel), Amadeus Cho (the Hulk)—superheroes of color. What the buttons showed in pictures, a prepared statement said in words. The Micro-Con was "a celebration of the diversity of comic book characters, creators, and their fans." One smiling librarian, a self-proclaimed nerdist and a woman of color, told me her name. "Erica," she said as she extended her hand. "Like, AMERICA." She winked.

I really dug the Mid City Micro-Con.

I was here because I, too, am a nerd. This is my local library. When I saw that the good folks of my local library were putting the Micro-Con together for a second annual event—2018's Micro-Con was "Welcome to Wakanda" in celebration of Marvel Studios' *Black Panther*, a blockbuster both at the box office and culturally—I sent an e-mail to the organizers begging them to let me speak about Zorro. They said: OK, great! So, I came prepared to explain the Latinx origins to Zorro, how they've been whitewashed over the years, and how Zorro's ghost is really about exposing a history of racial violence, exclusion, and cultural appropriation. But that would be later in the day. Now, I was here to enjoy and to learn from the amazing lineup they've put together of industry creators and critics.

I took my plastic tote and entered through the library's sliding glass doors. There were vendors, but what they were selling was their own work. "It's what I imagine the early comic conventions were," I heard one participant say. "Like, the creators are the main show; they're sharing their art and the worlds they've made." I thought that was a pretty good synopsis.

The vendor tables stretched from the library foyer to the inside, all the way back to where the Micro-Con faded into book stacks. But also, the creator tables wrapped around, from the foyer to the hallway on my right, and on into a large-ish makeshift exhibit hall.

I saw Keith Chow, creator of the pop culture blog *The Nerds of Color*, coeditor of two Asian American comics anthologies—*Secret Identities* (2009) and *Shattered* (2012)—as well as the host of not one, not two, but three podcasts: *Hard NOC Life*, *Southern Fried Asian*, and *DC TV Classics*.

I saw TaLynn Kel, author of two memoirs, avid essayist, cosplay guru, and educator. NORMAL IS A LIE read a bold vinyl banner skirting her table. The quote comes from one of Kel's essays. "Normal is a lie," she wrote. "It always has been. It's a curated reality that is often the depiction of aspirational whiteness . . . a reality that actively excludes races, bodies, sexualities, and ideologies that do not conform with the image whiteness seeks to have of itself."[1] Kel is passionate about the nerdy things she loves and about bringing justice and authentic representation to the fandom worlds she inhabits.

I saw Chip Reece, writer and creator of the comic book *Metaphase* (2015), the first graphic novel featuring a superhero with Down syndrome. The main character, Ollie, was inspired by Chip Reece's own son, who was born with the condition. "I was always a huge comic book fan," I heard Reece say later. "I wanted that for my kid too. Whether or not he likes comics when he gets older, I don't know. But I wanted him to be able to have that choice, that there would be a book that he could connect with and feel included."

I saw Jason Reeves, the Los Angeles–based owner and founder of 133art, an indie comics publishing company that promotes the work of artists of color. He's also the creator of the *OneNation* series of comics. It follows the adventures of Paragon, an African American superhero and ex-soldier who has to save the world by saving it from itself. Paragon uses a battle-tattered American flag as his mask and hood. Reeves's collaborator on *OneNation* is Luis Guerrero, a native of Guadalajara, Jalisco, Mexico. Guerrero wasn't at the Micro-Con, but I know his work. He's a rising star at DC Comics, working on the new line of *The Flash*.

And I saw other creators at the Micro-Con. There was Antoine GHOST Mitchell, a local artist and writer who's been crafting, for the past twenty years, in *Lord of the Rings*–style world-building thoroughness, an Afro-fantasy graphic novel called *Sankofa's Eymbrace*. There was a dynamic sister-brother duo—Lauren and Jason Reaves—working to publish their first comics series. And there was Shequeta Smith, a filmmaker presenting her new short movie, *The Takeover*, a story about what happens when best friends Ashley (a Caucasian fashion designer) and Tisha (an African American comics artist) swap bodies for twenty-four hours and have to experience the online dating scene in each other's shoes.

I saw a lot of really cool artists. Artists who, many explained later, never saw themselves represented in the worlds of fandom, but are now literally writing themselves into the comics narrative.

Lastly, I saw the Micro-Con's special guest, Ashley A. Woods. I introduced myself as she was setting up her table, laying out special prints of characters she was working on. Woods is a Chicago-born artist and illustrator who trained at the International Academy of Design and Technology. She received a degree in gaming and graphic design. Woods is a self-professed gaming nerd. She published her first comics series while still in school, *Millennia War* (2006). She spent time in Japan, showing her work in Kyoto. Her style reflects the manga/anime work she grew up loving. *Black Comix*, an anthology of African American comic book art, included some of her work.

Woods's big break came after actress Amandla Stenberg (*The Hunger Games*) saw her art at a comics convention. Stenberg and Sebastian Jones recruited Woods to illustrate their new series, *Niobe: She Is Life* (2015). It follows Niobe Ayutami, "an orphaned wild elf teenager and also the would-be savior of the vast and volatile world of Asunda." *Niobe: She Is Life* was the first comic book nationally distributed through the direct market that had a black woman as a protagonist, with black women both writing and illustrating the book.

And there's more. Woods did the line art for Dark Horse's *Tomb Raider: Survivor's Crusade* (2017), as well as illustrated the new *Ladycastle* comic, written by Delilah S. Dawson (of YA fiction and Star Wars' new canon novel fame). At this writing, Ashley Woods is doing design work for HBO's *Lovecraft Country* television show, produced by Jordan Peele and J. J. Abrams. Ashley Woods is kind of a big deal, in short. She's killing it. And, as I found out, she's super kind to boot.

"Ah, Zorro!" she told me. *Zft zft zft*—she made the sign of the *Z* in thin air. "I love Zorro!"

A young girl walked up as we were talking. Woods took a picture with the starry-eyed fan. After the picture was snapped, Woods turned and told me, "The Antonio Banderas movie was a favorite of mine!"

A six-foot, five-inch cosplay Gandalf sat comfortably in the far-left corner of the conference room waiting for the first panel to begin. It was not my Zorro panel. It was the panel that everyone, including me, wanted to see: "The Influence of Ink: How Comics Can Change the World." Ashley Woods was on it. And also, Jason Reeves, of 133art, as well as Keith Chow, of the *Nerds of Color* blog, and Chip Reece, *Metaphase* creator and writer. The cosplay Gandalf occasionally faux puffed on his long-stemmed church warden pipe, blowing imaginary smoke rings over the increasingly crowded room.

In addition to the panelists, I was excited to hear from the moderator, Rodneyna Hart. A local artist, an entrepreneur, an aesthetic kickstarter of the

Healthcare Gallery and Culture Candy, as well as the division director of the Regional Louisiana State Museums, Hart is basically a Baton Rouge celebrity. She has her finger on the pulse of all things art and culture in the city. "Talent is equally distributed around the world," she told me in an interview later, "but opportunity is not."[2]

That's Hart's mission: increasing opportunity for those individuals without access. Hart grew up in a family that loved art. Her mother read the dictionary for fun, she told me. Hart had her first solo forty-one-piece exhibition at the age of fifteen. She attended Baton Rouge's premier magnet school, operated as a self-professed "Afro-goth," and went on to study fine art in college. "I am fluent in art snob," she confessed. But for her, holding the worlds of high art and pop culture together comes naturally. She doesn't struggle with the multiple aspects to her identity as a black woman in America. "I interpret blackness," she later explained, "as an intrinsic birthright rather than some kind of performative act." Rodneyna Hart revels in her singular personality. It's a source of pride. "If I ever wanted to deny my 'nerd-dom,'" she said, "moderating a panel at a comic convention would not be the first step!"[3]

The panelists shuffled into place. I noticed that on the other side of the room from cosplay Gandalf was a teenager pulling off what was, to me, a spot-on Miles Morales Spider-Man. He had the red suit with black highlights that Spidey uses in the series—he had supercool kicks on his feet as well. And the teenager just so happened to be a person of color. Just as cosplay Gandalf—a white dude—identified with the *Lord of the Rings*, so, too, the cosplay Miles Morales identified with the new Spider-Man. It was obviously not just about race, it was about who that character represents and who that character was made for. Miles Morales is the Afro-Latinx alter ego to Spider-Man. The character came about, back in 2011, essentially because of a similar conversation to the one we were having at the Micro-Con: representation matters.

"Does Spiderman have to be white?" film critic and writer Marc Bernardin wrote, a sentiment rearticulated by actor Donald Glover, who had just been overlooked for the starring role in *The Amazing Spiderman* series of movies.[4] (The role went to Andrew Garfield, a white actor.)

The answer was no. Thousands of comics fans, and comics creators Brian Michael Bendis and Sara Pichelli, agreed. Bendis and Pichelli went on to introduce a new storyline for Spidey. Queens, the traditional hometown borough of Peter Parker, is an area of New York that has an African American and Puerto Rican population of over 50 percent. It made sense that Spider-Man would reflect that reality because it was, well, realistic.

A film take on the Miles Morales storyline hit theaters in 2018, *Spider-Man: Into the Spider-Verse*. It was sharply written and brilliantly animated with a comics aesthetic—Pow and BAM appear on screen during action sequences, mimicking the comic book tradition—and it made a ton of money. At this writing, the film has made over $375 million worldwide. They produced it for $90 million. It was a smash success. Miles Morales, like Black Panther, the Marvel comics superhero and protagonist of the blockbuster film of the same name, belies the tired industry argument that black and Latinx superheroes are not bankable. It's not true anymore.

And, perhaps, it's never been true. Consider that in 1998 Marvel Studios made *Blade*, starring Wesley Snipes as a superhero vampire killer. The character started in the comics. The movie version starred an African American lead. And the movie broke box office records at the time. It proved, way back in 1998, that a black comic book hero and a black comic book superhero movie had sufficient audience appeal. And yet, it took twenty years for Marvel to make another movie with a black superhero as its lead, *Black Panther* (2018).

The panel began as cosplay Gandalf and cosplay Miles Morales anchored both sides of the room. I thought of what one sage commentator had said of comics conventions. "Same passion, just dressed up in a different suit. And that's all that Comic-Con is: a whole lot of different suits."[5]

Rodneyna Hart, the moderator, gave the floor to the panelists to introduce themselves and their work. I noticed that each of the panelists was young, which seemed to root them in optimism. They wanted to create really cool work. And they were already doing it. And yet, all of them had stories about resistance from gatekeepers—many of those stories rooted in racism. "How did you get that previous job?" or "Did you really do that work?" were questions they'd heard from an older generation of mostly white, mostly male gatekeepers. "But you can't pay your bills," one panelist said, "if you're always triggered by who said what."

Jason Reeves saw this as proof that diversifying gatekeepers is key to inclusion and representation. "If you have brown people," Reeves said, "people of color, behind the scenes as well, you can green-light projects." And that's just why Jason Reeves founded 133art, his publishing company and creative incubator. There's no established channel to get the work of creators of color out to their audience—that is, without publishers and distributors who back the work. The industry needs, according to Reeves, more behind-the-scenes people who can promote inclusive comics.

Keith Chow agreed. "There needs to be people of color," he said, "marginalized folks doing the critiques, putting out the conversation, because that's what changes culture." The reason Keith Chow created the blog *The Nerds of Color* was because he loves the comics world, but often found when he'd say things like, "You know, here is what bothered me . . . ," he would get shut down. *Nerds of Color* provided a space where he could not only share his love for comics but also provide a critical eye based on his experience as an Asian American. "We love the stuff," he told the audience, "but we critique the stuff that we love too. We critique the stuff *because* we love it. We want it to be better. We want it to be representative. And that's really important to us. We need to see ourselves on the screen, on the pages."

Rodneyna Hart, the fearless moderator, keeping the panel on topic, intervened with a crucial question: "How many people in the audience feel that they see themselves on a regular basis in the media?"

Hands went up, but mostly my hand and the hands of other white members of the audience. I remembered that only 2 percent of mainstream media representations include Latinx people, even though Latinx people are the largest minority in the United States.[6] I thought about the irony of Zorro always being played by a white actor throughout the years. Even while Zorro represented a Latinx character in films and on television, he was usually played by a non-Latinx person.

Hart followed the question with an even more pointed one: "How many people see themselves in a positive light?"

Again, white hands went up. Laughs came from the audience. We all knew what Hart was talking about. Jason Reeves cracked a joke about why media representations of black men getting arrested always seemed to be so present. That's not the sort of media representation, obviously, that's positive, he said. Representation in comics is one thing, but also positive representations— authentic depictions that are done by and for people of color—are essential in order to create inclusive fandoms.

As the panelists talked, I couldn't help but think about how several sum-mers ago, near here, at the EBR Library on Goodwood Road, just a mile down the street, hundreds of protesters took to the street outside police headquarters. The protesters demanded that they be heard and that Black Lives Matter. It was the same here, in this panel discussion about comic books. Often the lives and personalities of people of color have not mattered in the worlds of comics and fandom.

Take, for instance, the Marvel Cinematic Universe (MCU), the name for the overarching link between, at this writing, twenty-three superhero films. Over a decade, from 2008 to 2019, one film in twenty-three starred a black superhero—again, *Black Panther*. And one film in twenty-three starred a female superhero, *Captain Marvel* (2019), played by Brie Larson, a white actress. To many panelists and audience members in this room, right now, the MCU has given scant proof to the idea that black lives do matter.

The opposite is often the case. The MCU was not made for people of color. Take a review posted on the internet by Kevin Smith, after he saw *Avengers: Endgame* (2019) for the first time. It's the film that culminated the first decade of the MCU's storyline. Kevin Smith is an indie filmmaker, a guy who has often promoted diversity and inclusion in the world of art and media. Marc Bernardin, the critic who got the "Does Spiderman have to be white?" conversation underway, cohosts a podcast with Kevin Smith. But what I mean by "the MCU was not created for people of color" was abundantly evident in Kevin Smith's raw one-hour YouTube stream-of-consciousness review of *Avengers: Endgame*. Smith weeps during this solo review. He rehashes the major plot points of the movie and what it means to him—although unstated, a white, middle-aged, heterosexual father. Smith can see himself in Tony Stark's final great sacrifice for humanity. Iron Man "saved everyone," Smith says holding back tears. Smith mentions the touching scene where director Jon Favreau, cast in the movie as a friend of Tony Stark, has to console Stark's now fatherless daughter. She asks for cheeseburgers. "I'll give you all the cheeseburgers you want," Favreau's character says. Smith wipes tears from his eyes. He can also see himself in Captain America, Steve Rogers, who finally gets a chance to live a life with his lost love, Peggy Carter. "Cap finally gets a win!" Smith tells the YouTube audience. The MCU was made for Kevin Smith.

Those movies were made for me, too, I realized. That's what representation means. That's what these panelists, right here at the Micro-Con, were saying.

If comics fandom is just the same passion—the power of storytelling—dressed up in different suits, what happens when there's no suit for your passion? Art, at its best, even sometimes not at its best, provides a narrative within which we find meaning. What does it say about our culture, about our nation, about our entertainment, when we've written out a significant portion of our people from the stories that we tell? Thanos's snap in *Avengers: Endgame* was not nearly so catastrophic.

"Batman could never be black," Keith Chow quipped to the audience, "because his superpower is his white privilege." The audience laughed because there was something deeply true about the statement. Intentional inclusion is not just about making all the existing superheroes into people of color. Rodneyna Hart provided some deeper insight. You have to look "at the core of the character to see how much of their identities are tied up in the social climate they were developed in." For Spider-Man, an outsider from Queens, there's nothing that would prevent a Miles Morales from being a representative character. Batman, on the other hand, is different. "Batman," Hart said, "is white. Super white. Read-any-book-and-never-question-the-race-of-the-protagonist white. He's also rich. Super rich. Inherited multigenerational wealth allows him enormous expendable income, the freedom to be a broadly innocuous playboy, and the ability to disappear in social situations."[7]

Zorro, I thought. The conversation is crucial to understanding Zorro's core character. Can Zorro be made into a representative, inclusive character? Does Zorro only work as a masked hero because of the last hundred years of whitewashing? Of forgetting his Latinx origins?

The answer is both yes and no. It's a yes because Don Diego de la Vega has a huge amount of rich, white privilege that enables Zorro to hide in plain sight. In fact, I've argued that it is this very white privilege part of the dual identity alter ego that was elemental in the superhero genre.

But the answer is also no—Zorro can be and, in many ways, has always been representative. Zorro, at his core, is a product of American collisions—of culture, of race, of violence, of class. Zorro is a product of American culture just as much as jazz is a product of American culture, or rock 'n' roll, or even comics in general. Zorro carries the Mexican American experience. And part of that Mexican American experience has always included racial violence and cultural appropriation. Zorro's part in developing the secret identity, the alter ego, is embedded in the superhero genre and it's also embedded in American history.

Minorities, especially, have always had to carry a "secret identity"— W. E. B. Du Bois called it a "double-consciousness"—to survive as people of color in America. "The superheroic alter ego is a fantastic analogy," Rodneyna Hart told me, "perfect for demonstrating the necessity of managing perceptions for [minority] safety, success, well-being and growth." "Superheroes," she continued, "also bear the burden of a cloaked identity; crossing that boundary is a heavy decision with great potential for personal loss but also holds a chance to reap a great gain. Minorities do this tirelessly, and with substantially less fanfare."[8]

One of the basic superhero tropes, then, the secret identity, finds perhaps its most culturally significant expression in the many varieties of minority experience in America. And so, even if superhero movies, or comics, are only now just beginning to be representative, the superhero genre itself—in secret identities, in code-switching, in the immigrant experience—is already deeply indebted to American diversity.

That's a place to start, I thought to myself as the panel ended. There was a whole lot more passion in this room than only that represented by cosplay Miles Morales in the corner. There's work to be done, and the work is already happening in the art the panelists in front of me are doing. Journalist Steve Rose argues, in a phrase he admits that Martin Luther King Jr. certainly wouldn't have said, that "the arc of nerdom is bending toward justice."[9] I would agree. But only because of those here, and people like them, these creators and critics, these fans, who make it so. We need to make more suits and we need to tell better stories.

The panelists returned to the Micro-Con vendors' tables. They were doing what they do best—sharing their art and their passion. Nerds aren't defined by the of a love a thing, as one writer puts it, but rather, "The true sign of a geek is a delight in *sharing* a thing."[10]

As I prepared to share my own research on the Latinx origins of Zorro, and how American diversity laid the foundation of the American superhero, I saw cosplay Gandalf introduce himself to cosplay Miles Morales. The two snapped a picture together. The arc of nerdom, I thought, at least on that day in this tiny corner of the nerdverse, was bending in the right direction.

ACKNOWLEDGMENTS

JOURNEYS ARE BEST MADE IN THE COMPANY OF FRIENDS. The same can be said of writing books. I have many friends to thank, both old and new.

Jason Glaspey, my traveling companion, let me ride shotgun in the "Vandit" for one of the greatest road trips of my life.

Janet Boyd shared with me out of her faith that Lena Boyd's voice should be heard. I hope I have done justice to her story.

Fred Wehling graciously lent me four irreplaceable tomes of *Zorro* TV scripts.

Richard Rodriguez, John Valadez, Rodneyna Hart, David Avallone, and Javier Hernández kindly allowed me to interview them for the book.

Aaron Sheehan-Dean, Charles Shindo, Julia Young, and James Wilkey read early versions of the manuscript. Their comments were always spot on.

Cody Hoesly, the eminent attorney, listened to my questions and gave excellent legal advice on court documents. Dusty Hoesly, the eminent religious studies scholar, made wonderful suggestions and saved me while I was in Beverly Hills.

A host of comics historians and borderlands scholars informed my thinking. Thank you: Frederick Luis Aldama, Brannon Costello, Blake Hausman, Robert McKee Irwin, Chris Gavaler, Mauricio Espinoza, Jose Ulloa, Carlos Velazquez Torres, William Anthony Nericcio, Ilan Stavans, Katlin Marisol Sweeney, Christopher Gonzalez, and J. P. Telotte.

The work of Yunte Huang and Jill Lepore was hugely influential in helping me to craft an approach to Zorro.

The archivists at the Margaret Herrick Library, especially Louise Hilton, were amazing to work with. The History Department at LSU provided generous funds for research and publication subventions. My agent, Britt Siess, held my hand through the whole process. I can't thank her enough. Jerome Pohlen, at Chicago Review Press, is a fantastic editor. Any mistakes that remain are my own.

In memory of Matthew Bennett—this is the kind of book you would've loved, brother.

And to Sarilyn, for whom I wear no masks.

NOTES

Preface: Who Is America's First Superhero?

1. I owe a debt to Jill Lepore's *The Secret History of Wonder Woman* (New York: Vintage, 2015). Lepore writes, "I've got the secret history of Wonder Woman!" in the introduction to her book. Lepore's approach to her superhero subject was both a creative inspiration and an intellectual aide for my investigation into Zorro.

1. The Statue

1. McCulley's original Zorro stories have recently been published in six volumes: *Zorro: The Complete Pulp Adventures by Johnston McCulley*, vols. 1–6 (Sunrise, FL: Bold Venture, 2016).

2. Robin S. Rosenberg and Peter Coogan, eds., *What Is a Superhero?* (New York: Oxford University Press, 2013), 8–9; Chris Gavaler, *On the Origin of Superheroes: From the Big Bang to Action Comics No. 1* (Iowa City: University of Iowa Press, 2015), 52–61.

3. Frank F. Latta, *Joaquín Murrieta and His Horse Gangs* (Sacramento: Bear State Books, 1980); Bruce Thornton, *Searching for Joaquín: Myth, Murieta, and History in California* (San Francisco: Encounter Books, 2003); Lori Lee Wilson, *The Joaquín Band: The History Behind the Legend* (Lincoln: University of Nebraska Press, 2011).

4. A. C. Baine, justice of the peace, affidavits, August 12, 1853, Joaquín Murrieta Papers, California State Archives.

5. Susan Lee Johnson, *Roaring Camp: The Social World of the California Gold Rush* (New York: W. W. Norton, 2000), 46–48.

6. Fabio Troncarelli, *El mito del 'Zorro' y la Inquisición en México: la aventura de Guillén Lombardo (1613–1659)* (Mexico City: Editorial Milenio, 2003).

7. The bulk of Lamport's process is in Archivo General de la Nación, Inquisición, vols. 1496–1498.

8. Tracey Goessel, *The First King of Hollywood: The Life of Douglas Fairbanks* (Chicago: Chicago Review Press, 2015), 227–228.

9. *The Curse of Capistrano* was published in novella form in 1919 but was later published as *The Mark of Zorro* (New York: Grosset & Dunlap, 1924). *The Sword of Zorro* (New York: L. Harper Allen, 1928) was another reprint of *The Curse of Capistrano*, but extremely scarce.

10. McCulley, *Complete Pulp Adventures*.

11. Eric Trautman et al., *Lady Rawhide: Sisters of the White Rose (Issues #1–#5)* (Mt. Laurel, NJ: Dynamite Entertainment, 2014), bonus materials, original script.

12. McCulley, *Complete Pulp Adventures*, vol. 1, *The Mark of Zorro*, 51–52.

13. James H. Creechan and Jorge de la Herrán Garcia, "Without God or Law: Narcoculture and Belief in Jesús Malverde," *Religious Studies and Theology* 24, no. 2 (2005): 5–57. The classic treatment of bandits as social avengers is Eric Hobsbawm, *Bandits* (New York: New Press, 2000; 1969), and his *Primitive Rebels* (New York: W. W. Norton, 1973). For a recent treatment of borderland folk heroes, see Robert McKee Irwin, *Bandits, Captives, Heroines, and Saints: Cultural Icons of Mexico's Northwest Borderlands* (Minneapolis: University of Minnesota Press, 2007).

14. Mauricio Tenorio-Trillo, *I Speak of the City: Mexico City at the Turn of the Twentieth Century* (Chicago: University of Chicago Press, 2013), 23–24.

2. The Pyre

1. Gerard Ronan, *The Irish Zorro: The Extraordinary Adventures of William of Lamport* (Dublin: Brandon Books, 2004), 280–283.

2. McCulley, "Zorro Deals with Treason," in *Complete Pulp Adventures*, 1:201.

3. "Rodrigo Ruíz de Zepeda Martínez, Auto general de la fe, 19 de noviembre 1659. Imprenta del Santo oficio, por la viuda de Bernardo Calderón en la calle de San Agustín, México, licencia del 20 de diciembre de 1659," Biblioteca Digital Mexicana, accessed November 2, 2018, http://bdmx.mx/documento/galeria/auto -general-fe-1659-imprenta-santo-oficio/fo_01, 53r.

4. Troncarelli, *El mito*, 284.

5. "Proclama por la liberación de la Nueva España de la sujeción a la Corona de Castilla y sublevación de sus naturales," Biblioteca Digital Mexicana, accessed November 2, 2018, http://bdmx.mx/documento/galeria/liberacion-nueva-espana, 40v.

6. Ronan, *Irish Zorro*, 165.

7. Ronan, 263–266.

8. Troncarelli, *El mito*, 283.

9. Ronan, *Irish Zorro*, 280–283.

3. The Legend of Don Guillén de Lampart

1. Theodore G. Vincent, "The Blacks Who Freed Mexico," *Journal of Negro History* 79, no. 3 (Summer 1994): 257–276.

2. Theodore G. Vincent, "The Contributions of Mexico's First Black Indian President, Vicente Guerrero," *Journal of Negro History* 86, no. 2 (Spring 2001): 148–159.

3. Vicente Riva Palacio, *Memorias de un impostor: D. Guillén de Lampart, rey de México* (Mexico City: Manuel C. de Villegas, 1872), v. My translation from the Spanish original here and following.

4. Riva Palacio, *Memorias*, v.

5. Vincent, "Contributions," 156.

6. Vincent, 154–155.

7. Riva Palacio, *Memorias*, vi.

8. Riva Palacio, viii.

9. Dolores Rangel, "El proyecto de nación e identidad de Vicente Riva Palacio en *Martín Garatuza*," *Espéculo: Revista de estudios literarios* (2009): 1–10.

10. Vicente Riva Palacio, *Martín Garatuza: memorias de la Inquisición* (Mexico City: J. Ballescá y C.a., Sucesores, 1904; 1868), 795.

11. Riva Palacio, *Memorias*, vi–vii.

12. Riva Palacio, vii.

13. See, for instance, the short work written in the early twentieth century, before the centenary of independence celebration, that touted Don Guillén as a precursor of Mexican independence: Alberto Lombardo, *D. Guillen Lombardo: estudio histórico* (Mexico City: Tipografía Económica, 1901), 1–23.

14. William Lamport wasn't the only Irishman to take up space in Mexican historical memory. During Mexico's war with the United States (1846–1848) a brigade of American Irish Catholics, called the San Patricios, actually fought for Mexico against the northern invader. Many of them remained in Mexico after the war. (Special thanks to Richard Rodriguez for reminding me of this Irish-Mexican link.)

15. Troncarelli, *El mito*, 302–306.

16. Personal e-mail correspondence with Julie Doellingen, M. W. Grand Lodge A.F & A.M. of Colorado, December 5, 2018.

17. Tom Reiss, *The Black Count: Glory, Revolution, Betrayal, and the Real Count of Monte Cristo* (New York: Broadway Books, 2013), 14.

18. Karl Bell, *The Legend of Spring-Heeled Jack: Victorian Urban Folklore and Popular Cultures* (Woodbridge, Suffolk, UK: Boydell, 2017), 19–33.

19. Baroness Orczy, *The Scarlet Pimpernel* (New York: Signet Classics, 2000), 216.

20. Don't worry! We'll get to the ways in which Kane's testimony is suspect, as recent research has uncovered the ways he didn't credit his collaborators—like Bill Finger.

But even Finger's own testimony points to many Zorro influences. Marc Tyler Nobleman and Ty Templeton, *Bill the Boy Wonder: The Secret Co-creator of Batman* (Watertown, MA: Charlesbridge, 2012).

4. Welcome to the Hotel Zorro!

1. A version of this chapter was published as "Welcome to the Hotel Zorro! Such a Lovely Place," *Post Script: Essays in Film and the Humanities* 38, no. 1 (Fall 2019): 52–55.
2. Framed newspaper article on said wall of history: "Lic. Roberto Balderrama Gomez premio nacional de turismo," *La Voz de Sinaloa*, May 10, 1995.
3. Another article mounted on said wall of history: Selene Baldenegro, "Invade a El Fuerte la fiebre por 'El Zorro,'" *La Moral*, January 20, 2008.

5. Back to the Desert

1. Robert McKee Irwin, *Bandits, Captives, Heroines, and Saints: Cultural Icons of Mexico's Northwest Borderlands* (Minneapolis: University of Minnesota Press, 2007); Blake Michael Hausman, "Becoming Joaquín Murrieta: John Rollin Ridge and the Making of an Icon" (unpublished PhD diss., University of California, Berkeley, 2011); Bruce Thornton, *Searching for Joaquín: Myth, Murieta, and History in California* (San Francisco: Encounter Books, 2003); Lori Lee Wilson, *The Joaquín Band: The History Behind the Legend* (Lincoln: University of Nebraska Press, 2011).
2. Frank F. Latta, *Joaquín Murrieta and His Horse Gangs* (Sacramento: Bear State Books, 1980).
3. Baine, affidavits, August 12, 1853.
4. Latta, *Joaquín Murrieta*.
5. Alberto Prago, *Stangers in Their Own Land: A History of Mexican-Americans* (New York: Four Winds, 1973).
6. Pablo Neruda, foreword to *Splendor and Death of Joaquín Murieta* (New York: Farrar, Straus and Giroux, 1972), viii.
7. Manuel Rojas, *Joaquín Murrieta, El Patrio*, 7th ed. (Tijuana, Baja California: Sociedad Histórica de Baja California, 2012).
8. Neruda, *Splendor and Death*, 180.

6. Mexican Argonaut

1. Joseph Henry Jackson, introduction to *Life and Adventures of Joaquín Murieta: Celebrated California Bandit*, by John Rollin Ridge, Western Frontier Library (Norman: University of Oklahoma Press, 1944).

2. Jackson, xii.
3. Jackson, xx.
4. Irwin, *Bandits*, xviii.
5. Brian DeLay, *War of a Thousand Deserts: Indian Raids and the U.S. Mexican War* (New Haven: Yale University Press, 2009), 9–10.
6. Rojas, *Joaquín Murrieta*, 20.
7. Brian Hamnett, *A Concise History of Mexico*, 2nd ed. (Cambridge: Cambridge University Press, 2006), 104–106.
8. McCulley, *Complete Pulp Adventures*, 1:150.
9. Daniel Fogel, *Junípero Serra, the Vatican, and Enslavement Theology* (San Francisco: Ism Press, 1988), 48.
10. Lee M. Penyak and Walter J. Petry, eds., *Religion in Latin American: A Documentary History* (Maryknoll, NY: Orbis Books, 2006), 73.
11. Justo L. González and Ondina E. González, *Christianity in Latin American: A History* (Cambridge: Cambridge University Press, 2007), 107–108.
12. Fogel, *Junípero Serra*, 70.
13. Fogel, 63.
14. González and González, *Christianity*, 109.
15. Fogel, *Junípero Serra*, 73.
16. Rojas, *Joaquín Murrieta*, 25–27. (Rojas actually prints a facsimile of both documents in his book.)
17. Irwin, *Bandits*, 41.

7. I Am Joaquín

1. Johnson, *Roaring Camp*, 27–28.
2. DeLay, *War of a Thousand Deserts*, 86–88.
3. Johnson, *Roaring Camp*, 53.
4. Johnson, 53.
5. Hamnett, *Concise History*, 154.
6. Amy S. Greenberg, *A Wicked War: Polk, Clay, Lincoln, and the 1846 U.S. Invasion of Mexico* (New York: Vintage, 2013), 76.
7. Greenberg, *Wicked War*, xiii.
8. Johnson, *Roaring Camp*, 30–31.
9. Johnson, 30–32.
10. Johnson, 30–32.
11. *Placer Herald* (Placer County, CA), February 3, 1853.
12. *Placer Herald*, February 3, 1853.
13. McCulley, *Complete Pulp Adventures*, 1:182.

14. Irwin, *Bandits*, 43.

15. Wilson, *Joaquín Band*, 156.

16. *Placer Herald*, May 21, 1853.

17. Wilson, *Joaquín Band*, 11.

18. McCulley, *Complete Pulp Adventures*, 1:31.

19. Wilson, *Joaquín Band*, 101.

20. Announcement, publication unknown, n.d., Joaquín Murrieta Papers.

21. McCulley, *Complete Pulp Adventures*, 1:113.

22. Baine, affidavits, August 12, 1853.

23. John Gumperz and Eduardo Hernández-Chavez, "Bilingual Code-Switching (1972)," in *The Language, Ethnicity, and Race Reader*, ed. Roxy Harris and Ben Rampton (New York: Routledge, 2003), 291–302.

24. W. E. B. Du Bois, *The Souls of Black Folk* (Mineola, NY: Dover, 1994), 2.

25. Harry Brod, *Superman Is Jewish? How Comic Book Superheroes Came to Serve Truth, Justice, and the Jewish-American Way* (New York: Free Press, 2012), 18.

26. One of the best expressions of this comes in Michael Chabon's novel *The Amazing Adventures of Kavalier and Clay* (New York: Random House, 2012).

8. The Return of the Head of Joaquín Murrieta

1. Richard Rodriguez, *Days of Obligation: An Argument with My Mexican Father* (New York: Penguin, 1993).

2. Rodriguez, *Days of Obligation*, 135. Italics in original here and following.

3. Rodriguez, 135.

4. Rodriguez, 135.

5. Rodriguez, 136.

6. Rodriguez, 144.

7. Rodriguez, 138.

8. Rodriguez, 141.

9. Alfredo Torres Jr., "The Noose Plagued Mexican-Americans, Too," *San Antonio Express-News*, November 25, 2017, https://www.mysanantonio.com/opinion /commentary/article/The-noose-plagued-Mexican-Americans-too-12381761 .php.

10. Nicholas Villanueva Jr., *The Lynching of Mexicans in the Texas Borderlands* (Albuquerque: University of New Mexico Press, 2017); William D. Carrigan and Clive Webb, *Forgotten Dead: Mob Violence Against Mexicans in the United States, 1848–1928* (Oxford: Oxford University Press, 2013).

9. Writer Behind the Mask

1. "The Builder's Creed," Forest Lawn Memorial Park, accessed June 20, 2018, https://forestlawn.com/2015/12/29/the-builders-creed.

2. State of Oregon v. Joe Doe McLaren or Johnston McCulley, reg. 1280, judgment 41497, in the Circuit Court of the State of Oregon for Multnomah County, November 1909 term, Records Unit, Multnomah County Court.

3. Ancestry.com, year: 1860; census place: Chillicothe, Peoria, Illinois; roll: M653_217; page: 447; family history library film: 803217.

4. Gary Fyke, "Chillicothe's Master Storyteller," *iBi*, Peoria Magazines, May 2013, https://www.peoriamagazines.com/ibi/2013/may/chillicothes-master-storyteller.

5. Fyke, "Chillicothe's Master Storyteller."

6. *Chillicothe (IL) Independent*, September 30, 1882.

7. Fyke, "Chillicothe's Master Storyteller."

8. *Chillicothe (IL) Independent*, December 31, 1881.

9. Fyke, "Chillicothe's Master Storyteller."

10. Seth Bailey, "Johnston McCulley, Alias," *Oakland (CA) Tribune*, May 20, 1923.

11. Bailey, "Johnston McCulley, Alias."

12. "Woos the Muse Out of Doors," *Los Angeles Sunday Times*, March 16, 1924.

13. "Woos the Muse," *Los Angeles Sunday Times*.

14. McCulley, *Complete Pulp Adventures*, vol. 3, *Zorro Rides Again*, 109.

15. McCulley, *Complete Pulp Adventures*, vol. 2, *The Further Adventures of Zorro*, 130.

16. *Daily Illini* (University of Illinois, Urbana-Champaign), April 13, 1900.

17. *Bureau County Tribune* (Princeton, IL), February 14, 1902.

18. Fyke, "Chillicothe's Master Storyteller."

19. Mansel G. Blackford, "The Lost Dream: Businessmen and City Planning in Portland, Oregon, 1903–1914," *Western Historical Quarterly* 15, no. 1 (January 1984): 39.

20. James Labosier, "From the Kinetoscope to the Nickelodeon: Motion Picture Presentation and Production in Portland, Oregon from 1894 to 1906," *Film History* 16, no. 3 (2004): 286–323.

21. Denise M. Alborn, "Crimping and Shanghaiing on the Columbia River," *Oregon Historical Quarterly* 93, no. 3 (Fall 1992): 262–291.

22. *Oregon Daily Journal* (Portland, OR), December 30, 1904.

23. Bailey, "Johnston McCulley, Alias."

24. Bailey, "Johnston McCulley, Alias."

25. Bailey, "Johnston McCulley, Alias."

26. *Oregon Sunday Journal* (Portland, OR), July 9, 1905.

27. Johnston McCulley, "Ga-Guin: The New Joss of Portland's Chinatown," *Sunday Oregonian* (Portland, OR), August 21, 1904.

28. Johnston McCulley, "Queer Scenes in Jap Theater," *Oregon Daily Journal* (Portland, OR), August 30, 1906.
29. Johnston McCulley, "The Play," *Oregon Daily Journal* (Portland, OR), November 23, 1906.
30. Karl Jacoby, *The Strange Career of William Ellis: The Texas Slave Who Became a Mexican Millionaire* (New York: W. W. Norton, 2017), 116.
31. Bailey, "Johnston McCulley, Alias."

10. The Blood of Lolita Pulido

1. *Henry (IL) Republican*, November 14, 1907.
2. Claire Dederer, "What Do We Do with the Art of Monstrous Men?" *Paris Review*, November 20, 2017, https://www.theparisreview.org/blog/2017/11/20/art-monstrous-men.
3. This and all other quotes from her letter were taken from Zylpha McCulley to Robert H. Davis, January 15, 1909, Robert H. Davis Papers, Manuscripts and Archives Division, New York Public Library. (Hereafter cited as Davis Papers.)
4. "Reporter Elopes with His Affinity," *Peoria (IL) Star* and *Peoria (IL) Evening Journal*, January 14, 1909, Davis Papers.
5. "Reporter Elopes," Davis Papers.
6. "Reporter Elopes," Davis Papers.
7. *Morning Oregonian* (Portland, OR), January 15, 1909.
8. *Morning Oregonian* (Portland, OR), January 15, 1909.
9. Zylpha McCulley v. Johnston McCulley, record #46809, case #9510, divorce, Clackamas County, 1909, Oregon State Archives.
10. Robert H. Davis to Mrs. Johnston McCulley, January 21, 1909, Davis Papers.
11. *Macomb (IL) Journal*, January 28, 1909.
12. Johnston McCulley to Robert H. Davis, February 7, 1909, Davis Papers.
13. Robert H. Davis to Johnston McCulley, February 5, 1909, Davis Papers.
14. Davis to McCulley, February 5, 1909.
15. McCulley to Davis, February 7, 1909.
16. Robert H. Davis to Johnston McCulley, February 13, 1909, Davis Papers.
17. "Reporter Elopes," Davis Papers.
18. *Morning Oregonian* (Portland, OR), June 2, 1909.
19. *Morning Oregonian* (Portland, OR), September 25, 1909.
20. *Morning Oregonian* (Portland, OR), October 2, 1909.
21. *Morning Oregonian* (Portland, OR), October 2, 1909.
22. *Oregon v. McLaren or McCulley.*
23. *Morning Oregonian* (Portland, OR), November 12, 1909.

24. *Oregon Daily Journal* (Portland, OR), November 11, 1909.

25. *Oregon v. McLaren or McCulley.*

26. *Oregon v. McLaren or McCulley.*

27. *Morning Oregonian* (Portland, OR), November 19, 1909.

28. *Morning Oregonian* (Portland, OR), November 12, 1909.

29. *Sunday Oregonian* (Portland, OR), August 8, 1909.

30. Ancestry.com, "U.S. City Directories, 1822–1995" (online database), Provo, UT.

31. Janet Boyd, e-mail to author, May 15, 2019.

32. Boyd, e-mail, May 15, 2019.

33. *Oregon Daily Journal* (Portland, OR), November 11, 1909.

34. "Perpetrators of Sexual Violence: Statistics," RAINN, accessed May 7, 2019, https://www.rainn.org/statistics/perpetrators-sexual-violence.

35. Ancestry.com, "U.S. City Directories, 1822–1995" (online database), Provo, UT.

36. Ancestry.com, "1920 United States Federal Census" (online database), Provo, UT.

37. McCulley, *Complete Pulp Adventures*, 1:106.

38. Dederer, "Art of Monstrous Men."

39. Ari Shapiro, "How People Are Grappling with Art from 'Monstrous Men,'" *All Things Considered*, National Public Radio, November 24, 2017, https://www.npr.org/2017/11/24/566387340/how-people-are-grappling-with-art-from-monstrous-men.

40. McCulley, *Complete Pulp Adventures*, 1:242.

41. McCulley, 1:227.

42. McCulley, 1:229.

11. Becoming Zorro

1. Carey McWilliams, *North from Mexico: The Spanish-Speaking People of the United States* (Westport, CT: Praeger, 1990 [1948]), 43

2. McWilliams, 44

3. McWilliams, 44–45.

4. Bailey, "Johnston McCulley, Alias."

5. Brian Steele, *Thomas Jefferson and Nationhood* (Cambridge: Cambridge University Press, 2012), 96.

6. Walter LaFeber, *Inevitable Revolutions: The United States in Central America* (New York: W. W. Norton, 1993), 23.

7. Amy S. Greenberg, *A Wicked War: Polk, Clay, Lincoln, and the 1846 U.S. Invasion of Mexico* (New York: Vintage, 2013), 76.

8. Greenberg, *Wicked War*, 68.

9. McCulley, *Complete Pulp Adventures*, 1:24.

10. Sandra R. Curtis, "Zorro's California," in McCulley, *Complete Pulp Adventures*, 1:18.

11. Richard L. Kagan, *The Spanish Craze: America's Fascination with the Hispanic World, 1779–1939* (Lincoln: University of Nebraska Press, 2019), 6.

12. Sunny Yang, "Fictions of Territoriality: Legal and Literary Narratives of US Imperial Contestation Zones, 1844–1914" (unpublished PhD diss., University of Pennsylvania, 2014).

13. Kagan, *Spanish Craze*, 85–86.

14. Phoebe S. Kropp, *California Vieja: Culture and Memory in a Modern American Place* (Berkeley: University of California Press, 2008), 55–56.

15. Yunte Huang, *Charlie Chan: The Untold Story of the Honorable Detective and His Rendezvous with American History* (New York: W. W. Norton, 2011), 194.

16. Bailey, "Johnston McCulley, Alias."

17. Irwin, *Bandits*, 56.

18. Irwin, 55–56.

19. *San Francisco Call*, August 1, 1910.

20. Johnson, *Roaring Camp*, 46.

21. *Daily Alta California* (San Francisco), May 20, 1858; Irwin, *Bandits*, 55–56.

22. Irwin, 59.

23. *San Francisco Call*, August 8, 1911.

24. *Morning Press* (Santa Barbara, CA), June 14, 1883.

25. Carl Gray, *A Plaything of the Gods* (Boston: Sherman, French, 1912), 6.

26. *Publishers Weekly*, July 6, 1912, 14.

27. *Morning Union* (Grass Valley and Nevada City, CA), July 28, 1916.

28. On these individuals, see, Carlos Manuel Salomon, *Pío Pico: The Last Governor of Mexican California* (Norman: University of Oklahoma Press, 2011), and John Boessenecker, *Bandido: The Life and Times of Tiburcio Vázquez* (Norman: University of Oklahoma Press, 2010).

29. Edward Childs Carpenter, *Captain Courtesy* (Philadelphia: G. W. Jacobs, 1906), 25.

30. Carpenter, 17, 20.

31. Carpenter, 25.

32. Carpenter, 25.

33. Carpenter, 26.

34. *Morning Press* (Santa Barbara, CA), January 6, 1917.

35. *Santa Ana (CA) Register*, June 12, 1915.

36. *Washington (DC) Times*, May 25, 1916.

37. Johnston McCulley, *Captain Fly-by-Night* (Rockville, MD: Wildside, 2013), 115.

12. The Mark of Douglas Fairbanks

1. Douglas Fairbanks, *Laugh and Live* (New York: Britton, 1917), 11.

2. Tracey Goessel, *The First King of Hollywood: The Life of Douglas Fairbanks* (Chicago: Chicago Review Press, 2015), 376n.

3. Goessel, *First King*, 79n.

4. George Grant, *Carry a Big Stick: The Uncommon Heroism of Theodore Roosevelt* (Nashville: Cumberland House, 1996), 83.

5. Goessel, *First King*, 70.

6. Eileen Whitfield, *Pickford: The Woman Who Made Hollywood* (Lexington: University Press of Kentucky, 2007), 100–105.

7. Scott Eyman, *Mary Pickford, America's Sweetheart* (New York: Dutton, 1990), 52–57.

8. Huang, *Charlie Chan*, 148.

9. Huang, 148–150.

10. Wheeler Winston Dixon and Gwendolyn Audrey Foster, *A Short History of Film*, 3rd ed. (Piscataway, NJ: Rutgers University Press, 2018), 21–25.

11. Roger Ebert, "The Birth of a Nation," March 30, 2003, https://www.rogerebert.com/reviews/great-movie-the-birth-of-a-nation-1915.

12. Thomas Dixon, *The Clansman: An Historical Romance of the Ku Klux Klan* (New York: A. Wessels, 1907), 365.

13. Dixon, 321–322.

14. Dixon, 344.

15. Gavaler, *On the Origin*, 179.

16. Gavaler, 190.

17. Blake M. Hausman, "Zorro's Ancestor: Connections Between Zorro and Joaquín Murrieta," *Post Script: Essays in Film and the Humanities* 38, no. 1 (Fall 2019): 8–19.

18. Gavaler, *On the Origin*, 190.

19. At the time, D. W. Griffith worked for Triangle Films, but Fairbanks wasn't directed by him. Fairbanks was slated to star in the strictly entertainment films, while Griffith did his epics.

20. Goessel, *First King*, 86.

21. McCulley, *Complete Pulp Adventures*, 1:260.

22. Goessel, *First King*, 336.

23. Kathleen Feeley, *Mary Pickford: Hollywood and the New Woman* (Boulder, CO: Westview, 2016), 53–54.

24. Charles Shindo, *1927 and the Rise of Modern America* (Lawrence: University Press of Kansas, 2015), 135–139.

25. Goessel, *First King*, 157.

26. Anne Helen Peterson, *Scandals of Classic Hollywood: Sex, Deviance, and Drama from the Golden Age of American Cinema* (New York: Plume, 2014), 5–13.

27. Eyman, *Mary Pickford*, 128.

28. Goessel, *First King*, 241.

29. Goessel, 246.

30. McCulley, *Complete Pulp Adventures*, 1:243.

31. Goessel, *First King*, 251.

32. *Brooklyn Life*, November 27, 1920, 16.

33. Goessel, *First King*, 248–249.

34. John C. Tibbetts and James M. Welsh, *Douglas Fairbanks and the American Century* (Jackson: University Press of Mississippi, 2014), 190.

35. Goessel, *First King*, 244.

36. Lucy Fischer, *American Cinema of the 1920s: Themes and Variations* (Paskataway, NJ: Rutgers University Press, 2009), 41.

37. Goessel, *First King*, 250n, 252.

38. Harriette Underhill, "Fairbanks Is Entertaining and Amusing in 'The Mark of Zorro,'" *New York Tribune*, November 29, 1920.

39. *New York Times*, November 29, 1920.

40. *Philadelphia Evening Public Ledger*, November 15, 1919.

41. *New York Times*, November 29, 1920.

42. Wilson, *Joaquín Band*, 102.

43. Tibbetts and Welsh, *Douglas Fairbanks*, 191.

44. Goessel, *First King*, 252n.

13. Zorro in La La Land

1. Merry Ovnick, "The Mark of Zorro: Silent Film's Impact on 1920s Architecture in Los Angeles," *California History* 86, no. 1 (2008): 28–64.

2. Ovnivk, 47.

3. Ovnick, 43.

4. Ovnick, 43.

5. *Salt Lake Telegram*, January 15, 1922.

6. Robert H. Davis to Johnston McCulley, January 5, 1922, Davis Papers.

7. *Photoplay*, January–June 1922, 442–443.

8. Johnston McCulley to Mitchell Gertz, April 22, 1939, Rudy Behlmer Papers, folder 221 ("The Mark of Zorro Research"), Margaret Herrick Library, Academy of Motion Picture Arts and Sciences.

9. *Oakland (CA) Tribune*, August 27, 1922.

10. *Film Year Book*, 1925.

11. Michael G. Ankerich, "Maurine Powers: How the Actress Became Zorro's Daughter," *Close-Ups and Long-Shots* (blog), May 17, 2014, https://michaelgankerich.wordpress.com/2014/05/17/maurine-powers-how-the-actress-became-zorros-daughter.

12. Tibbetts and Welsh, *Douglas Fairbanks*, 193.

13. Goessel, *First King*, 333.

14. Goessel, 334.

15. Goessel, 333.

16. Goessel, 250.

17. Goessel, 335.

18. *Photoplay*, January–June 1927, 44.

19. *Brooklyn Daily Eagle*, May 9, 1927.

20. Catherine Williamson, "'Draped Crusaders': Disrobing Gender in 'The Mark of Zorro,'" *Cinema Journal* 36, no. 2 (Winter 1997): 3–16.

21. *Billings (MT) Gazette*, August 23, 1929.

22. Louella O. Parsons, "'Mark of Zorro' Is Sold at Record Price!" *San Francisco Examiner*, January 27, 1936.

23. James Bawden and Ron Miller, *Conversations with Classic Film Stars: Interviews from Hollywood's Golden Era* (Lexington: University Press of Kentucky, 2016), 96.

14. The Lone Ranger: Or, How Zorro Gets Whitewashed

1. Zane Grey, *The Lone Star Ranger: A Romance of the Border* (New York: Grosset & Dunlap, 1915).

2. "Hughes, John Reynolds," Texas State Historical Association, June 15, 2010, https://tshaonline.org/handbook/online/articles/fhu18.

3. Jim Harmon and Donald E. Glut, *The Great Movie Serials: Their Sound and Fury* (Milton Park, Abingdon, UK: Routledge, 2014), 301.

4. George W. Trendle to Mary Pickford, June 9, 1947, Mary Pickford Papers, folder 984 ("The Lone Ranger"), Margaret Herrick Library, Academy of Motion Picture Arts and Sciences.

5. Jim Harmon, *The Great Radio Heroes* (Jefferson, NC: McFarland, 2001), 159–160.

6. Dick Osgood, *Wyxie Wonderland: An Unauthorized 50-Year Diary of WXYZ Detroit* (Bowling Green, OH: Bowling Green University Popular Press, 1981), 48.

7. Harmon, *Radio Heroes*, 160.

8. Osgood, *Wyxie Wonderland*, 49.

9. Harmon, *Radio Heroes*, 160.

10. Harmon, 161.

11. Harmon, 161.

12. Harmon, 161.
13. The correspondence between Jewell and Striker has been published online in Martin Grams Jr., "Bass Reeves and the Lone Ranger: Debunking the Myth," 2018, https://docs.wixstatic.com/ugd/41b57b_65fd2f2e944846ddbfa937d8449a43cf.pdf.
14. Grams, "Debunking the Myth."
15. Harmon, *Radio Heroes*, 162.
16. Harmon, 156–157.
17. Grams, "Debunking the Myth."
18. Jack Mathis, *Republic Confidential: The True Story Inside the Valley of the Cliffhangers* (Northbrook, IL: Jack Mathis Publishing, 1992), 37, 176.
19. *Daily News* (New York), April 18, 1937.
20. Mathis, *Republic Confidential*, 102.
21. David Ray Carter, "Frozen in Ice: Captain America's Arduous Journey to the Silver Screen," in *Marvel Comics into Film: Essays on Adaptations Since the 1940s*, ed. Matthew J. McEniry, Robert Moses Peaslee, and Robert G. Weiner (Jefferson, NC: McFarland, 2016), 131.
22. Buck Rainey, *Serial Film Stars: A Biographical Dictionary, 1912–1956* (Jefferson, NC: McFarland, 2013), 712–715.
23. Jack Mathis, *Valley of the Cliffhangers* (Northbrook, IL: Jack Mathis Publishing, 1975), 279.
24. Mathis, 279.
25. William C. Cline, *In the Nick of Time: Motion Picture Sound Serials* (Jefferson, NC: McFarland, 1997), 87–88.
26. Rainey, *Serial Film Stars*, 712–715.
27. Johnston McCulley, "Zorro Saves an American," in *Complete Pulp Adventures*, vol. 5, *A Task for Zorro*, 227–242.
28. Antoinette Girgenti Lane, *Guy Williams: The Man Behind the Mask* (Albany, GA: Bear Manor Media, 2005), 191.
29. Republic did two final generic Zorro-like serials in the 1950s (*Don Daredevil Rides Again*, 1951, and *Man with the Steel Whip*, 1954), but their lease from McCulley of the Zorro character had ended by that time. Extensive stock footage was used from previous Zorro serials.
30. George W. Trendle to Mary Pickford, June 23, 1947, Mary Pickford Papers, folder 984 ("The Lone Ranger"), Margaret Herrick Library, Academy of Motion Picture Arts and Sciences.
31. Rainey, *Serial Film Stars*, 442–444.
32. Jerry Blake, "George J. Lewis," *The Files of Jerry Blake* (blog), accessed July 25, 2019, https://filesofjerryblake.com/serial-character-actors-2/george-j-lewis.

15. Fox Does the Fox

1. Walter Noble Burns, *The Robin Hood of El Dorado: The Saga of Joaquín Murrieta, Famous Outlaw of California's Age of Gold* (New York: Coward-McCann, 1932).

2. "The Robin Hood of El Dorado (1936)," Turner/MGM Scripts, R-712, Margaret Herrick Library, Academy of Motion Picture Arts and Sciences.

3. "Robin Hood of El Dorado," Turner/MGM Scripts.

4. Frank S. Nugent, The Screen, *New York Times*, March 14, 1936.

5. Johnston McCulley to Mitchell Gertz, April 22, 1939, Rudy Behlmer Papers, folder 221 ("The Mark of Zorro Research"), Margaret Herrick Library, Academy of Motion Picture Arts and Sciences.

6. Mathis, *Valley of the Cliffhangers*, 59.

7. Rudy Behlmer, ed., *Memo from Darryl F. Zanuck: The Golden Years at Twentieth Century Fox* (New York: Grove, 1995), 28–29.

8. Peter Lev, *Twentieth Century-Fox: The Zanuck-Skouras Years, 1935–1965* (Austin: University of Texas Press, 2013), 43.

9. Lev, 48.

10. Lev, 46.

11. David Luhrssen, *Mamoulian: Life on Stage and Screen* (Lexington: University Press of Kentucky, 2012), 91–92.

12. Luhrssen, 99.

13. Luhrssen, 99–100.

14. Luhrssen, 100.

15. Behlmer, *Darryl F. Zanuck*, 26–27.

16. Behlmer, 27.

17. Luhrssen, *Mamoulian*, 100–101.

18. "On the Set with 'The Californian,'" *Modern Screen*, November 1940, 40–41.

19. Daniel Eagan, *America's Film Legacy, 2009–2010: A Viewer's Guide to the 50 Landmark Movies Added to the National Film Registry in 2009–2010* (New York: Bloomsbury, 2011), 67.

20. Luhrssen, *Mamoulian*, 100.

21. Bosley Crowther, The Screen, *New York Times*, November 4, 1940.

22. Brian O'Neil, "The Demands of Authenticity: Addison Durland and Hollywood's Latin Images During World War II," in *Classic Hollywood, Classic Whiteness*, ed. Daniel Bernardi (Minneapolis: University of Minnesota Press, 2001), 359.

23. O'Neil, 360–361.

24. O'Neil, 359–362.

25. Addison Durland to Colonel Jason S. Joy, December 6, 1943, Motion Picture Association of America, Production Code Administration Records, Margaret Herrick Library, Academy of Motion Picture Arts and Sciences.

26. Durland to Joy, December 6, 1943.

27. Pancho Kohner, *Lupita Tova: The Sweetheart of Mexico* (Bloomington, IN: Xlibris, 2010), 32.

28. "'The Californian,'" *Modern Screen*, 40–41.

29. "'The Californian,'" 40–41.

30. "'The Californian,'" 40–41.

31. *Chillicothe (IL) Constitution-Tribune*, November 23, 1940.

32. Mae Tinee, "Swashbuckling 'Zorro' Is Fine Entertainment," *Chicago Tribune*, November 24, 1940.

33. *Albuquerque Journal*, December 1, 1940.

34. *Albuquerque Journal*, December 1, 1940.

35. Kate Cameron, "Roxy Showing New 'Zorro,'" *New York Daily News*, November 3, 1940.

36. Bosley Crowther, The Screen, *New York Times*, November 4, 1940.

37. *Hollywood Reporter*, November 4, 1940.

38. *Nebraska State Journal* (Lincoln, NE), November 17, 1940.

39. *Ogden (UT) Standard-Examiner*, November 3, 1940.

40. *El Siglo de Torreón* (Comarca Lagunera, Mexico), January 1, 1941. My translation from the Spanish original.

41. Anne Rubenstein, "Mass Media and Popular Culture in the Postrevolutionary Era," in *The Oxford History of Mexico*, ed. William Beezley and Michael Meyer (Oxford: Oxford University Press, 2010), 648.

42. Ignacio M. Sánchez Prado, "The Golden Age Otherwise: Mexican Cinema in the Mediations of Capitalist Modernity in the 1940s and 1950s," in *Cosmopolitan Film Cultures in Latin America, 1896–1960*, ed. Rielle Navitski and Nicolas Poppe (Bloomington: Indiana University Press, 2017), 241–266.

43. Dolores Tierney, "Latino Acting on Screen: Pedro Armendáriz Performs Mexicanness in Three John Ford Films," *Revista Canadiense de Estudios Hispanicos* 37, no. 1 (2012): 111–134.

44. Sánchez-Prado, "Golden Age Otherwise," 244–251.

45. James Wilkey, "Truth, Justice, and the Mexican Way: Lucha Libre, Film, and Nationalism in Mexico," in *Race and Cultural Practice in Popular Culture*, ed. Domino Renee Perez and Rachel González-Martin (Paskataway, NJ: Rutgers University Press, 2018), 59–75.

46. Mauricio Espinoza, "'Latinizing' Zorro: Domestication and Resistance in Three Cinematic Portrayals of America's First Superhero," *Post Script: Essays in Film and the Humanities* 38, no. 1 (Fall 2019): 20–31.

47. Edwin Schallert, "From Refined to Ruffian—That's Barbara Britton," *Los Angeles Times*, October 22, 1950.

16. Disneylandia

1. Marshall William Fishwick, *The Hero, American Style* (New York: D. McKay, 1969), 220.

2. Ralph G. Giordano, *Pop Goes the Decade: The Fifties* (Santa Barbara, CA: Greenwood, 2017), 37.

3. "Kevin Corcoran," Internet Movie Database, accessed July 25, 2019, www.imdb .com/name/nm0002019.

4. *Walt Disney Treasures: Zorro; Season 1* (Walt Disney Studios Home Entertainment, 2009), DVD.

5. Steven Miles, *Consumerism: As a Way of Life* (Thousand Oaks, CA: Sage, 1998), 64–66.

6. Heather L. Holian, "Animators as Professional Masqueraders: Thoughts on Pixar," in *Masquerade: Essays on Tradition and Innovation*, ed. Deborah Ball (Jefferson, NC: McFarland, 2014), 234–240.

7. Michael Barrier, *The Animated Man: A Life of Walt Disney* (Berkeley: University of California Press, 2007), 138.

8. Neal Gabler, *Walt Disney: Triumph of the Imagination* (New York: Vintage, 2007), 15–18.

9. J. P. Telotte, *The Mouse Machine: Disney and Technology* (Champaign: University of Illinois Press, 2008), 104.

10. Douglas Brode, *Multiculturalism and the Mouse: Race and Sex in Disney Entertainment* (Austin: University of Texas Press, 2006), 90–91.

11. Brode, *Multiculturalism*, 91.

12. James R. Parish, *Pirates and Seafaring Swashbucklers on the Hollywood Screen: Plots, Critiques, Casts and Credits for 137 Theatrical and Made-for-Television Releases* (Jefferson, NC: McFarland, 1995), 186.

13. Barrier, *Animated Man*, 135.

14. Barrier, 242.

15. Barrier, 242.

16. Johnston McCulley to Leo Margulies, December 6, 1957, Leo Margulies Collection, correspondence (incoming) 8/4, University of Oregon Libraries, Special Collections and University Archives.

17. Beatrix Maurine McCulley v. Estate of Mitchell Gertz / Walt Disney Productions, 1961/1965, #C768884, Superior Court of the State of California for the County of Los Angeles, Archives and Records Center.

18. Barrier, *Animated Man*, 237.
19. Leonard Mosley, *Disney's World* (Chelsea, MI: Scarborough House, 1990), 231.
20. Mosley, 232.
21. Mosley, 233.
22. Barrier, *Animated Man*, 141.

17. Guy Williams Becomes Zorro

1. Girgenti Lane, *Guy Williams*, 1.
2. Girgenti Lane, 44.
3. Girgenti Lane, 62–68.
4. Girgenti Lane, 68.
5. Girgenti Lane, 70.
6. Girgenti Lane, 88.
7. Girgenti Lane, 84.
8. Gabler, *Walt Disney*, 496.
9. Girgenti Lane, *Guy Williams*, 88.
10. Alfred Richard, *The Hispanic Image on the Silver Screen: An Interpretive Filmography from Silents into Sound, 1898–1935* (Santa Barbara, CA: Greenwood, 1992), xxvii.
11. Girgenti Lane, *Guy Williams*, 88.
12. Girgenti Lane, 88.
13. Girgenti Lane, 98–99.
14. Girgenti Lane, 86.
15. Fred Wehling, telephone interview with author, March 26, 2019.
16. Bob Wehling and Norman Foster, "Presenting Señor Zorro" (prod. no. 5850-004), *Zorro*, season 1, episode 1, first draft, April 4, 1957, personal archive of Fred Wehling.
17. Wehling and Foster, "Presenting Señor Zorro."
18. Wehling and Foster, "Presenting Señor Zorro."
19. It's a four-episode arc from season 1, episodes 31–34: "The Man with the Whip," May 8, 1958; "The Cross of the Andes," May 15, 1958; "The Deadly Bolas," May 22, 1958; "The Well of Death," May 29, 1958.
20. Season 2, episodes 6–9: "The New Order," November 13, 1958; "An Eye for an Eye," November 20, 1958; "Zorro and the Flag of Truce," November 27, 1958; "Ambush," December 4, 1958.
21. Bob Wehling, "The New Order," (prod. no. 7206), *Zorro* season 2, episode 6, shooting script, April 25, 1958, personal archive of Fred Wehling.
22. Girgenti Lane, *Guy Williams*, 204–205.

23. Girgenti Lane, 200.

24. Gabler, *Walt Disney*, 568.

25. Girgenti Lane, *Guy Williams*, 202.

26. Girgenti Lane, 205.

27. Girgenti Lane, 219.

28. Girgenti Lane, 205.

29. "Zooming Zorros," *Life*, August 18, 1958, 69–75.

18. Zorro, Alias Batman

1. Special thanks to Aaron Sheehan-Dean for providing the reminder.

2. Larry Tye, *Superman: The High-Flying History of America's Most Enduring Hero* (New York: Random House, 2013), 5; Brad Ricca, *Super Boys: The Amazing Adventures of Jerry Siegel and Joe Shuster—The Creators of Superman* (New York: St. Martin's Griffin, 2014), 126.

3. Tye, *Superman*, 32.

4. Aljean Harmetz, "The Life and Exceedingly Hard Times of Superman," *New York Times*, June 14, 1981, Warner Bros. production files, *Superman* (1978), Margaret Herrick Library, Academy of Motion Picture Arts and Sciences.

5. John Tibbetts, "Bob Kane: 'Batman and Me,'" June 14, 1989, *Over the Rainbow: The John C. Tibbetts Archive of Conversations in the Arts and Humanities (1980–Present)*, KU Scholar Works, Oral Histories and Interviews, https://kuscholarworks.ku.edu/handle/1808/25146.

6. Glen Weldon, *The Caped Crusade: Batman and the Rise of Nerd Culture* (New York: Simon and Schuster, 2017), 80.

7. Weldon, *Caped Crusade*, 12–16.

8. Tim Hanley, *The Many Lives of Catwoman: The Felonious History of a Feline Fatale* (Chicago: Chicago Review Press, 2017), 4–5.

9. Antony Tollin, "Batman Foreshadowed," in *Detective Comics: 80 Years of Batman Deluxe Edition* (Burbank, CA: DC Comics, 2019), 22.

10. Roy Thomas, "Yet Another Year of the Bat," in *Alter Ego: The Comic Book Artist Collection* (Raleigh, NC: TwoMorrows, 2001), 122–123.

11. Johnston McCulley, *The Bat Strikes Again and Again!* (CreateSpace, 2009), 16.

12. Robert Sampson, *Yesterday's Faces: A Study of Series Characters in the Early Pulp Magazines*, vol. 6, *Violent Lives* (Madison, WI: Popular Press, 2005), 35.

13. Kenneth Lowe, "The Fox and the Batman: How Zorro Shaped a Century of Heroes," *Escapist Magazine*, April 5, 2019, https://www.escapistmagazine.com/v2/2019/04/05/the-fox-and-the-batman-how-zorro-shaped-a-century-of-heroes.

19. Zorro Reborn

1. A version of this chapter was published online in "Zorro Turns 100: Fights the Undead!" December 11, 2018; "Django and Zorro Fight Together!" December 20, 2018; and "Zorro Slays the Myth of Forced Diversity," January 3, 2019, https://medium.com/@steveandes.

2. C. O. "Doc" Erickson (Producer), oral history, Academy Oral History Project, OH137, Margaret Herrick Library, Academy of Motion Picture Arts and Sciences.

3. Hal Dresner, *Zorro: The Gay Blade*, revised final draft, October 3, 1980, 64, Herman A. Blumenthal Papers, folder 141 ("Script"), Margaret Herrick Library, Academy of Motion Picture Arts and Sciences.

4. Dresner, *Zorro: The Gay Blade*, 112.

5. Paramount production files, *S.O.B.* (1981), Margaret Herrick Library, Academy of Motion Picture Arts and Sciences.

6. Cary Elwes with Joe Layden, *As You Wish: Inconceivable Tales from the Making of "The Princess Bride"* (New York: Atria Books, 2016), 35.

7. Steven Spielberg bio, Biography Files, Margaret Herrick Library, Academy of Motion Picture Arts and Sciences.

8. Steven Spielberg bio, Biography Files

9. Alex Toth, *The Complete Classic Adventures of Zorro* (Image Comics, 2001); *Zorro: The Complete Dell Pre-Code Comics Adventures* (Hermes Press, 2014).

10. Don McGregor and Tom Yeates, *Dracula Versus Zorro* #1–#2 (Topps, October and November 1993; Image Comics, 1998).

11. Don McGregor and Mike Mayhew, *Zorro* #0–#11 (Topps, 1993–1994).

12. A comic book censorship code (Comics Code Authority) was put into place in 1954, but by the 1990s only DC Comics, Archie Comics, and Bongo Comics still adhered to it. Bradford W. Wright, *Comic Book Nation: The Transformation of Youth Culture in America* (Baltimore: Johns Hopkins University Press, 2003), 155ff.

13. Carolyn Cocca, *Superwomen: Gender, Power, and Representation* (New York: Bloomsbury, 2016), 40–41; George A. Khoury, *Image Comics: The Road to Independence* (Raleigh, NC: TwoMorrows, 2007), 221.

14. Trina Robbins, *From Girls to Grrlz: A History of Women's Comics from Teens to Zines* (San Francisco: Chronicle Books, 1999), 113.

15. Zachary Ingle, *Robert Rodríguez: Interviews* (Jackson: University Press of Mississippi, 2012), 50.

16. Sean Connery bio, Biography Files, Margaret Herrick Library, Academy of Motion Picture Arts and Sciences.

17. Frederick Luis Aldama and Christopher González, *Reel Latinxs: Representation in U.S. Film and TV*, Latinx Pop Culture (Tucson: University of Arizona Press, 2019), 64.

18. Hausman, "Zorro's Ancestor," 8–19.

19. Espinoza, "'Latinizing' Zorro," 20–31.

20. Hausman, "Zorro's Ancestor," 8–19.

21. Graeme McMillan, "Zorro Marking 100th Anniversary with Comic Book Horror Series," *Hollywood Reporter*, November 21, 2018, https://www.holly woodreporter.com/heat-vision/zorro-100th-anniversary-celebrated-comic-book -horror-series-1163419.

22. At this writing, Mike Wolfer is writing *Zorro: Sacrilege*, a new four-part horror series for American Mythology Productions.

23. David Avallone, telephone interview with author, January 3, 2019.

24. Avallone, telephone interview.

25. Avallone, telephone interview.

26. Javier Hernández, e-mail to author, July 13, 2019.

27. Note that, like Zorro, Latinx characters of the 1970s such as White Tiger and El Diablo still carried many of the same stereotypes—for instance, the "Latin lover" mystique. On this point, see, Allan W. Austin and Patrick L. Hamilton, *All New, All Different? A History of Race and the American Superhero* (Austin: University of Texas Press, 2019), 160.

28. Javier Hernández, *Daze of the Dead: Special Dia de Los Muertos Edition* (Los Angeles: Los Comex, 2018), 10.

29. Frederick Luis Aldama, *Latinx Superheroes in Mainstream Comics* (Tucson: University of Arizona Press, 2017), 179.

Epilogue: Zorro in an Alternate Nerdverse

1. TaLynn Kel, *Breaking Normal: Essays About My Fat, Black, Geek Life* (CreateSpace, 2017).

2. Rodneyna Hart, e-mail interview with author, April 2, 2019.

3. Hart, e-mail interview.

4. Marc Bernardin, "The Last Thing Spider-Man Should Be Is Another White Guy," *Gizmodo*, April 28, 2010, https://io9.gizmodo.com/the-last-thing-spider-man -should-be-is-another-white-gu-5549613.

5. Weldon, *Caped Crusade*, 8.

6. Frederick Luis Aldama and William Anthony Nericcio, introduction to *Talking #browntv: Latinas and Latinos on the Screen* (Columbus: Ohio State University Press, 2019), 3–7.

7.   Hart, e-mail interview.

8.   Hart, e-mail interview.

9.   Steve Rose, "The New Nerds: How Avengers and Game of Thrones Made Everyone Geek Out," *Guardian*, May 1, 2019, https://www.theguardian.com/film/2019/may/01/the-new-nerds-how-avengers-and-game-of-thrones-made-everyone-geek-out.

10. Rose, "New Nerds."

INDEX